This book is a spec

Name:

....

Date:

....

From:

....

Message:

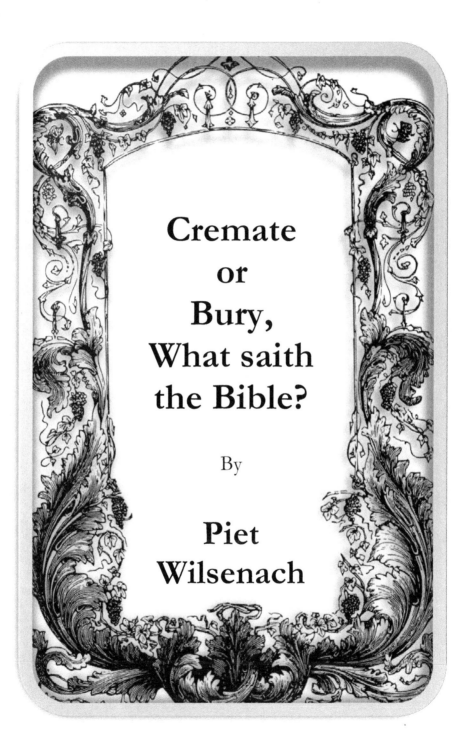

Cremate
or
Bury,
What saith
the Bible?

By

Piet
Wilsenach

Author - Publisher:
Piet Wilsenach

First Edition: (HC0)
31 July 2014

ISBN:
978-0-620-55257-8

Contact Details:
Web: www.pietwilsenach.com
Email: piet@pietwilsenach.com

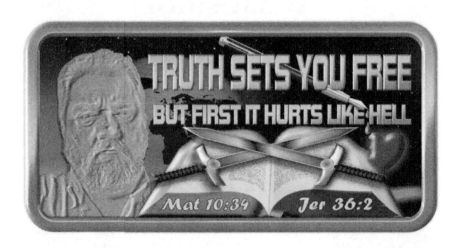

I am indebted to:
My Creator and Heavenly Father

and:

AW, RM, MS, NRK, BH, CEM, DW, JH, GA, SP, PK, BM and WS.

May our Father bless each person mentioned, whether they are aware of their contribution or not.

****

This book is lovingly dedicated to:
Riaan & Desiré

Thank you for your love that we cherish, your friendship, hospitality, support, understanding, dedication, all the late nights and most of all, your perseverance in choosing truth before man… you are truly not ashamed of the Word of God. May our Father bless you abundantly.

Important!
HYPOTHESIS

My Oxford Dictionary[1] declares the term "hypothesis" as follows:

"an idea that has not yet been proved to be true or correct"

Herewith, I then declare, because I am an unlearned and ignorant man, that every word in this book is subjected to the term as described above.

Excluded is the following:
Every scripture quoted in this book, which I regard as undeniable fact, true, imperishable, everlasting, incorruptible Holy and inspired by God.

Furthermore I declare that every reader of this book, not merely accept the writings of the author, but search and investigate as we are commanded to do by the scriptures and then only decide on their conviction, persuasion and belief, based on their own findings and research, with their knees on the floor and their Bible in their hands.

****

THIS BOOK IS WRITTEN FOR THE:
GOD SEEKER and TRUTH SEEKER

THIS BOOK WAS WRITTEN BY A FUNDAMENTALIST!

This is a person whose base principal is founded in scripture, which reads what is written in scripture and understands, what is written in scripture. This is a person of whom the highly educated theological professors say, he does not understand the scriptures for if you read that what is written in scriptures, you cannot understand that which is written is scripture. (Don't worry, I don't understand this either!!!)

I, the author, am not infallible:

- *I do not declare that my interpretation of the scriptures is infallible*
- *I do not declare that my knowledge of the truth is infallible*
- *I do not declare that my way of serving God or my obedience to Him is infallible*

Furthermore: every person in this book who I call by their name, who is still among the living, I call by their name for the following reason:

> _Eze 3:17_ _Son of man, I have made thee a watchman unto the house of Israel: therefore hear the word at my mouth, and give them warning from me._
> _Eze 3:18_ _When I say unto the wicked, Thou shalt surely die; and thou givest him not warning, nor speakest to warn the wicked from his wicked way, to save his life; the same wicked man shall die in his iniquity; but his blood will I require at thine hand._
> _Eze 3:19_ _Yet if thou warn the wicked, and he turn not from his wickedness, nor from his wicked way, he shall die in his iniquity; but thou hast delivered thy soul._

****

CORE MESSAGE

> _2Cor 4:2_ _But have renounced the hidden things of dishonesty, not walking in craftiness, nor handling the word of God deceitfully; but by manifestation of the truth commending ourselves to every man's conscience in the sight of God._
> _2Cor 4:3_ _But if our gospel be hid, it is hid to them that are lost:_
> _2Cor 4:4_ _In whom the god of this world hath blinded the minds of them which believe not, lest the light of the glorious gospel of Christ, who is the image of God, should shine unto them._

Dear friend, as you read through the pages of this book I ask that you constantly ponder over these thoughts:

- _Who handles the Word of God deceitfully?_
- _For whom is the gospel hidden?_
- _Whose minds are blinded?_
- _And who manifests the truth?_

****

All Scriptures quoted in this book are from the 1769 King James Version of the Holy Bible (also known as the Authorized Version) unless otherwise noted.

Contents

Chapter 1

Introduction

"A nation of well-informed men who have been taught to know and prize the rights which **God** has given them cannot be enslaved."

Benjamin Franklin

Destroyed for lack of knowledge

God says:

> *Hos 4:6 My people are destroyed for lack of knowledge: because thou hast rejected knowledge, I will also reject thee, that thou shalt be no priest to me: seeing thou hast forgotten the law of thy God, I will also forget thy children.*

In our day and age this is an excruciating and distressful, but painful reality, with dire consequences not only to God's children, but the world in general. It's difficult to grasp as in this day and age we have 24 hour gospel programs on TV and radio, millions of books and publications and millions of churches around the globe – we even have smart phones with daily devotions, as well as bibles on our mobile phones. At no time in history were we subjected to such a vast amount of communication channels and dispersal of information, especially related to the preaching of the gospel, interpretation of prophecy and Christian theology.

Some would argue that God is referring to the age where man did not have all these avenues which are used to distribute such a vast amount of information, knowledge if you will. But…. yes there is a BUT – The truth is, one can literally be bombarded with spiritual information, 24 hours a day, but all this information may be totally void of any "knowledge" in the true meaning of the word.

God tells us:

> *Amo 8:11 Behold, the days come, saith the Lord GOD, that I will send a famine in the land, not a famine of bread, nor a thirst for water, but of hearing the words of the LORD:*
> *Amo 8:12 And they shall wander from sea to sea, and from the north even to the east, they shall run to and fro to seek the word of the LORD, and shall not find it.*

God shall send a famine, not of food and water, **but of His Words.** I believe this is the time we are living in now. This vast ocean of so-called knowledge, which in actual fact contains no knowledge at all, has conditioned our minds to such an extent, we cant tell Arthur from Mather anymore – we have lost our ability to discern between good and evil, because we have lost our ability to discern bogus bull-dust from real knowledge and pure truth. Like God tells us; we will wander from sea to sea, from north to east, but we will not find….and this leads to His people being in captivity, imprisoned by high walls of worthless information and not even realising it!

> *Isa 5:13 Therefore my people are gone into captivity, because they have no knowledge: and their honourable men are famished, and their multitude dried up with thirst*

We are today in that very same captivity of which God speaks! Ask yourself, if you are a congregation member, when last did you truly learn something new from the puppet behind the pulpit. Yes, we are prisoners in a bogus cesspool of theology where the puppet behind the pulpit will loose his job, the moment he dares bringing you the true Word of God. The truth however is out there, but it takes some effort to find it and in our brainwashed minds we are too happy when we have access to the theologically qualified so-called man-of-God; he will always tell us the truth, we are led to believe, but dear reader, this unfortunately is not the case. I am not referring to the proverbial truth of "milk", but of "strong meat" - quoting the Apostle Paul. The "strong meat" – truth, is not even far, its right there in our homes, in a book called: The Holy Bible!

> *Heb 5:12 For when for the time ye ought to be teachers, ye have need that one teach you again which be the first principles of the oracles of God; and are become such as have need of milk, and not of strong meat.*

My job then, as with very few other lonely soldiers fighting to restore God's truth, is simply to bring you the undiluted, unaltered Word of God, teaching again the first principals from the scriptures which He gave us. I am not a soul winner, nor am I tainted by theology and I don't take heed to Jewish fables or commandments of men, so-called "truth" which I guarantee, will never, ever set you free!

> *Tit 1:14 Not giving heed to Jewish fables, and commandments of men, that turn from the truth.*

And I most definitely love the praise of God, more than the praise of men!

> *Joh 12:43 For they loved the praise of men more than the praise of God.*

Therefore, I humbly place the unspoiled and uncorrupted knowledge of scripture before you – for you to decide…..

"TRUTH WITHOUT COMPROMISE"

> *Jer 36:2 Take thee a roll of a book, and write therein all the words that I have spoken unto thee...*

"None are more hopelessly enslaved than those who falsely believe they are free."

Johann Wolfgang von Goethe

The qualifying factor

There are literally millions of preachers, ministers and pastors, so-called shepherds of Gods flock, as well as church members who believe that when they speak, it is the Holy Spirit speaking through them, but when they speak, they contradict every word in the bible! How do we know that our declarations of faith, our teachings and that which we believe are from the Holy Spirit? It sounds like a daunting question, but is it really? What do the scriptures say?

> *Heb 5:12 For when for the time ye ought to be teachers, ye have need that one teach you again which be the first principles of the oracles of God; and are become such as have need of milk, and not of strong meat.*
> *Heb 5:13 For every one that useth milk is unskilful in the word of righteousness: for he is a babe.*
> *Heb 5:14 But strong meat belongeth to them that are of full age, even those who by reason of use have their senses exercised to discern both good and evil.*

We are simply commanded to discern (differentiate) good from evil. How do we achieve this?

> *Act 17:11 These were more noble than those in Thessalonica, in that they received the word with all readiness of mind, and searched the scriptures daily, whether those things were so.*

We simply search the scriptures to see if in fact, what they tell us to be true is actually true according to scriptures. It is true that there are many interpretations when it comes to the Word of God, but you will find that for the most part, it is written in very clear and comprehensible language. However, a precondition is required:

YOU HAVE TO BELIEVE THE WORD OF GOD

> *Psa 10:3* *For the wicked boasteth of his heart's desire, and blesseth the covetous, whom the LORD abhorreth.*
> *Psa 10:4* *The wicked, through the pride of his countenance, will not seek after God: God is not in all his thoughts.*

> *Ecc 1:13* *And I gave my heart to seek and search out by wisdom concerning all things that are done under heaven: this sore travail hath God given to the sons of man to be exercised therewith.*

Billions declare openly and publically that they believe in the Bible, but they refuse to accept what is written in the Bible. You will be astonished regarding the multitude of the highly educated theologians, whom teaches that the Bible is a mere fairy tale. The worst is -it is usually theologians with titles such as "Doctor" and "Professor". Yes, you did not misread the latter;

they are not atheists or even evolutionists, but highly respected theologians, people who teach your ministers and pastors at universities and colleges.

Then we have the average person whom "believes" in God and "believes" in the Bible, but do they really? No, he believes in his pastor and his church and where scripture differs with his pastor or church or even his own conviction, his pastor, church and his own belief system triumphs, every single time. We can observe this daily, why? The answer is very simple indeed: The person believes that his pastor studied for 2, 7 or even 40 years and therefore the authority of the pastor overrides the scriptures every time. If the Bible states that a tree is green, but the pastor says: "No, the tree is red" we immediately believe the pastor over what the Bible so clearly teaches in comprehensible language. Why is this? We have gradually been dumbed down to believe that the Bible is locked; inaccessible and too complicated for the non-theologian to understand and this my friend is utter nonsense, as you will come to see in this book.

This is why God tells us the following in no uncertain terms, but clearly and comprehensibly:

> *Hos 4:6* *My people are destroyed for lack of knowledge: because thou hast rejected knowledge, I will also reject thee, that thou shalt be no priest to me: seeing thou hast forgotten the law of thy God, I will also forget thy children.*
> *Hos 4:7* *As they were increased, so they sinned against me: therefore will I change their glory into shame.*

The very first step then to differentiate the good from the bad is, we must believe and accept what the Bible teaches us. There is no middle highway to heaven! There are only two sides, God and Satan. There is no grey area as the churches and pastors so skilfully would have us believe. There is no road to heaven where everything is acceptable, as long as I "believe".

If you truly believe the Word of God, we are on the right path. If you don't believe the Word of God then this book will mean absolutely nothing to you and you may as well put it down now.

There are so many people and preachers who teach that as long as you believe, you are saved. In addition you have the people who swore their allegiance to the majority. The majority can never be wrong. As long as I follow the majority, I cannot be wrong. And so the conscience is lulled and put to rest.

Let's do like we are commanded and search the scriptures. Do we only have to believe to be saved?

> **Jas 2:19 Thou believest that there is one God; thou doest well: the devils also believe, and tremble.**

In other words, if you declare personally as well as publically that you believe in God, you achieved absolutely nothing at all. Satan and his angels (demons) also believe in God. To be more specific, Satan's "belief" in God is greater than ours because he knows God very well. Satan even knows the Bible better than us. Satan even quoted scriptures to Jesus, saying: "for it is written…"

> **Mat 4:5 Then the devil taketh him up into the holy city, and setteth him on a pinnacle of the temple,**
> **Mat 4:6 And saith unto him, If thou be the Son of God, cast thyself down: for it is written…1**

What does the Bible teach regarding the majority or "multitude"?

> **Exo 23:2 Thou shalt not follow a multitude to do evil…**

Why would God tell us not to follow the majority?

> **Mat 7:14 Because strait is the gate, and narrow is the way, which leadeth unto life, and few there be that find it.**

It's kind of ironic when we consider how scripture tells us time and time again that a very small minority will enter the narrow gates, but people and especially the church, believes that their salvation is in fact vested in being part of the majority or multitude. The opposite is true, if you are part of the majority, a red light should already be flashing for you. You should do as God commands and start searching the scriptures. There are people who have been deceived to such a degree that they truly believe their false religion to be their salvation.

> **1Tim 6:3 If any man teach otherwise, and consent not to wholesome words, even the words of our Lord Jesus Christ, and to the doctrine which is according to godliness;**
> **1Tim 6:4 He is proud, knowing nothing, but doting about questions and strifes of words, whereof cometh envy, strife, railings, evil surmisings,**

> *1Tim 6:5 Perverse disputings of men of corrupt minds, and destitute of the truth, supposing that gain is godliness: from such withdraw thyself.*

The qualifying factor then, required to read this book is:

Believe the Word of God
No matter what any man says!

Remember this very important appeal, no preacher, minister, pastor, priest, doctor or professor, nor confessions of faith or creed of no church is going to judge you. You will be judged by:

> *Joh 12:48 He that rejecteth me, and receiveth not my words, hath one that judgeth him: the word that I have spoken, the same shall judge him in the last day.*

It does not matter whether you reject what is written in scriptures now, you will be judged by those same scriptures in the last day!

> *"The difference between a child of God and a Christian is: God's child obeys God, but the Christian god obeys the Christian"*
> - **Piet Wilsenach**

Goal and Structure

We are going to study scripture to try and find answers to our question. Is there something in scripture in terms of God's law, ordinances, preferences or examples which directs us to whether we should cremate or bury? I have heard, and I am sure you have heard the following statement as well:

"There is nothing in the Bible that explicitly prohibits…this, that or the other"

It is such a pity that it is mostly the highly qualified, so-called spiritual leaders whom freely shoots off these kinds of statements from the hip. We must however be on guard with this deceit. We can formulate a long list of things which the Bible does not "explicitly" prohibit, but this does not make the deed or action acceptable, for example:

The Bible does not "explicitly" prohibit:

- *Cigarettes - does this mean we can smoke?*
- *Cocaine - does this mean we can start sniffing?*
- *Gambling - does this mean we can gamble away?*
- *Pornography - does this mean we can indulge in it?*
- *Abortion - does this mean it carries God's consent?*
- *Speeding - does this mean driving recklessly is acceptable?*

The list is endless, but the above will suffice. The truth is if we are just a little prepared to study the Bible in conjunction with prayer, we find very quickly that scriptures do condemn all of the above, even though not explicitly by name.

Furthermore we should consider another very important issue. If I was a painter and you instructed me to paint your wall white and in a couple of days you return only to find that I had painted your wall red, you would say; "But I specifically told you to paint it white". And I would say – (due to my theological training) – "You did not **explicitly** say I am not allowed to paint it red". Would you be happy with my defence? If not, ask yourself if God will be happy with your defence, on the day of reckoning, in this regard!

It is with sadness as well as pity and sometimes even irony to observe how people corrupt the Word of God.

> *2Cor 2:17 For we are not <u>as many, which corrupt the word of God:</u> but as of sincerity, but as of God, in the sight of God speak we in Christ.*

For example: Maybe you have noticed the wristbands people wear these days with the words "WWJD". This is:

"What Would Jesus Do"

There may be people whose intention with the wearing of the wristband is honest and they try to walk the talk and it is not my intention to judge them. The problem is the vast majority of people I observed, wearing that same wristband, are a scandalous testimony of:

"What Jesus would NEVER DO!"

But, maybe we should also, related to our question, consider: "What would Jesus have done". If He was here on earth today, would he have cremated or buried? How can we be sure? This dear reader is so easy to find. We simply consult the Great Manual, the Guidebook of guidebooks which He gave us, which is everlasting, God inspired and the purest form of undiluted truth you have ever encountered, to distinguish right from wrong.

Please forgive me for not being able to remember where I have read or heard the following, but it goes like this:

"Bible" stands for:

B - Basic
I - Instructions
B - Before
L - Leaving
E - Earth

In our case, related to our question, it has great significance. We can even state that to cremate or bury is the very last "say" or "choice" we have on this earth, "***before leaving earth***".

Because most of the spiritual leaders today tell us that the Bible does not explicitly prohibit cremation, we are going to "search" like scripture tells us to do and particularly in the following manner:

- **Which practises were in use, from Genesis to Revelation?**
- **What does His Word teach related to our question?**
- **Does God have a preference for one or the other?**
- **What does secular history and facts teach us?**
- **What is the nature of the resurrected body?**

When we completed our study, we have to decide how strongly the one is, compared to the other, based on the scriptures and then decide which one of the two is scripturally sound. We have to decide whether both are acceptable or if one or the other is unscriptural. After this follows the very easy or very painful task, to make a decision, based on the facts, with all the cards on the table.

Please be aware that I bring you nothing new from scriptures! The more than 800 verses we quote are the same verses which were written in your Bible, thousands of years ago. I don't present you with new revelations nor any "fresh" information from scripture; however you will be shocked with the majority of scriptures. How is this possible, you may ask? The answer is very simple. We quote scriptures which the churches avoid like the black plague! Very soon you will find that Gods Word is an embarrassment for the churches and when you start seeing this truth, it may feel like our study originates from an unfamiliar Bible, but it is indeed the very same Bible that you have in your home today!

May God be with you in this decision...

The Author

Chapter 2

Why Cremate?

"When a well-packaged web of lies has been sold gradually to the masses over generations, the truth will seem utterly preposterous <u>and it's speaker a raving lunatic.</u>"

Dresden James

Arguments in favour of cremation

When we research the subject, we find the following arguments promoting cremation as the better alternative. I list the arguments which I found, but I don't comment now as we will look at each one of these in depth later in the book.

Economical

Cremation is cheaper than the traditional method of burial. Costs excluded from cremation are alleged to be as follows:

- **A coffin (Though most are cremated with coffin and all).**
- **The cost of the grave.**
- **The cost of the gravestone (which can be very expensive).**
- **The maintenance costs of the gravesite.**

Hygienic

A body which decomposes posts the following dangers:

- **Spreading of diseases and epidemics.**
- **Polluting of underground water sources.**

Aesthetical value

It is said that cremation does not include the thought of a decomposing body and therefore it is clean, from an aesthetical perspective and thus more acceptable.

The Time factor

A traditional burial must be organised, planned and executed in a very short period of time. We are all familiar with the proverbial "running around like headless chickens" when it comes to making the necessary arrangements for a traditional funeral. With cremation however we can have the "memorial service" long after the actual cremation, with the following benefits:

- A time and place which suits everyone involved.
- The "service" can be held a month or three after the passing of the loved one.
- Enough time for family to prepare their last tributes.
- More family and friends can become involved in the arrangements.
- There is enough time for someone like me who would need to get a new suit, one that fits. :-)
- The loved ones "ashes" can be kept until the holidays, when we again visit that place where grandma requested her ashes to be scattered.

The list may be longer, but this will suffice.

Cold character

The graveyard always brings a sombre feeling, "a cold place", even in summertime. One always gets a grisly feeling due to your awareness of all the "dead people" around you. In contrast, a cremation service may be held at any venue without this "cold" character of a cemetery. Later visits to the grave are also very different from the traditional cemetery. The ash container may be stored anywhere we choose. The grave also deteriorates, unlike the memorial wall for the cremated. The grave is also scarcely visited.

In the old days on the farms, we had family graveyards. The idea was that the farms would be in family possession for ages to come and thus be cared for and nurtured. Well, the graves are still there on the farms, but the farms have long since been either sold or expropriated. Some of these once beautiful farm houses are now in little less than ruins and houses a multitude, not even to mention the dismal state of the once productive farms, now overgrown with wild grass and shrubs. The two pictures which follow are the graves of my great-great grandma and grandpa on my grandma's side. These graves are still on the farm today. Grandpa Wilsenach is also buried there in the same farm cemetery.

Just as the sold or expropriated farm cemeteries degrades, public cemeteries also falls in decay. I would just like to give credit to one of my uncles who visit the graves on the farm every year and he has done so for 31 years already, well done! Old cemeteries even get sold to developers whom then build shopping centres and such on top of the graves. Some years ago I saw on television how a multitude of squatters made themselves at home on top of an old cemetery and once they were settled in, became upset and paraded because they "had to live on top of the dead". These problems are of course absent when cremation is embraced as an alternative.

Grave Pillaging

Grave plundering is an age old practice. Bodies are dug up during the night and stripped of any items of value. Bodies are even dug up to extract gold from the teeth of the dead. Legislation does exist with regards to the desecration of graves, but the following occurred recently in my own hometown.

They dig up the coffin and check if the coffin was manufactured from any form of metal. If so, the remains in the coffin is thrown back into the hole without ceremony and the coffin is skilfully placed on a wheeled trolley, after which it is manually hauled, in broad daylight, through the streets of the town, to the nearest scrap metal dealer in exchange for a bit of money.

By contrast, the only possible mishap with grandma's ashes could be when the vase is cleaned by the domestic worker, because of the dust inside the vase. :-)

Property

The space required for a traditional grave is obviously a huge argument in favour of cremation. World population figures for 2011 is estimated at 6.97 billion, according to the *World Bank* The figure for South Africa[2] (same year) is estimated at 50,58 million. (Some interesting figures for South Africa - SA 1960 = 17,39m. 1970 = 22,08m. 1980 = 27.57m. 1990 = 35,2m. 2000 = 44m. 2010 = 49.99m)

We also have to consider the mortality rate per capita. This figure is calculated with the amount of deaths per 1000 people, by country. Our source[3] supplies the top ten highest figures by country. A shot in the dark as to who wins, globally? None other than our good old South Africa with a figure of 17.23 deaths per 1000, per year. This figure comes from the **"2012 CIA World Fact book"**.

(Yes, our new and improved South Africa does not take second place to any other country! A few months ago when the Olympic Games were being held, one of the radio hosts made the following announcement:
"Three South Africans have taken five gold medals at the Olympic Games this morning, but luckily security caught them before they could get away with it". Just a bit of humour, nothing more :-)

The point is, such a high rate of deaths do contribute a lot in favour of cremation. My personal opinion? Cremation is headed our way like an avalanche and the spiritual leaders of today are preparing us in advance, in order to lessen any protest actions against cremation, when legislation is passed that cremation is to become compulsory. It may first be legislated in certain geographical areas and then sweep like a tidal wave through the entire globe. Maybe you will disagree, but the church and its leaders are first in line to pave the way towards the achievement of political goals, and the churches prepare the "flock" to achieve those goals. Whether the goal is totally against scripture or not, does not matter in the slightest degree!

Technology

I've heard the following statement: "The traditional burial is out-dated and old-fashioned". It suggests that we have to embrace the new technology i.e. cremation, and let go of the traditional method of burial. There were no crematoriums in biblical times, therefore the only logical way to dispose of bodies were the traditional way of a ground burial. We now have advanced, computerised crematoriums and we should utilise this, rather than be old fashioned and out-dated. Get with the programme, so to speak!

The Majority

Humanity always has the tendency to follow the majority like lemmings. According to our source[4], the cremation figure for America up to 1965 was approximately 4%. This figure for 2012 is estimated at around 40%. This is a growth rate that will give any investor goose bumps on his toenails! Of course we have to always consider the population growth over the same period, but together with this we have to remember that there are cultures that never bury their dead, but cremated them from almost the beginning of time.

Maybe there are more alleged arguments to promote cremation, but we suffice with the primary arguments as listed up to now. When we have completed our study, we will revisit each one of these so-called arguments in light of scriptures, facts and current reality which came to the forefront in our study.

Chapter 3

The Origen of Cremation

If the world hate you, ye
know that it hated me before
it hated you.

Joh 15:18

What is Cremation?

The Oxford dictionary gives the following definition:
Cremate = **"Disposal of a dead body by burning it"**

My translation:[5]
Cremation is the use of high temperature burning, evaporation and oxidisation to reduce animals and people to a basic chemical substance in the form gasses and mineral fragments, with an appearance of dried bone.

Cremation serves as an alternative to the traditional body in a coffin. The remains of a cremated body hold no health or hygienic risk, can be buried or stored at a dedicated place of memorial. The remains may legally be in possession of the family or they can scatter it where and how they please. Cremation, in the true sense of the word is not an alternative for a traditional burial, but rather an alternative method of body disposal.

Years ago, we had a loving female Rottweiler.

She was eleven years old when she was diagnosed with cancer. It was so bad that the veterinarian told us, the best possible most humane thing we could do was to put her to sleep. We were given some time to say goodbye and while my wife was at Sheila's cage, crying her eyes out, I was in the waiting room, doing everything a man can possibly do to disguise his tears and sadness.

A young man was seated nearby and after some time had passed, one of the vet's employees came and handed the young man a beautiful little wooden box. At first I could not fathom what the little box was for. I mean, the young man could not possibly bring his pet-silkworms in for "deworming" now, would he? Through the constant, undercover wiping of my tears, I started to gather the meaning of it all. This little box contained the last remains, "ashes" of this young man's pet bird. This makes me wonder, did he also scatter the ashes in the sea? I mean, birds can't swim, can they?

The Crematorium

A Cremation is normally executed in a crematorium which is basically just a building, housing a large, modern oven. There are however many countries where "open air" cremations are still practiced today.

Pre- Industrial Revolution

My translation from our previous source:

Prior to the industrial revolution, all cremations were performed in "open air". The primary fuel was wood and to a lesser degree, coal was also used. The relatively low heat generated by these fuels caused people not to support cremation, especially in highly populated areas.

These "open air" cremations are still being practiced today in certain countries where it is a requirement of religion or culture, as we can see from the following image.

The First Modern Crematorium

During 1873, a certain Professor Brunetti unveiled the first modern crematorium oven in Vienna. This device found huge support in Great Britain from Queen Victoria's surgeon, Sir Henry Thompson. Thompson, together with a few colleagues, founded the **Cremation Society of England** in 1874.

The first modern crematorium was erected at *Woking, Surrey*, in England during 1878. In the same year, another crematorium was erected at Gotha, Germany. (North America at LeMoyne, however had a crematorium 2 years prior to this, in 1876 and later another was erected during 1877 at Washington, Pennsylvania.)

The first cremation was executed in England at *Woking* on 26th of March 1886. Legislation was only passed in 1902 in the form of the *Cremation Act of 1902*.

Where did it all begin?

My translation from our source:[6]
A certain Doctor William Price from England was the first person to perform a "legal" cremation according to his eccentric religious beliefs. Price was born in the country town of *Pontypridd*. As a young man he loved running around naked in the rural areas to great dismay of the inhabitants of the town. Price later became an apprentice, working for a doctor by the name of *Caerphilly*, whom encouraged Price to study the medical profession. After some years, Price started studying medicine at the University of London. After he completed his studies, he accepted a position as the company doctor of a coal mine in *Rhonda*. He started his own practice in 1846 in his hometown of *Pontypridd* and later relocated to *Llantrisant*.

Price believed the only true god is nature itself and because of this, he appointed himself Chief Celtic Priest of Druidism, a religion he wanted to revive. Price and his housemaid had a child together and Price baptised this baby as **"*Jesus Christ Price*"**. Price firmly believed that this child will become a sort of messiah of druidism and that he would revive this religion.

Druidism

Before we delve further into the life of Price, let's first get an understanding of what exactly Druidism is.

My translation from our source:[7]
A *Druid* was a member of a priestly class in England, Ireland, Gaul (France) and possibly other parts of "Celtic Europe". Very little is known with regards to ancient druidism. The Druids did not leave any written historical records and the only information known to us is through Greek and Roman authors and artists, which were preserved. Some later records originated from Irish authors as well.

The first reference to druidism dates to about 200 BC. A few themes seems to surface, originating from Greek- Roman records indicating that the Druids believed in reincarnation and they practised human sacrifice. They held an elevated position in the Gallic community, which they also enforced. The *Gauls*[8] believed and practised animism.

The Oxford Dictionary defines "animism" as follows:
"The belief that all things in nature have a soul"

They had, for example accredited a "godly status" to streams, lakes, mountains and other elements of nature. They even prayed to animals. Their most holy animal was the wild boar which was also the symbol of their military strength.

In addition, they also had "culture" and "house" gods.
From our source:

> *"Perhaps the most intriguing facet of Gallic religion is the practice of the Druids. There is no certainty concerning their origin, but it is clear that they vehemently guarded the secrets of their order and held sway over the people of Gaul. Indeed they claimed the right to determine questions of war and peace, and thereby held an "international" status. In addition, the Druids monitored the religion of ordinary Gauls and were in charge of educating the aristocracy. They also practiced a form of excommunication from the assembly of worshippers, which in ancient Gaul meant a separation from secular society as well. Thus the Druids were an important part of Gallic society"*

The Romans invaded Gaul, conquered it and roman emperors Tiberius en Claudius, started to suppress Druidism in the first century after Christ. By the second century after Christ, Druidism disappeared from the written record.

Of interest to us is the fact that Druid's, practised human sacrifice.

Back with Jesus Christ Price

Dr Price baptises his baby "Jesus Christ Price" because he believes that little Jesus will be the messiah who is going to resurrect Druidism.

> *Jer 22:30 Thus saith the LORD, <u>Write ye this man childless</u>, a man that shall not prosper in his days: for no man of his seed shall prosper, sitting upon the throne of David, and ruling any more in Judah.*

I am not suggesting that Jeremiah's words are applicable here, but the little boy, Jesus Christ Price, the so called messiah of Druidism, only lived for five months. What I do suggest as a fact though is that this religion can never ever be compatible with our God, nor our scriptures!

Jesus Christ Price is cremated

Dr William Price believed that nature is the true god; therefore he firmly believed that it would be a sin against god (the nature god) to bury a deceased person in the earth. He built a pyre on a hill near his home with coal as fuel, in order to free the soul of his deceased son of five months. Only in this manner (by burning the body i.e. cremation) is the soul free for the sky to accept the soul, or so he believed. After Price performed the necessary rituals according to druidism (which he had compiled himself) did he set the pyre alight with the body of little Jesus Christ Price on it. A short time later, the ceremony was cut short when an English policeman snatched the half burnt body of the infant from the fire. The police arrested Price and charged him with:

"The illegal disposition of a body"

The Trial

After some time, the courts decision was as follows:

"No practise is unlawful unless the law specifically declares the act to be unlawful by such law."

Doctor Price was acquitted on account of there was no law at the time which prohibited the act of cremation; therefore the cremation was ruled as being legal. (I am not sure what happened to the half-burned body of little Jesus Christ Price after the incident though). The first legislation is this regard was passed in 1902 in the form of the *"Cremation Act"*. Price died some years after the incident and it should be no surprise that he was cremated. The ceremony took place on a hill which overlooks the town *Llantrisant*. The *Times* reported on the front page that approximately twenty thousand people attended the cremation.

Cremation and Church History

When the cremation of Price was declared as being legal by the court, Wales followed suit. The cremation act of 1902 was however not accepted in Ireland at the time because Ireland insisted on a few requirements before any cremation could be performed:

- **Some procedures must be executed and confirmed prior to the commencement of any cremation.**

- Cremation venues had to be approved, prior to the cremation.
- Only certain approved people were allowed to carry out a cremation.

Some protestant churches accepted cremation without any reservations. Their argument was stated as follows:

> *"God can resurrect a bowl of ash just as easily as a bowl of dust."*

(See what I am telling you about theology and church? Scriptures isn't worth one iota to them! And this is not even the Catholics; it's the Protestant's for Pete sake!)

Although I agree with this statement due to the following verse, we will later see that unfortunately it is not that simple and there are major problems with this argument.

Mat 3:9 And think not to say within yourselves, We have Abraham to our father: for I say unto you, that God is able of these stones to raise up children unto Abraham.

The Catholic Encyclopaedia of 1908 was critical toward people who accepted cremation. It suggested that these people are evil and linked them with freemasonry, although they declared that there is nothing in their Catholic dogma which condemns cremation. Pope Paul VI lifted the ban on cremation in 1963 and in 1966 he allowed catholic priests to perform cremation services.

Sources allege that some people specifically chose cremation because they believed that one would not be resurrected, once cremated to ashes. This is, as you will see later, a huge blunder.

Heb 10:26 For if we sin wilfully after that we have received the knowledge of the truth, there remaineth no more sacrifice for sins,
Heb 10:27 But a certain fearful looking for of judgment and fiery indignation, which shall devour the adversaries.

Let's just quickly have a look at the dynamics of the device itself so that we can distinguish between the huge differences of cremation versus the traditional burial.

From a previous source:

Although cremation pyres used to be open air in the past, we now have advanced ovens in industrialised countries. These ovens are in buildings called crematoriums and they are designed for maximum heat, but also to emit minimum smoke and gasses as well as "unfriendly odours".

(However disgusting it may sound, this is flesh – human flesh – which is first cooked, then charred and subsequently burnt to charcoal. All of us are aware what happens when a piece of meat is left unattended on a normal kitchen stove or campfire and what it smells like. Can you imagine 100kg's of human flesh going through the same or even a worse process?)

The human body has a negative *caloric* (warmth) which simply means, energy is required to make it combust, to light up, in order for the cremation process to start. This is due to the high water content of the human body. This water must first evaporate before physical burning can take place and to achieve this requires enormous heat.

A 68kg body consists of approximately 65% water which requires 100MJ (Mega Jules) of energy before any burning will take place. 100MJ is approximately 3 cubic meters of natural gas. Additional energy is also required to preheat the oven. The average oven has both a primary as well as a secondary burning chamber. These chambers are lined with heat reflective ceramic bricks, specially designed to resist the high temperatures achieved during the cremation process.

The body is placed in the primary burning chamber, usually inside a coffin or other flammable container. This chamber consists of a burner which generates the necessary heat to first evaporate all the water content from the body and later to burn the flesh, organs and such. The temperature in this chamber starts at 760°C, but can reach temperatures as high as 1150°C. The average temperature though fluctuates between 870°C and 980°C. Higher temperatures can speed up the cremation process, but this requires more energy, causes more gasses and the oven deteriorates faster, which increases maintenance frequencies and of course operational costs.

The secondary chamber may be installed at the top or behind the primary chamber. This secondary burner burns and oxidises any organic material which escapes the primary chamber. This is to minimise pollution and reduce smoke before the gasses are released into the atmosphere. The secondary burner usually operates at a temperature of 900°C. There are some ideas to utilise these waste products in future. There are also plans to re-channel and utilise the heat energy for other purposes before it is released into the atmosphere.

The modern crematorium oven of today is computerised. It consists of oxygen and temperature sensors which monitors and regulates the cremation process. The open- and closing as well as the feed mechanism are automated. The system only needs the weight of the deceased's body and there you have it, practically no "living" body is required for the rest of the process!

How long does it take?

The duration of a cremation can be anywhere between 70 and 200 minutes (One hour, ten minutes or three hours and twenty minutes). Computer software calculates the required time duration by using the weight of the body. Older crematorium ovens have timers and some only have a start and stop button. The operator ends the process when he observes the cremation to be complete.

This is enough basic information regarding the cremation oven. Later on we will delve a little deeper into the practice of cremation.

Chapter 4

Religion and Culture

Beware of false prophets, which come to you in sheep's clothing, but inwardly they are ravening wolves.

Mat 7:15

Cremation – Early history

Why is it necessary to delve into other religions if the purpose of this book is to supply a biblical answer? It is important to see that the first "lawful" cremation was in fact not performed by Doctor Price as we have learned so far. It may well have been the first cremation in Britain and possibly even the first cremation in the west, but positively end unequivocally not the first, that I can assure you!

Cremation or "body burning" has come a long way, in fact long before Price inhaled his first breath. We are all familiar with the term "heathen", which in our context means: "non-Christian". You will be thunderstruck when you find the multitude of heathen (pagan) practises we practise in our churches today, shamefully under the banner of "Christianity". I don't want to elaborate on it here, but it is covered in detail in my other book I referred to earlier. Be that as it may, when we consult the Word of God for answers, we also have to look at the world around us, especially people's customs, cultures and religions. This helps us identify what is pure scripture and what has been imported into our religion as Paganism, practiced as Christianity.

I translate from our source:[9]
Scholars seem to agree that the burning of bodies probably started as a serious practice during the Stone Age, approximately 3000 years before Christ. Cremation seems to have spread during the late Stone Age to Europe, which is confirmed by archaeological discoveries of "ash" containers in the west of Russia as well as in Slavic cultures.

During the Bronze Age, 2500 to 1000 before Christ, it is believed that the act of cremation migrated to the British islands and -what we know today as Spain and Portugal. Cemeteries for cremation developed in Hungary and North Italy and then migrated to North Europe and even Ireland.

By 1000 BC, cremation became an integral part of the versatile *Grecian* "burial" culture. Later it developed into the dominant or preferred method of body disposal during the time of Homer by 800 BC. It was especially popular with the disposal of soldier's bodies that died on the battle field. The first Romans accepted cremation to such a degree that by 600 BC, cremations within city limits had to be banned.

When Constantine paganised the Christians and Christianised the pagans in his roman empire, the traditional ground burial replaced cremation and remained like this for approximately 1500 years. In spite of the fact that cremation was not supported for over 1500 years, people like Price proverbially lit the cremation flame again. By 1999, the cremation figure for the USA was at 25.4% of all deaths.

Cremation as Religious Obligation

I translate from our source:[10]

Religions like Hinduism, Jainism, Sikhism and Buddhism has cremation as an integral part of their religious creed. In these religions, the body is regarded as in instrument or vessel that conveys or transports the soul. There are many examples of this in the *Bhagavad Gita*.[11] Also known as the *Gita*, it is a 700 verse *Dharmic* writing which is part of the ancient *Sanskrit epic Mahabharata*. These writings are from a dialogue between *Pandava*, prince *Arjuna* and his guide, *Krishna* which covers a number of philosophical subjects. The *Bhagavad Gita* has inspired many leaders of the Indian freedom organisations, for example *Mohandas Karamchand Gandhi* referred to it as his "spiritual dictionary".

Hinduism

According to Hinduism tradition, the purpose of cremation is to free the soul from the body, as well as "encouragement" for the soul to start its journey to its next destination. If cremations do not take place, the soul risks remaining too close to the body and not starting its journey.

A Hindu is subjected to sixteen rituals or ceremonies during his life. (Christianity may call these "sacraments"). Which is of importance to us is the last sacrament which is of course the soul which is being released on its journey, through the "last right" – i.e. cremation. It is called *antim-sanskara* and means "the last right".

At the time of the "last right", a *Puja* is also performed which is a type of prayer ritual. The "holy scripture", *Rigveda* is one of the oldest Hindu scriptures and consists of a multitude of "poems", related to cremation. These scriptures state that the god Agni (god of fire) will cleanse the body. (Please keep this in mind as you progress through the book – "**Agni (god of fire) will cleanse the body**")

There are different cultures within Hinduism. The Balinese Hindu buries its dead for a month or even a year before the act of cremation is performed and this is for the following two reasons:

- It drains the body of fluids, which in turn makes the cremation process easier.

- To perform the cremation ceremony on dates that coincides with their holy calendar.

Islam

On the other hand, Islam forbids cremation in the strongest possible form. This religion prescribes specific practices regarding the dead. Normally, the remains are covered in a sheet or shroud only and buried without a coffin.

Christendom

Personally, I think Christen**DUM** would be a more suitable description, with emphasis on <u>DUM</u>! The reason? Everything is fine, everything is acceptable and everybody is going to heaven. God is love, He loves us and He loves everybody else. Therefore we do everything that suits us, because God loves us anyhow. Cremate or Bury? Which one is scriptural? Which one carries God's approval? We do both! In this way we are sure that we will not offend or upset anyone. Indeed, it is our choice to select which is suitable and comfortable for us. If this choice is totally against scripture it does not matter at all, because just as with Rome, all roads lead to "god" and heaven!

Theological Arguments in favour of Cremation

A few so-called theological arguments which are taken from scripture to supposedly "justify" cremation are provided by theologians. We will look at a substantial list of arguments here, but later when we get to scripture, we will scrutinise the arguments under the biblical magnifying glass.

Theological Arguments:

No	Quoted Scripture	Argument
1	*1Cor 6:19 What? know ye not that your body is the temple of the Holy Ghost which is in you, which ye have of God, and ye are not your own?*	The body is the temple of the Holy Ghost, but this is only applicable to the living body. When the body dies, it is no longer a temple for the Holy Ghost.
2	*1Cor 15:44 It is sown a natural body; it is raised a spiritual body. There is a natural body, and there is a spiritual body.*	Due to the resurrection of a spiritual body, there is nothing wrong with the natural body being consumed by fire.

3	*1Cor 15:50 Now this I say, brethren, that flesh and blood cannot inherit the kingdom of God; neither doth corruption inherit incorruption.*	Flesh and blood cannot inherit the kingdom of God; therefore it makes no difference whether the body is cremated or not.
4	*2Cor 5:8 We are confident, I say, and willing rather to be absent from the body, and to be present with the Lord.*	"Absent from the body" is self-explanatory.
5	*Luk 9:59 And he said unto another, Follow me. But he said, Lord, suffer me first to go and bury my father.* *Luk 9:60 Jesus said unto him, Let the dead bury their dead: but go thou and preach the kingdom of God.*	The argument here is that Jesus did not attach any importance to the dead; therefore the method of disposal is of no importance.
6	*Mat 23:27 Woe unto you, scribes and Pharisees, hypocrites! for ye are like unto whited sepulchres, which indeed appear beautiful outward, but are within full of dead men's bones, and of all uncleanness.*	This supposedly suggests that Jesus compares a grave and dead man's bones to something unclean, hence cremation is acceptable.
7	*Exo 24:17 And the sight of the glory of the LORD was like devouring fire on the top of the mount in the eyes of the children of Israel.* *Exo 13:21 And the LORD went before them by day in a pillar of a cloud, to lead them the way; and by night in a pillar of fire, to give them light; to go by day and night:* *Exo 13:22 He took not away the pillar of the cloud by day, nor the pillar of fire by night, from before the people.*	"Fire" in the Bible symbolises the "good" as the "presence" of God. Therefore, the "fire" used to cremate may also symbolise the good.

	Exo 3:2 And the angel of the LORD appeared unto him in a flame of fire out of the midst of a bush: and he looked, and, behold, the bush burned with <u>fire</u>, and the bush was not consumed.	
8	*<u>Gen 3:19</u> In the sweat of thy face shalt thou eat bread, till thou return unto the ground; <u>for out of it wast thou taken: for dust thou art, and unto dust shalt thou return.</u>*	Cremation merely speeds up the process of "returning" to dust.
9	Cremation is not explicitly forbidden is scriptures.	
10	The last argument is that Christen**DUM** accepts cremation more and more on a daily basis as an alternative to the traditional burial.	

At face value, it would seem that these arguments are sufficient and therefore we can, based on these arguments, accept the following:

- **God cannot be against cremation**
- **Cremation is not forbidden**
- **Christians may cremate without any reservation.**

This may be so, but… one of the biggest problems in the world today (and I am talking specifically to people who calls themselves children of the Living God) is that there is a command that we have to execute. This command is addressed to you and me, not the preacher, minister, priest, pastor or the spiritual leader, but **YOURS and MINE!!!**

<u>Act 17:11</u> These were more noble than those in Thessalonica, in <u>that they received the word with all readiness of mind, and searched the scriptures daily, whether those things were so.</u>

<u>Take Note:</u>
They received the word (lowercase "w") in all readiness. In other words they heard and paid attention to the word of the spiritual leaders, just as Christians today listen and accept what their preachers tell them.

However, when did these people ACCEPT the "word" as TRUE and JUST? When they "heard", like we hear the word in church, TV or radio from the preachers? NO, they did not! First they searched the scriptures to establish "whether those things were so", if it was indeed the truth.

Now you can say: "If my preacher states I only have to believe in Christ in order to receive everlasting life" and your preacher quotes the following scripture:

> *Joh 3:16* *For God so loved the world, that he gave his only begotten Son, that whosoever believeth in him should not perish, but have everlasting life.*

Then you can say: "I have searched scriptures and found that it is written in my Bible, just as my preacher said, therefore I believe my preacher". No, you have not searched the scriptures, you merely read what the preacher told you to read and therefore you accept it as true, notwithstanding the fact that it is taken totally out of context, related to scriptures as a whole.

If you searched the scriptures, you will find that the preacher's statement is totally false. Why? There are numerous conditions to this promise which the preacher does not teach. If the preacher's statement that you only have to believe to be saved is true, then the devil is also saved and he is also going to heaven! Let's see what scripture say when we "search the scriptures":

> *Jas 2:19* *Thou believest that there is one God; thou doest well: the devils also believe, and tremble.*
> *Jas 2:20* *But wilt thou know, O vain man, that faith without works is dead?*

You see dear reader; the spiritual church leader will always follow the majority, will always make socially acceptable statements and will always scrape, cut and saw scriptures so that the teaching of the church paves the way for the ideologies of politics and human rights!

In the next chapter then, we are going follow the very good advice of scriptures:

> **_Act 17:11_** **_These were more noble than those in Thessalonica, in that they received the word with all readiness of mind, <u>and searched the scriptures daily, whether those things were so.</u>_**

Mat 7:13 Enter ye in at the strait gate: for wide is the gate, and broad is the way, that leadeth to destruction, and many there be which go in thereat:
Mat 7:14 Because strait is the gate, and narrow is the way, which leadeth unto life, and few there be that find it.
Mat 7:15 Beware of false prophets, which come to you in sheep's clothing, but inwardly they are ravening wolves.
Mat 7:16 Ye shall know them by their fruits. Do men gather grapes of thorns, or figs of thistles?

Chapter 5

Searching Scriptures

These were more noble than those in Thessalonica, in that they received the word with all readiness of mind, and searched the scriptures daily, whether those things were so.

Act 17:11

We are going to look at practices used in scripture, related to the disposal of the dead.

To "HIDE"

The very first place in the Bible where we find the word "Buried" is here:

> **_Gén 15:15_** **_And thou_**[H859] **_shalt go_**[H935] **_to_**[H413] **_thy fathers_**[H1] **_in peace;_**[H7965] **_thou shalt be buried_**[H6912] **_in a good_**[H2896] **_old age._**[H7872]

The word "buried" in Hebrew is: "qâbar"
buried
H6912

קָבַר

BDB Definition:[12]
to bury
to be buried
to bury, bury (in masses)

The oxford dictionary defines the word "bury" as follows:
"Place or hide something underground"

According to me, the very first burial in scripture is found as follows:

> *Gen 4:9 And the LORD said unto Cain, Where is Abel thy brother? And he said, I know not: Am I my brother's keeper?*
> *Gen 4:10 And he said, What hast thou done? the voice of thy brother's blood crieth unto me from the ground.*
> *Gen 4:11 And now art thou cursed from the earth, which hath opened her mouth to receive thy brother's blood from thy hand;*

I do realise that the word "bury" is not used in these verses, but I read in an Apocryphal book that, after Cain had slayed Abel, he did not know how to "hide" the body. Cain then covered Abel with soil in an attempt to hide the body.

This is however only my opinion and an Apocryphal book, but let's look at a few verses which clearly describe the practice of "burial" in order to "hide":

> *Amo 9:3 And though they hide themselves in the top of Carmel, I will search and take them out thence; and though they be hid from my sight in the bottom of the sea, thence will I command the serpent, and he shall bite them:*

(In other words, underneath water)

> *Gen 37:26 And Judah said unto his brethren, What profit is it if we slay our brother, and conceal his blood?*

(In other words, just as Cain did with Abel)

> *Rev 6:16 And said to the mountains and rocks, Fall on us, and hide us from the face of him that sitteth on the throne, and from the wrath of the Lamb:*

(In other words, to be buried underneath the mountains and rocks)

We will now look at a few verses to comprehend the term "bury" from a scriptural perspective.

Just for interest sake, in the Bible:

- *"Burial" is used 6 times in 6 verses*
- *"Bury" is used 39 times in 36 verses*
- *"Buried" is used 106 times in 102 verses*

We will reference a few of these as follows:

> *Gen 23:4 I am a stranger and a sojourner with you: give me a possession of a buryingplace with you, that I may bury my dead out of my sight.*
> *Gen 23:6 Hear us, my lord: thou art a mighty prince among us: in the choice of our sepulchres bury thy dead; none of us shall withhold from thee his sepulchre, but that thou mayest bury thy dead.*
> *Gen 23:7 And Abraham stood up, and bowed himself to the people of the land, even to the children of Heth.*
> *Gen 23:8 And he communed with them, saying, If it be your mind that I should bury my dead out of my sight; hear me, and intreat for me to Ephron the son of Zohar,*
> *Gen 23:9 That he may give me the cave of Machpelah, which he hath, which is in the end of his field; for as much money as it is worth he shall give it me for a possession of a buryingplace amongst you.*

We see that a grave (burying place) for the dead was a very important issue, although in this case it was a cave.

> *Gen 23:13 And he spake unto Ephron in the audience of the people of the land, saying, But if thou wilt give it, I pray thee, hear me: I will give thee money for the field; take it of me, and I will bury my dead there.*
> *Gen 23:14 And Ephron answered Abraham, saying unto him,*
> *Gen 23:15 My lord, hearken unto me: the land is worth four hundred shekels of silver; what is that betwixt me and thee? bury therefore thy dead.*
> *Gen 23:16 And Abraham hearkened unto Ephron; and Abraham weighed to Ephron the silver, which he had named in the audience of the sons of Heth, four hundred shekels of silver, current money with the merchant.*

> *Gen 23:17 And the field of Ephron, which was in Machpelah, which was before Mamre, the field, and the cave which was therein, **and all the trees that were in the field, that were in all the borders round about, were made sure***

This piece of land, to serve as a family graveyard or cemetery is purchased by Abraham for 400 shekels. (It is quite difficult to determine the value of a shekel in today's currency. There were different shekels, silver, gold, bronze and the value also varied at different times and with different "governments". We are all aware that Judas betrayed Jesus for 30 shekels, but this unfortunately does not aid us in calculating the value of Abrahams purchase in today's currency.) The point is: It sounds like a lot of money and the fact that it is used to buy a piece of land for the purpose of burying the dead means that one cannot dispute, disregard nor deny the absolute importance of the last resting place of Abrahams loved ones.

> *Gen 23:19 And after this, Abraham buried Sarah his wife in the cave of the field of Machpelah before Mamre: the same is Hebron in the land of Canaan.*
> *Gen 23:20 And the field, and the cave that is therein, were made sure unto Abraham for a possession of a buryingplace by the sons of Heth.*

Here we see that the "grave site" becomes a "family grave site", just as some of used to have, and some still have, on the family farms.

> *Gen 25:8 Then Abraham gave up the ghost, and died in a good old age, an old man, and full of years; and was gathered to his people.*
> *Gen 25:9 And his sons Isaac and Ishmael buried him in the cave of Machpelah, in the field of Ephron the son of Zohar the Hittite, which is before Mamre;*
> *Gen 25:10 The field which Abraham purchased of the sons of Heth: there was Abraham buried, and Sarah his wife.*

Abraham himself is then also buried at the same grave site as his wife Sarah. We learn from this that the remains were not thrown away or discarded, or even disrespected, but taken care of with great honour and respect.

> *Gen 35:8 But Deborah Rebekah's nurse died, and she was buried beneath Bethel under an oak: and the name of it was called Allonbachuth.*

Deborah was buried underneath an oak tree, thus in the ground. Even Isaac was buried with his people, in other words, at the family grave site.

> *Gen 35:29* *And Isaac gave up the ghost, and died, and was gathered unto his people, being old and full of days: and his sons Esau and Jacob buried him.*

Next we read about the wishes of Israel (Previously Jacob). Take note how intensely important it is for Jacob to ensure that his sons deals kindly and truly with his remains according to his last wishes.

> *Gen 47:29* *And the time drew nigh that Israel must die: and he called his son Joseph, and said unto him, If now I have found grace in thy sight, put, I pray thee, thy hand under my thigh, and deal kindly and truly with me; bury me not, I pray thee, in Egypt:*
> *Gen 47:30* *But I will lie with my fathers, and thou shalt carry me out of Egypt, and bury me in their buryingplace. And he said, I will do as thou hast said.*
> *Gen 47:31* *And he said, Swear unto me. And he sware unto him. And Israel bowed himself upon the bed's head.*

Jacob made his son Joseph, swear an oath that he will not bury his father is Egypt, but at the family grave site, with his fathers. Jacob was satisfied only once Joseph vowed total adherence to Jacobs wishes, regarding the treatment of his remains. This truly indicates the utmost importance of the matter, doesn't it? Please take note once again of the absolute importance attached to the remains, in other words, the dead body, in these verses. After Jacob blessed his sons, he again stipulated in great detail how his body must be disposed of, exactly where he must be buried with a detailed description and history of the grave site.

> *Gen 49:28* *All these are the twelve tribes of Israel: and this is it that their father spake unto them, and blessed them; every one according to his blessing he blessed them.*
> *Gen 49:29* *And he charged them, and said unto them, I am to be gathered unto my people: bury me with my fathers in the cave that is in the field of Ephron the Hittite,*
> *Gen 49:30* *In the cave that is in the field of Machpelah, which is before Mamre, in the land of Canaan, which Abraham bought with the field of Ephron the Hittite for a possession of a buryingplace.*

> *Gen 49:31   There they buried Abraham and Sarah his wife; there they buried Isaac and Rebekah his wife; and there I buried Leah.*
> *Gen 49:32   The purchase of the field and of the cave that is therein was from the children of Heth.*
> *Gen 49:33   And when Jacob had made an end of commanding his sons, he gathered up his feet into the bed, and yielded up the ghost, and was gathered unto his people.*

We see further that Joseph executed his father's wishes to the letter. This was not just an empty promise to make his father feel comfortable on his death bed, but an extremely sensitive and important matter.

> *Gen 50:5   My father made me swear, saying, Lo, I die: in my grave which I have digged for me in the land of Canaan, there shalt thou bury me. Now therefore let me go up, I pray thee, and bury my father, and I will come again.*
> *Gen 50:6   And Pharaoh said, Go up, and bury thy father, according as he made thee swear.*
> *Gen 50:7   And Joseph went up to bury his father: and with him went up all the servants of Pharaoh, the elders of his house, and all the elders of the land of Egypt,*
> *Gen 50:8   And all the house of Joseph, and his brethren, and his father's house: only their little ones, and their flocks, and their herds, they left in the land of Goshen.*
>
> *Gen 50:13   For his sons carried him into the land of Canaan, and buried him in the cave of the field of Machpelah, which Abraham bought with the field for a possession of a buryingplace of Ephron the Hittite, before Mamre.*

We learn that the remains (the dead body), were utterly important to Jacob as well as Joseph. Now, let's ask ourselves a question: If it was permitted to dispose of the remains as we please and there are no biblical prescriptions, why was this history from Abraham to Jacob recorded so meticulously and in such detail in scripture? If it was not important to God, He would not have it recoded in scriptures, especially in such detail, not so? The fact that it appears in scriptures in the finest detail and that it is repeated a number of times, must be the first indication that a dead body is not simply "remains" as we call it today.

One can possibly argue that the following is an attempt to hide a body, but even Moses buried the Egyptian whom he killed.

> *Exo 2:11 And it came to pass in those days, when Moses was grown, that he went out unto his brethren, and looked on their burdens: and he spied an Egyptian smiting an Hebrew, one of his brethren.*
> *Exo 2:12 And he looked this way and that way, and when he saw that there was no man, <u>he slew the Egyptian, and hid him in the sand.</u>*

Another very significant commandment:

> <u>*Deu 21:22*</u> *And if a man have committed a sin worthy of death, and he be to be put to death, and thou hang him on a tree:*
> <u>*Deu 21:23*</u> *<u>His body shall not remain all night upon the tree, but thou shalt in any wise bury him that day;</u> (for he that is hanged is accursed of God;) that thy land be not defiled, which the LORD thy God giveth thee for an inheritance.*

This law was also adhered to with the crucifixion of Jesus. He was hung on a tree and subsequently had to be buried before sundown.

Here we have it recorded that the only part of Ishbosheth's remains David had, was his head, but even this had to be buried. Does this not once again clearly portray the prescriptive care taken with remains, even if it just a skull?

> *2Sam 4:7 For when they came into the house, <u>he lay on his bed in his bedchamber, and they smote him, and slew him, and beheaded him, and took his head,</u> and gat them away through the plain all night.*
> *2Sam 4:8 And they brought the head of Ishbosheth unto David to Hebron, and said to the king, <u>Behold the head of Ishbosheth</u> the son of Saul thine enemy, which sought thy life; and the LORD hath avenged my lord the king this day of Saul, and of his seed.*
> *2Sam 4:12 And David commanded his young men, and they slew them, and cut off their hands and their feet, and hanged them up over the pool in Hebron. <u>But they took the head of Ishbosheth, and buried it in the sepulchre of Abner in Hebron.</u>*

Later, we shall look more closely at the connotation attached to the bones of a dead cadaver, but here we also see how important the bones of the dead are. Again we have a body, discarded alongside the road, yet it is not left there like "road kill", but great care is taken to bury it according to the method, scriptures so clearly indicates.

> *1Kin 13:28 And he went and found his carcase cast in the way, and the ass and the lion standing by the carcase: the lion had not eaten the carcase, nor torn the ass.*
> *1Kin 13:29 And the prophet took up the carcase of the man of God, and laid it upon the ass, and brought it back: and the old prophet came to the city, to mourn and to bury him.*
> *1Kin 13:30 And he laid his carcase in his own grave; and they mourned over him, saying, Alas, my brother!*
> *1Kin 13:31 And it came to pass, after he had buried him, that he spake to his sons, saying, When I am dead, then bury me in the sepulchre wherein the man of God is buried; lay my bones beside his bones:*

> *Job 5:26 Thou shalt come to thy grave in a full age, like as a shock of corn cometh in in his season.*

Lastly, we are all aware that Jesus was also "buried" in a sepulchre.

> *Act 13:29 And when they had fulfilled all that was written of him, they took him down from the tree, and laid him in a sepulchre.*

What about Babies

We are familiar with Job who found himself in such dismal circumstances that he did not want to live anymore, but even so, he says that even the (still born) baby must be carried to the grave.

> *Job 10:19 I should have been as though I had not been; I should have been carried from the womb to the grave.*

God-Fearing Men

> *Act 8:2 And devout men carried Stephen to his burial, and made great lamentation over him.*

This is yet again a very important verse. Devout, in other words, God-fearing men buried Stephen. This is another indicator that the burial practice of the Bible is not merely a tradition or custom. It was practiced by **DEVOUT** men, people who loved God, served God and obeyed His commandments, statutes, and laws. The argument that the biblical burial is merely a tradition, custom or old-fashioned practice does not hold any water when we study the scriptures!

Uncleanliness related to remains

> **Num 19:16** *And whosoever toucheth one that is slain with a sword in the open fields, or a dead body, or a bone of a man, or a grave, shall be unclean seven days.*
> **Num 19:18** *And a clean person shall take hyssop, and dip it in the water, and sprinkle it upon the tent, and upon all the vessels, and upon the persons that were there, and upon him that touched a bone, or one slain, or one dead, or a grave:*

A person, who came in contact with a dead body or bones of the dead, had to cleanse themselves according to the law. We must however not read this verse out of context and assume that to bury someone is "unclean" or that we can do with the remains however we please. We must remember that death was never part of God's original creation plan for us; this was brought about by Eve's disobedience. She also listened to a "false prophet" and was deceived by him, the supreme master of all the false prophets, and every false prophet is under his authority, **SATAN!**

To Bury is to cleanse the land

> **Eze 39:11** *And it shall come to pass in that day, that I will give unto Gog a place there of graves in Israel, the valley of the passengers on the east of the sea: and it shall stop the noses of the passengers: and there shall they bury Gog and all his multitude: and they shall call it The valley of Hamongog.*
> **Eze 39:12** *And seven months shall the house of Israel be burying of them, that they may cleanse the land.*
> **Eze 39:13** *Yea, all the people of the land shall bury them; and it shall be to them a renown the day that I shall be glorified, saith the Lord GOD.*

We learn from this verse that it makes the land unclean if the dead are not buried. Can we assume by implication, to scatter the ashes of the dead also falls squarely into this category? Maybe, maybe not, but later we shall see exactly how God feels about cremation of the dead.

The Grave Marker or Tombstone

Before we look at the "tombstone", allow me to share something with you. In my first book, I quote the following verse:

> **_Rev 12:9 And the great dragon was cast out, that old serpent, called the Devil, and Satan, which deceiveth the whole world: he was cast out into the earth, and his angels were cast out with him._**

And then I make the following statement:

Satan, which deceives the whole world, most definitely includes me, the author of this book. I am not immune to this deception. I go on to say that as I grow spiritually, I will most probably have to also revise my own convictions, as the scriptures become more clear to me. Well, with this study, a case like this has surfaced.

In said book, I leave what may be called a last will and testament related to how I would like to be buried. One of the stipulations is that I don't want my loved ones to erect a tombstone for me, as I am not there anymore. With our current study however, we will learn that a tombstone is a scriptural requirement. Therefore I have to revise my previous statement, in light of what I have learned during this study, and state that I was incorrect in saying that there is no need for a tombstone. (More will follow later in the book regarding the tombstone or grave marker)

> **_Gen 35:20 And Jacob set a pillar upon her grave: that is the pillar of Rachel's grave unto this day._**

Have you ever, like me, attended a funeral or even visited the grave of a loved one and had a conscious feeling not to walk over a grave? I can't remember that I was ever taught not to walk over a grave. We may very well be born with this instinct. Nonetheless, it seems that it is scriptural not to walk over a grave. One of the purposes of a tombstone or marker is in fact to indicate the position of the grave, so that people don't walk over it.

> **_Luk 11:44 Woe unto you, scribes and Pharisees, hypocrites! for ye are as graves which appear not, and the men that walk over them are not aware of them._**

(For those who are not aware, Pharisees and Scribes are the pastors, preachers, priests and ministers, the so-called learned theologians of those days.)

Moses was buried in an unknown place without any marker (tombstone). I have no idea what the reason for this is and I don't want to speculate. It may have something to do with the fact that Moses were not granted entry into the promised land or it could be because of the dispute between the archangel Michael and the devil related to the body of Moses. We will look at this dispute a little later in the book. (If you know the answer to this question, please be so kind as to let me know. Some say it was to prevent people from worshipping the body of Moses, but I am unable to justify this from scripture)

> *Deu 34:5 So Moses the servant of the LORD died there in the land of Moab, according to the word of the LORD.*
> *Deu 34:6 And he buried him in a valley in the land of Moab, over against Bethpeor: but no man knoweth of his sepulchre unto this day.*

Graves in the time of Jesus

> *Luk 11:47 Woe unto you! for ye build the sepulchres of the prophets, and your fathers killed them.*
> *Luk 11:48 Truly ye bear witness that ye allow the deeds of your fathers: for they indeed killed them, and ye build their sepulchres.*

These verses are significant, as it contains some hidden meaning as well, but let's concentrate on the fact that graves were also built in the time of Jesus. In other words, from the beginning of time, up until the time of Jesus, the scriptural tomb or grave was still practised.

Who were not buried?

So far we have learned that the burial process and marking of the grave is a scriptural practise and not merely old-fashioned tradition. We shall now look at instances where people were deprived of a proper burial and under what conditions it happened.

> *Psa 79:1 A Psalm of Asaph. O God, the heathen are come into thine inheritance; thy holy temple have they defiled; they have laid Jerusalem on heaps.*
> *Psa 79:2 The dead bodies of thy servants have they given to be meat unto the fowls of the heaven, the flesh of thy saints unto the beasts of the earth.*
> *Psa 79:3 Their blood have they shed like water round about Jerusalem; and there was none to bury them.*

These people were not buried according to scripture, but given as meat to the creatures. Was this act from God? No! Take note: The heathen came into 'thine' inheritance and they defiled the temple. We can therefore derive the following: Not to bury is a heathen practice! Notwithstanding the fact that we will later see that God also used this method, but only where the people were "heathen".

> *Jer 14:15   Therefore thus saith the LORD concerning <u>the prophets that prophesy in my name, and I sent them not</u>, yet they say, Sword and famine shall not be in this land; By sword and famine shall those prophets be consumed.*
> *Jer 14:16   <u>And the people to whom they prophesy shall be cast out in the streets of Jerusalem because of the famine and the sword; and they shall have none to bury them</u>, them, their wives, nor their sons, nor their daughters: for I will pour their wickedness upon them.*

Again, God warns against the false prophets who prophesied in His Name which He has not sent. This is also a warning that needs to be taken very seriously by God's true children whom so easily believe and almost worships their false prophets whom prophesied falsely in God's Name! These people, who place their convictions in the false prophets, will not be buried, but serve as food to the creatures. (I can't help but to think how many people believed their false prophets in church and as a result, did not get an honoured scriptural burial, but instead were cremated) Take head to what God says:

"I will pour their wickedness upon them"

God's anger in this case, does not allow for an honoured scriptural burial. Thus, not to bury is most definitely a form punishment.

> *Jer 16:3   For thus saith the LORD concerning the sons and concerning the daughters that are born in this place, and concerning their mothers that bare them, and concerning their fathers that begat them in this land;*
> *Jer 16:4   <u>They shall die of grievous deaths; they shall not be lamented; neither shall they be buried; but they shall be as dung upon the face of the earth</u>: and they shall be consumed by the sword, and by famine; and their carcases shall be meat for the fowls of heaven, and for the beasts of the earth.*
> *Jer 16:5   For thus saith the LORD, <u>Enter not into the house of mourning, neither go to lament nor bemoan them: for I have*

> *taken away my peace from this people, saith the LORD, even lovingkindness and mercies.*
> *Jer 16:6 Both the great and the small shall die in this land: they shall not be buried, neither shall men lament for them, nor cut themselves, nor make themselves bald for them:*

Yet again we see a direct link between **no burial** and the **anger of God** with regards to these people.

> *Jer 22:17 But thine eyes and thine heart are not but for thy covetousness, and for to shed innocent blood, and for oppression, and for violence, to do it.*

Firstly, the heart of Jehoiakim the son of Josiah is far from God. He is being accused of shedding innocent blood, oppression and violence. As part of his punishment, he is deprived of a scriptural burial.

> *Jer 22:18 Therefore thus saith the LORD concerning Jehoiakim the son of Josiah king of Judah; They shall not lament for him, saying, Ah my brother! or, Ah sister! they shall not lament for him, saying, Ah lord! or, Ah his glory!*
> *Jer 22:19 He shall be buried with the burial of an ass, drawn and cast forth beyond the gates of Jerusalem.*

Jehoiakim is being drawn and disposed of like a dead donkey, without a scriptural burial as a direct result of his disobedience and sin.

God's Anger = "No Burial" as Punishment

We continue to list a multitude of scriptures where the person(s) is deprived of an honourable scriptural burial, without comment, but to emphasise the relationship between "no burial" and God's anger and punishment.

> *1Kin 13:22 But camest back, and hast eaten bread and drunk water in the place, of the which the LORD did say to thee, Eat no bread, and drink no water; thy carcase shall not come unto the sepulchre of thy fathers.*

> *2Kin 9:34 And when he was come in, he did eat and drink, and said, Go, see now this cursed woman, and bury her: for she is a king's daughter.*
> *2Kin 9:35 And they went to bury her: but they found no more of her than the skull, and the feet, and the palms of her hands.*

2Kin 9:36 Wherefore they came again, and told him. And he said, This is the word of the LORD, which he spake by his servant Elijah the Tishbite, saying, In the portion of Jezreel shall dogs eat the flesh of Jezebel:
2Kin 9:37 And the carcase of Jezebel shall be as dung upon the face of the field in the portion of Jezreel; so that they shall not say, This is Jezebel.

Jer 36:30 Therefore thus saith the LORD of Jehoiakim king of Judah; He shall have none to sit upon the throne of David: and his dead body shall be cast out in the day to the heat, and in the night to the frost.

Lev 26:30 And I will destroy your high places, and cut down your images, and cast your carcases upon the carcases of your idols, and my soul shall abhor you.

Num 14:29 Your carcases shall fall in this wilderness; and all that were numbered of you, according to your whole number, from twenty years old and upward, which have murmured against me,
Num 14:32 But as for you, your carcases, they shall fall in this wilderness.
Num 14:33 And your children shall wander in the wilderness forty years, and bear your whoredoms, until your carcases be wasted in the wilderness.

Deu 28:25 The LORD shall cause thee to be smitten before thine enemies: thou shalt go out one way against them, and flee seven ways before them: and shalt be removed into all the kingdoms of the earth.
Deu 28:26 And thy carcase shall be meat unto all fowls of the air, and unto the beasts of the earth, and no man shall fray them away.

1Sam 17:46 This day will the LORD deliver thee into mine hand; and I will smite thee, and take thine head from thee; and I will give the carcases of the host of the Philistines this day unto the fowls of the air, and to the wild beasts of the earth; that all the earth may know that there is a God in Israel.

Isa 34:2 For the indignation of the LORD is upon all nations, and his fury upon all their armies: he hath utterly destroyed them, he hath delivered them to the slaughter.
Isa 34:3 Their slain also shall be cast out, and their stink shall come up out of their carcases, and the mountains shall be melted with their blood.

Isa 66:24 And they shall go forth, and look upon the carcases of the men that have transgressed against me: for their worm shall not die, neither shall their fire be quenched; and they shall be an abhorring unto all flesh.

(Almost sounds like either hell or… cremation, doesn't it?)

Jer 9:22 Speak, Thus saith the LORD, Even the carcases of men shall fall as dung upon the open field, and as the handful after the harvestman, and none shall gather them.

Jer 41:9 Now the pit wherein Ishmael had cast all the dead bodies of the men, whom he had slain because of Gedaliah, was it which Asa the king had made for fear of Baasha king of Israel: and Ishmael the son of Nethaniah filled it with them that were slain.

Heb 3:16 For some, when they had heard, did provoke: howbeit not all that came out of Egypt by Moses.
Heb 3:17 But with whom was he grieved forty years? was it not with them that had sinned, whose carcases fell in the wilderness?

Isa 14:18 All the kings of the nations, even all of them, lie in glory, every one in his own house.
Isa 14:19 But thou art cast out of thy grave like an abominable branch, and as the raiment of those that are slain, thrust through with a sword, that go down to the stones of the pit; as a carcase trodden under feet.
Isa 14:20 Thou shalt not be joined with them in burial, because thou hast destroyed thy land, and slain thy people: the seed of evildoers shall never be renowned.
Isa 14:21 Prepare slaughter for his children for the iniquity of their fathers; that they do not rise, nor possess the land, nor fill the face of the world with cities.

> *Rev 11:7 And when they shall have finished their testimony, the beast that ascendeth out of the bottomless pit shall make war against them, and shall overcome them, and kill them.*
> *Rev 11:8 And their dead bodies shall lie in the street of the great city, which spiritually is called Sodom and Egypt, where also our Lord was crucified.*
> *Rev 11:9 And they of the people and kindreds and tongues and nations shall see their dead bodies three days and an half, and shall not suffer their dead bodies to be put in graves.*

Please take note that this relationship between "no burial" and God's punishment, stretches from the Old Testament into the last book of the Bible, Revelation.

We look at just a few more verses where a scriptural burial is not allowed, directly linked to God's anger or wrath.

> *Jer 19:10 Then shalt thou break the bottle in the sight of the men that go with thee,*
> *Jer 19:11 And shalt say unto them, Thus saith the LORD of hosts; Even so will I break this people and this city, as one breaketh a potter's vessel, that cannot be made whole again: and they shall bury them in Tophet, till there be no place to bury.*
> *Jer 19:12 Thus will I do unto this place, saith the LORD, and to the inhabitants thereof, and even make this city as Tophet:*
> *Jer 19:13 And the houses of Jerusalem, and the houses of the kings of Judah, shall be defiled as the place of Tophet, because of all the houses upon whose roofs they have burned incense unto all the host of heaven, and have poured out drink offerings unto other gods.*

Later we will have a closer look at the name **"Tophet"**.

Here we have a very serious warning indeed from the Almighty God. The bones, not of the heathen, but of Israel, will be taken from the graves and dishonoured. What angers God so heavily? None other than idolatry!

> *Jer 8:1 At that time, saith the LORD, they shall bring out the bones of the kings of Judah, and the bones of his princes, and the bones of the priests, and the bones of the prophets, and the bones of the inhabitants of Jerusalem, out of their graves:*

> *Jer 8:2 And they shall spread them before the sun, and the moon, and all the host of heaven, whom they have loved, and whom they have served, and after whom they have walked, and whom they have sought, and whom they have worshipped: they shall not be gathered, nor be buried; they shall be for dung upon the face of the earth.*

You may think that we are not like this, we go to church and do not practice any form of idolatry, and therefore this warning is not intended for us churchgoing folk. I can tell you dear friend, the contrary is true. We are busy with a multitude of idolatrous acts in our so called holy churches every day! We believe the things we do, like certain sacraments and rituals are part of our religion, ordained by God; indeed we are taught by our spiritual leaders that these acts are performed according to God's will, but this is far from the truth. In my previous book I discuss a good few of these pagan practices we so dearly hold to our heart as obligatory acts required by God.

Take note to whom exactly this warning is addressed to:

> **"the kings of Judah, and the bones of his princes, and the bones of the priests, and the bones of the prophets,"**

Take head:
The kings, the princes and the priests and prophets.
The church leaders of today!

A few last examples from scripture

> *Jer 26:23 And they fetched forth Urijah out of Egypt, and brought him unto Jehoiakim the king; who slew him with the sword, and cast his dead body into the graves of the common people.*

> *2Chr 34:4 And they brake down the altars of Baalim in his presence; and the images, that were on high above them, he cut down; and the groves, and the carved images, and the molten images, he brake in pieces, and made dust of them, and strowed it upon the graves of them that had sacrificed unto them.*

> *2Kin 23:16 And as Josiah turned himself, he spied the sepulchres that were there in the mount, and sent, and took the bones out of the sepulchres, and burned them upon the altar,*

and polluted it, according to the word of the LORD which the man of God proclaimed, who proclaimed these words.

Dear reader, I trust you are taking note of the fact that
"burning of bones is to pollute the bones, according to the Word of God"
Shall I say that again?
"burning of bones is to pollute the bones, according to the Word of God"
Once more?

"burning of bones is to pollute the bones according to the Word of God"

The Bone – Unbelievably Important!

Next we look at the "bone" and the unbelievable importance attached to human bones. It was a revelation to me in this study to find just how important and valuable the human bone, after death is, and this from God's Word. For me personally it was an immensely important discovery. We will look at a few scriptures in this regard in a moment.

In my other book, I mentioned briefly that the word "ashes" in terms of the remains after a cremation, is very deceiving. An outright blatant lie may be more appropriate, because there are virtually no ashes, but only bones which are crushed and ground which is passed off as the "ashes" of the deceased. We look at this later in the book, but please keep this fact in mind when we read through the following scriptures.

> *Eph 5:30 For we are members of his body, of his flesh, and of his bones.*

I don't want to elaborate on the following, but we are literally and physically the generation of God, just as scripture declares, "of his body, of his flesh, and of his bones". Note that not all two legged creatures are from the generation of God.

> *Gen 2:23 And Adam said, This is now bone of my bones, and flesh of my flesh: she shall be called Woman, because she was taken out of Man.*

Just as Eve's bones is part of Adam's, so are our bones part of God's bones.

> *Psa 35:10 All my bones shall say, LORD, who is like unto thee,*
> *which deliverest the poor from him that is too strong for him,*
> *yea, the poor and the needy from him that spoileth him?*

> *Psa 141:7 Our bones are scattered at the grave's mouth, as*
> *when one cutteth and cleaveth wood upon the earth.*

Our **BONES** are scatted at the grave's mouth, not our **ASHES!**

> *Eze 6:4 And your altars shall be desolate, and your images*
> *shall be broken: and I will cast down your slain men before*
> *your idols.*
> *Eze 6:5 And I will lay the dead carcases of the children of*
> *Israel before their idols; and I will scatter your bones round*
> *about your altars.*
> *Eze 6:6 In all your dwellingplaces the cities shall be laid waste,*
> *and the high places shall be desolate; that your altars may be*
> *laid waste and made desolate, and your idols may be broken*
> *and cease, and your images may be cut down, and your works*
> *may be abolished.*

"Images" refers to "sun-pillars", which by the way is used by the majority of churches! Blatant paganism and idolatry without the congregation member ever finding the truth regarding these objects and symbols, hidden in plain view right in front of our eyes…

> *Eze 39:15 And the passengers that pass through the land, when*
> *any seeth a man's bone, then shall he set up a sign by it, till the*
> *buriers have buried it in the valley of Hamongog.*

There can be no doubt as to the importance of the bones of the dead when we consider this verse. Why can't these bones not just be left alone? After all, the person who discovered the bones did not have anything to do with them. These "passengers" however are fully aware of what scripture requires, therefore they mark the bones and bury it. Unlike us today, taking the bones and grinding and crushing it to small pieces!

> *Gen 50:24 And Joseph said unto his brethren, I die: and God*
> *will surely visit you, and bring you out of this land unto the*
> *land which he sware to Abraham, to Isaac, and to Jacob.*

Joseph comes to terms with the fact his passing is close. What is one of the most important issues for Joseph, after his death? It is of such importance that he requires his brethren to take an oath that they will comply with his wishes. What is so utterly important to him? They must not bury his bones in Egypt, but they must take it with them and bury it at the family grave site.

> **Gen 50:25** *And Joseph took an oath of the children of Israel, saying, God will surely visit you, and ye shall carry up my bones from hence.*

All of us know the story of Moses very well. He was born in Egypt, grew up in the king's palace and later fled because he had killed and buried an Egyptian. Many years later, Moses led the Israelites out of Egypt and they subsequently spent at least 40 years in the desert. We also need to be aware that Moses was in hiding for ± 40 years after he fled from Egypt. After these 40 years he encountered the burning bush and then went back to Egypt. Calculations indicate a period of ± 180 years between the deaths of Joseph and Moses.

When Moses fled he was ± 40 years old.
He spent ± 40 years in the vicinity of Median.
He was ± 80 years old when he led the Israelites from Egypt.
The Israelites spent ± 40 years in the desert.
Moses was 120 years when he died.

> **Deu 34:7** *And Moses was an hundred and twenty years old when he died: his eye was not dim, nor his natural force abated.*

Although it is an estimate, when we calculate the time it took for the remains (bones) of Joseph to eventually be laid to (final) rest, according to the wishes of Joseph, it took approximately 100 years. Joseph's bones were carted through the desert for 40 years! Yes, Josephs last will regarding the final resting place of his bones was in fact this important. Moses himself gave this instruction to the Israelites and took it to heart that the remains (bones) of Joseph be dealt with according to his wishes.

> **Exo 13:19** *And Moses took the bones of Joseph with him: for he had straitly sworn the children of Israel, saying, God will surely visit you; and ye shall carry up my bones away hence with you.*

It was so important an issue that Moses had the children of Israel swore as well as a warning that God will surely visit them if they do not fulfil this task. And so, eventually Joseph's bones were laid to rest with his father, Jacob's bones at the family grave site. This is such a significant issue that it is repeated in the New Testament, specifically so that we don't miss the importance of this event.

> *Jos 24:32 And the bones of Joseph, which the children of Israel brought up out of Egypt, buried they in Shechem, in a parcel of ground which Jacob bought of the sons of Hamor the father of Shechem for an hundred pieces of silver: and it became the inheritance of the children of Joseph.*

> *Heb 11:22 By faith Joseph, when he died, made mention of the departing of the children of Israel; and gave commandment concerning his bones.*

This, dear reader is an appropriate opportunity to ask yourself a very important question. Considering the above events, and if you believe that the Word of God is inspired by God and that ALL SCRIPTURE is profitable for correction and instruction, how in seven blue blazing hells can we justify taking the bones of a loved one and after burning the body to oblivion, crush and grind the bones to a fine powder? You have to make a decision. Either you believe that ALL SCRIPTURE is profitable for correction and instruction or you believe that scripture should be read like little red riding hood, when compared to our "human rights, likes and dislikes"!

> *2Tim 3:16 All scripture is given by inspiration of God, and is profitable for doctrine, for reproof, for correction, for instruction in righteousness:*
> *2Tim 3:17 That the man of God may be perfect, throughly furnished unto all good works.*

If the bones of the children of God are not important, why on earth would they be carted around in the desert for 40 years? No sir/madam, our bones are not the same as a chicken bone which is discarded in a refuse bin, much less grind it to fine pulp!!!

The bones are of such high value that it even caused a dead body to come alive. Yes, when a dead body came into contact with Elisha's bones, the person was revived and stood up on his feet.

> *2Kin 13:20 And Elisha died, and they buried him. And the bands of the Moabites invaded the land at the coming in of the year.*

> *2Kin 13:21 And it came to pass, <u>as they were burying a man,</u> that, behold, they spied a band of men; and they cast the man into the sepulchre of Elisha: and <u>when the man was let down, and touched the bones of Elisha, he revived, and stood up on his feet.</u>*

(I have to state categorically that this is not the case with all human bones, in fact the scripture do not teach this. Please don't go and start a new church or doctrine where people rub themselves with dead men's bones on Sundays now! Or Saturdays for the others :-)

Our bones (substance) are not hidden from our Creator.

> *Psa 139:15 My <u>substance was not hid from thee, when I was made in secret,</u> and curiously wrought in the lowest parts of the earth.*

Here we see the bones are not to be moved. Does this contradict the events surrounding Joseph's bones? Not at all, in fact, the bones must be moved until it reaches its final resting place, and then it must never again be moved.

> *2Kin 23:18 And he said, Let him alone; <u>let no man move his bones.</u> So they let his bones alone, with the bones of the prophet that came out of Samaria.*

Do you remember the practice of the roman soldiers where they had to break the legs of the crucified to speed up the death of the person? This was due to the commandment that someone, hung on a tree, must be buried before sundown. Do you remember when the soldier came to break the legs of Jesus, only to find that Jesus had already died? The reason for this was so that prophesies could be fulfilled with regards to "no bone of the Lam shall be broken". A few related verses to follow:

> *Psa 34:20 <u>He keepeth all his bones: not one of them is broken.</u>*

> *Exo 12:5 <u>Your lamb shall be without blemish,</u> a male of the first year: ye shall take it out from the sheep, or from the goats:*

> *Joh 19:31 The Jews therefore, because it was the preparation, <u>that the bodies should not remain upon the cross</u> on the sabbath day, (for that sabbath day was an high day,) besought*

> *Pilate that their legs might be broken, and that they might be taken away.*
> *Joh 19:32 Then came the soldiers, and brake the legs of the first, and of the other which was crucified with him.*
> *Joh 19:33 But when they came to Jesus, and saw that he was dead already, they brake not his legs:*
>
> *Joh 19:36 For these things were done, that the scripture should be fulfilled, A bone of him shall not be broken.*

Very clearly and comprehensibly, we learn from scriptures the utter importance of the BONE. Whether it is symbolic or not, the bone has great undisputable value. Whichever way you prefer to look at scripture, there is absolutely no way you can refute the significance of the bone! If bones are carried through a desert for 40 years, if even the Passover lam must be free from any broken bones and we take the bones and destroy it in an industrial blender and scatter it anywhere we please, how on earth can you my friend, reconcile this with scripture?

The bone is so important that even if you were to have a broken leg (foot) or a broken arm (hand), you were not even allowed to approach to offer to God, and we take the bone and do what with it.........? And yet, "the man of the cloth saith: Thou may doest whatever pleases thou". Absolutely preposterous!

> *Lev 21:17 Speak unto Aaron, saying, Whosoever he be of thy seed in their generations that hath any blemish, let him not approach to offer the bread of his God.*
> *Lev 21:18 For whatsoever man he be that hath a blemish, he shall not approach: a blind man, or a lame, or he that hath a flat nose, or any thing superfluous,*
> *Lev 21:19 Or a man that is brokenfooted, or brokenhanded,*

We look at this issue more closely later in the book, but there are also another side to the coin, or should I say bone?

God's Wrath - directed at the Bone

We have learned FROM SCRIPTURE – GOD'S WORD, which we claim to believe, with what utter respect, honour and veneration dead men's bones must be dealt with. The other side to this is exactly the opposite. To desecrate or defile the bones, even after the person has been buried is a form of punishment, enacted by God as we shall see shortly...

God scattered the bones of those He despised! God did exactly the opposite of what he sanctions in scripture for His people. We shall see that God's wrath also reaches beyond the grave in terms of the bones.

> *Psa 53:5 There were they in great fear, where no fear was: for God hath scattered the bones of him that encampeth against thee: thou hast put them to shame, because God hath despised them.*

God shall break their bones!

> *Num 24:8 God brought him forth out of Egypt; he hath as it were the strength of an unicorn: he shall eat up the nations his enemies, and shall break their bones, and pierce them through with his arrows.*

As punishment, this woman's bones were not dealt with as per the scriptures, but sent into different directions in Israel.

> *Jdg 19:29 And when he was come into his house, he took a knife, and laid hold on his concubine, and divided her, together with her bones, into twelve pieces, and sent her into all the coasts of Israel.*
> *Jdg 19:30 And it was so, that all that saw it said, There was no such deed done nor seen from the day that the children of Israel came up out of the land of Egypt unto this day: consider of it, take advice, and speak your minds.*

(Incidentally, the same fate also befell Nimrod)

God is talking about the good versus the bad. One of the bad things here is specifically, amongst others, bones which are broken, chopped into pieces. God will even hide His face from these people, which means their prayers will go unanswered! (I wonder if there are people who cremated their loved ones, had their bones chopped in pieces and feel that God is not answering their prayers?)

> *Mic 3:1 And I said, Hear, I pray you, O heads of Jacob, and ye princes of the house of Israel; Is it not for you to know judgment?*
> *Mic 3:2 Who hate the good, and love the evil; who pluck off their skin from off them, and their flesh from off their bones;*

> *Mic 3:3* *Who also eat the flesh of my people, and flay their skin from off them; and they break their bones, and chop them in pieces, as for the pot, and as flesh within the caldron.*
> *Mic 3:4* *Then shall they cry unto the LORD, but he will not hear them: he will even hide his face from them at that time, as they have behaved themselves ill in their doings.*

Another instance is where God has none other than priests bones burned on their idolatrous altars. Please don't make the mistake of thinking that these priests were heathens or pagans. They were Israelites, part of God's people. In addition, please don't make the mistake of thinking that this is not happening today, and please don't make the mistake of thinking that this is not happening in your own church of todays day and age!

> *2Chr 34:4* *And they brake down the altars of Baalim in his presence; and the images, that were on high above them, he cut down; and the groves, and the carved images, and the molten images, he brake in pieces, and made dust of them, and strowed it upon the graves of them that had sacrificed unto them.*
> *2Chr 34:5* *And he burnt the bones of the priests upon their altars, and cleansed Judah and Jerusalem.*

Please take note that the bones of these priests were burned because of the wrath of God, in punishment, just like the crematoriums do today!

Again, the following verse indicates the importance of the bones. Earlier we read about the man who encountered bones along the road which had to be marked and buried. Here we totally see the opposite, but note that once again, it is as a direct result of God's wrath. Bones are taken from the grave, burned and polluted (desecrated).

> *2Kin 23:16* *And as Josiah turned himself, he spied the sepulchres that were there in the mount, and sent, and took the bones out of the sepulchres, and burned them upon the altar, and polluted it, according to the word of the LORD which the man of God proclaimed, who proclaimed these words.*

Now we have to ask the obvious question: Why doesn't Josiah just leave the bones in the grave? The person is dead and has been dead for a long time. How much vengeance must one possess to exhume dead people's bones and burn them? In today's day and age I am sure we will have such a person admitted to a mental facility for the rest of his life, wont we? Also take note that the absolute majority of church leaders today teach that there is absolutely nothing wrong with burning the bones of a loved one!

Here we have the prophecy concerning Josiah's actions. God prophesied before the birth of Josiah that he (Josiah) would in future burn the bones of the priests. This is proof that Josiah did not merely do this from rage or revenge because he lost his temper, but under direct authority and instructions from God!

> *1Kin 13:1 And, behold, there came a man of God out of Judah by the word of the LORD unto Bethel: and Jeroboam stood by the altar to burn incense.*
> *1Kin 13:2 And he cried against the altar in the word of the LORD, and said, O altar, altar, thus saith the LORD; Behold, a child shall be born unto the house of David, Josiah by name; and upon thee shall he offer the priests of the high places that burn incense upon thee, and men's bones shall be burnt upon thee.*
> *1Kin 13:3 And he gave a sign the same day, saying, This is the sign which the LORD hath spoken; Behold, the altar shall be rent, and the ashes that are upon it shall be poured out.*

Not surprisingly, in our day and age, the same so called "priests" of the so called "church of god", teaches that there is nothing wrong with burning a body, crushing and grinding the bones of children of God, and so they also fulfil the warning which Jesus gave us, i.e. ravenous wolves in sheep's clothing!

Furthermore, Josiah did not do this once only, he did it more than once i.e. slaughtering and burning these false priests.

> _2Kin 23:19_ *And all the houses also of the high places that were in the cities of Samaria, which the kings of Israel had made to provoke the LORD to anger, Josiah took away, and did to them according to all the acts that he had done in Bethel.*
> _2Kin 23:20_ *And he slew all the priests of the high places that were there upon the altars, and burned men's bones upon them, and returned to Jerusalem.*

We look at one more occurrence where the bones of men, woman and children were broken in pieces, as punishment for their sins.

> *Dan 6:24 And the king commanded, and they brought those men which had accused Daniel, and they cast them into the den of lions, them, their children, and their wives; and the lions had the mastery of them, and brake all their bones in pieces or ever they came at the bottom of the den.*

The Dust of Cremation

Let's see how God feels about burning bones to ashes (lime).

> *Amo 2:1 Thus saith the LORD; For three transgressions of Moab, and for four, I will not turn away the punishment thereof; because he burned the bones of the king of Edom into lime:*
> *Amo 2:2 But I will send a fire upon Moab, and it shall devour the palaces of Kerioth: and Moab shall die with tumult, with shouting, and with the sound of the trumpet:*
> *Amo 2:3 And I will cut off the judge from the midst thereof, and will slay all the princes thereof with him, saith the LORD.*

In addition we have to consider the fact that Edom is an eternal enemy of God. If God then casts this horrible punishment onto someone who burnt the bones of Gods enemies to ashes, how in seven blue blazing hells can we justify cremation? Read these verses again and ask yourself how it is possible to teach that God has no problem whatsoever with cremation? This is a tremendously significant revelation regarding God's feeling related to the burning of bodies my friend!

The Resurrection

This is where things start to get very interesting indeed. Note that we will not jump out from ash containers, also note that God will not resurrect the "ashes", but the bones will be resurrected from the graves!

> *Eze 37:12 Therefore prophesy and say unto them, Thus saith the Lord GOD; Behold, O my people, I will open your graves, and cause you to come up out of your graves, and bring you into the land of Israel.*

> *Eze 37:13 **And ye shall know that I am the LORD, when I have
> opened your graves, O my people, and brought you up out of
> your graves,**
> *Eze 37:14 **And shall put my spirit in you, and ye shall live,** and
> I shall place you in your own land: then shall ye know that I the
> LORD have spoken it, and performed it, saith the LORD.*

I do realise that some readers may at this stage of our study think that we
have dwelt a lot in the Old Testament and everything changes in the New
Testament. This reasoning is yet another misconception and falsehood,
taught by the spiritual leaders of today. Anyhow, we will later delve into the
New Testament a little more, please be patient…

Note:
New Testament – Jesus's own Words: Everyone **IN THE GRAVES** shall
hear his voice. Note: Not scattered ashes or crushed bones!

> *Joh 5:28 **Marvel not at this: for the hour is coming, in the
> which all that are in the graves shall hear his voice,**
> *Joh 5:29 **And shall come forth; they that have done good, unto
> the resurrection of life; and they that have done evil, unto the
> resurrection of damnation.**

Note: "together with **MY DEAD BODY** shall they arise" – Also note that
the "**EARTH** shall cast out the dead", and not ash urns!

> *Isa 26:19 **Thy dead men shall live, together with my dead body
> shall they arise.** Awake and sing, ye that dwell in dust: for thy
> dew is as the dew of herbs, and **the earth shall cast out the
> dead.***

Look at the following lengthy section regarding the resurrection. Take head
of the bones which will receive sinews, flesh and also a spirit. Some will
come from the graves and some will just rise from the dry bones. Note
there is no mention of "ashes" or crushed and ground bone powder! When
you read this section of scripture, ask yourself how on earth it is possible to
associate this with the ashes of cremation…

> *Eze 37:1 **The hand of the LORD was upon me, and carried me
> out in the spirit of the LORD, and set me down in the midst of
> the valley which was full of bones,**

~ 82 ~

Eze 37:2 And caused me to pass by them round about: and, behold, there were very many in the open valley; and, lo, they were very dry.

Eze 37:3 And he said unto me, Son of man, can these bones live? And I answered, O Lord GOD, thou knowest.

Eze 37:4 Again he said unto me, Prophesy upon these bones, and say unto them, O ye dry bones, hear the word of the LORD.

Eze 37:5 Thus saith the Lord GOD unto these bones; Behold, I will cause breath to enter into you, and ye shall live:

Eze 37:6 And I will lay sinews upon you, and will bring up flesh upon you, and cover you with skin, and put breath in you, and ye shall live; and ye shall know that I am the LORD.

Eze 37:7 So I prophesied as I was commanded: and as I prophesied, there was a noise, and behold a shaking, and the bones came together, bone to his bone.

Eze 37:8 And when I beheld, lo, the sinews and the flesh came up upon them, and the skin covered them above: but there was no breath in them.

Eze 37:9 Then said he unto me, Prophesy unto the wind, prophesy, son of man, and say to the wind, Thus saith the Lord GOD; Come from the four winds, O breath, and breathe upon these slain, that they may live.

Eze 37:10 So I prophesied as he commanded me, and the breath came into them, and they lived, and stood up upon their feet, an exceeding great army.

Eze 37:11 Then he said unto me, Son of man, these bones are the whole house of Israel: behold, they say, Our bones are dried, and our hope is lost: we are cut off for our parts.

Eze 37:12 Therefore prophesy and say unto them, Thus saith the Lord GOD; Behold, O my people, I will open your graves, and cause you to come up out of your graves, and bring you into the land of Israel.

Eze 37:13 And ye shall know that I am the LORD, when I have opened your graves, O my people, and brought you up out of your graves,

Eze 37:14 And shall put my spirit in you, and ye shall live, and I shall place you in your own land: then shall ye know that I the LORD have spoken it, and performed it, saith the LORD.

We do have a few sources which indicate some people to have motivated their cremation with a belief that the cremated will not be resurrected. I would hypothesise that this belief may have had its origin from the passage we have just reviewed i.e. no bones, no resurrection! This is however not true, or is it? We look at this a little later in the book.

Again, note the "body" and "those who dwell in the dust – graves" and "the earth (graves) will cast out the dead"…

> **_Isa 26:19_** _Thy dead men shall live, together <u>with my dead body shall they arise</u>. Awake and sing, <u>ye that dwell in dust:</u> for thy dew is as the dew of herbs, and <u>the earth shall cast out the dead.</u>_

Some theologian will probably refer to "the dust" and claim that this refers to the ashes and there you have it, nothing wrong with cremation, case closed! Please note however what scripture says and what it does not say. "**_ye that dwell in the dust_**" and not "**_ye who are dust_**"! God uses this phrase or description regarding people dwelling (sleeping) in the dust, numerous times in the Bible and this simply refers to the dead IN THE GROUND, not the cremated!

To explain "sleeping in the dust", here is one example:

> **_Dan 12:2_** _And many of <u>them that sleep in the dust of the earth shall awake,</u> some to everlasting life, and some to shame and everlasting contempt._

The Resurrection of Jesus

> **_Luk 24:38_** _And he said unto them, Why are ye troubled? and why do thoughts arise in your hearts?_
> **_Luk 24:39_** _Behold my hands and my feet, that it is I myself: <u>handle me, and see; for a spirit hath not flesh and bones, as ye see me have.</u>_
> **_Luk 24:40_** _And when he had thus spoken, he shewed them his hands and his feet._
> **_Luk 24:41_** _And while they yet believed not for joy, and wondered, he said unto them, Have ye here any meat?_
> **_Luk 24:42_** _And they gave him a piece of a broiled fish, and of an honeycomb._
> **_Luk 24:43_** _And he took it, and did eat before them._

What do we learn from this? After Jesus's resurrection, from His tomb, He had flesh and very importantly, BONES! He even ate after he was resurrected from His tomb! The next logical question must be: What would have happened if Jesus was cremated and His bones were ground to fine powder? This dear reader, must be one of the most important thoughts in your decision making process if you are in fact considering cremation!

How in seven blue blazing hells can any person of sane mind and body, of whom Satan did not rob them from their senses and logic, consider cremation when Jesus, after his resurrection, says:

TOUCH ME!
I have flesh and bone.

Please remember what I said in the beginning of the book, I believe in God's Word – fundamentally, deeply and profoundly! The rest, including the non-fundamentalists, can do just as they please, but please do not tell me you believe in God's Word!

King Saul

History with regards to King Saul is extremely significant when we discover the manifestation of God's wrath, even after death and also in the method of death. We shall look briefly at King Saul's life and subsequent death.

> ***1Sam 9:3** And the asses of Kish Saul's father were lost. And Kish said to Saul his son, Take now one of the servants with thee, and arise, go seek the asses.*

> ***1Sam 9:14** And they went up into the city: and when they were come into the city, behold, Samuel came out against them, for to go up to the high place.*
> ***1Sam 9:15** Now the LORD had told Samuel in his ear a day before Saul came, saying,*
> ***1Sam 9:16** To morrow about this time I will send thee a man out of the land of Benjamin, and thou shalt anoint him to be captain over my people Israel, that he may save my people out of the hand of the Philistines: for I have looked upon my people, because their cry is come unto me.*
> ***1Sam 9:17** And when Samuel saw Saul, the LORD said unto him, Behold the man whom I spake to thee of! this same shall reign over my people.*

God revealed to Samuel, the day before Saul's arrival, that Saul would be the king of Israel. It is clear from this that God was very pleased with Saul. In addition, Saul was a very modest and humble man.

> *1Sam 9:21 And Saul answered and said, Am not I a Benjamite, of the smallest of the tribes of Israel? and my family the least of all the families of the tribe of Benjamin? wherefore then speakest thou so to me?*

Saul is anointed as king of Israel. We again clearly see that Saul is a chosen one, elected by God, because there is none like him (Saul) among all the people. The Spirit of God will come upon him and he will be transformed into a different man.

> *1Sam 10:1 Then Samuel took a vial of oil, and poured it upon his head, and kissed him, and said, Is it not because the LORD hath anointed thee to be captain over his inheritance?*
> *1Sam 10:6 And the Spirit of the LORD will come upon thee, and thou shalt prophesy with them, and shalt be turned into another man.*
> *1Sam 10:7 And let it be, when these signs are come unto thee, that thou do as occasion serve thee; for God is with thee.*
> *1Sam 10:24 And Samuel said to all the people, See ye him whom the LORD hath chosen, that there is none like him among all the people? And all the people shouted, and said, God save the king.*
> *1Sam 10:25 Then Samuel told the people the manner of the kingdom, and wrote it in a book, and laid it up before the LORD. And Samuel sent all the people away, every man to his house.*

Later in Saul's life, he completely looses his modesty and now only thinks of himself. When he is terrified, he prays to God, but God refuses to answer him.

> *1Sam 28:5 And when Saul saw the host of the Philistines, he was afraid, and his heart greatly trembled.*
> *1Sam 28:6 And when Saul enquired of the LORD, the LORD answered him not, neither by dreams, nor by Urim, nor by prophets.*

How many children of God attend church every Sunday (and Saturday for others) and experience or feels as though God is not answering their prayers. They may even ask questions like: "why is God punishing me?" One of the biggest reasons for this is the false church with her false teachers whom make you practise and believe in a religion which is totally in vain!

> *Jas 1:26 If any man among you seem to be religious, and bridleth not his tongue, but deceiveth his own heart, <u>this man's religion is vain.</u>*
> *Jas 1:27 <u>Pure religion and undefiled before God and the Father is this, To visit the fatherless and widows in their affliction, and to keep himself unspotted from the world.</u>*

(These practises are thoroughly discussed in my first book.)
Anyhow, the great King Saul goes on to do the unthinkable!

> *1Sam 28:7 Then said Saul unto his servants, <u>Seek me a woman that hath a familiar spirit, that I may go to her, and enquire of her.</u> And his servants said to him, Behold, there is a woman that hath a familiar spirit at Endor.*
> *1Sam 28:8 And Saul disguised himself, and put on other raiment, and he went, and two men with him, and they came to the woman by night: and he said, I pray thee, <u>divine unto me by the familiar spirit, and bring me him up, whom I shall name unto thee.</u>*
> *1Sam 28:9 And the woman said unto him, <u>Behold, thou knowest what Saul hath done, how he hath cut off those that have familiar spirits, and the wizards, out of the land: wherefore then layest thou a snare for my life, to cause me to die?</u>*

Saul himself had all the people with "familiar spirits" (mediums) "cut off" from the land. This was a scriptural thing to do, because we may never have anything to do with "familiar spirits" or "mediums", however now in his dry spell with God, he visits a medium which is a grievous sin and abomination!

> *1Sam 28:18 <u>Because thou obeyedst not the voice of the LORD,</u> nor executedst his fierce wrath upon Amalek, therefore hath the LORD done this thing unto thee this day.*
> *1Sam 28:19 Moreover the LORD will also deliver Israel with thee into the hand of the Philistines: <u>and to morrow shalt thou and thy sons be with me:</u> the LORD also shall deliver the host of Israel into the hand of the Philistines.*

"And tomorrow shalt thou and thy sons be with me" means that Saul and his sons will die the next day. This inconceivable sin of Saul is the proverbial last straw and so he seals, not only his own fate, but also that of his sons.

Saul started to sin to such an extent where God did not answer his prayers and he goes and commits even bigger sins. How many of us do exactly the same in our lives today?

Let's look at the events surrounding Saul's death.
The Philistines surrounded Saul and his men. His sons are killed, just as the "familiar spirit" told him the previous night. Saul is terrified and requests his arm bearer to kill him, but the arm bearer refuses. Saul then commits suicide (or rather attempts to commit suicide).

> *1Sam 31:2 And the Philistines followed hard upon Saul and upon his sons; and the Philistines slew Jonathan, and Abinadab, and Malchishua, Saul's sons.*
> *1Sam 31:3 And the battle went sore against Saul, and the archers hit him; and he was sore wounded of the archers.*
> *1Sam 31:4 Then said Saul unto his armourbearer, Draw thy sword, and thrust me through therewith; lest these uncircumcised come and thrust me through, and abuse me. But his armourbearer would not; for he was sore afraid. Therefore Saul took a sword, and fell upon it.*
> *1Sam 31:5 And when his armourbearer saw that Saul was dead, he fell likewise upon his sword, and died with him.*
> *1Sam 31:6 So Saul died, and his three sons, and his armourbearer, and all his men, that same day together.*

And so, the prophecy of the familiar spirit is fulfilled. Saul and his sons perish on the same day. During the Philistines quest to collect the spoils of war, they came across the bodies of Saul and his sons. They beheaded Saul and affixed his and his son's bodies to the wall of Bethlehem as a symbol of the Philistines victory for all to witness.

> *1Sam 31:8 And it came to pass on the morrow, when the Philistines came to strip the slain, that they found Saul and his three sons fallen in mount Gilboa.*
> *1Sam 31:9 And they cut off his head, and stripped off his armour, and sent into the land of the Philistines round about, to publish it in the house of their idols, and among the people.*
> *1Sam 31:10 And they put his armour in the house of Ashtaroth: and they fastened his body to the wall of Bethshan.*

(In my other book I explain the origin of Easter which is absolutely pagan and has nothing to do with the God of Abraham, Isaac and Jacob, but celebrated religiously with all the other false rituals by Christians – note "***the house of Ashtaroth***" in verse 10 above)

> ***1Sam 31:11 And when the inhabitants of Jabeshgilead heard of that which the Philistines had done to Saul;***
> ***1Sam 31:12 All the valiant men arose, and went all night, and took the body of Saul and the bodies of his sons from the wall of Bethshan, and came to Jabesh, and burnt them there.***

Even after the wrath of God was poured onto Saul, his body remains to have great value for his people. Amidst great risk and danger, some valiant men go in the night and remove, (steal) Saul's body and that of his sons from the wall. These courageous men have no other option but to burn the bodies, in other words, cremate the remains of Saul and his sons.

We may reason that circumstances left the brave men very little option, but to burn the bodies. If we however consider what we have learned thus far from scriptures with regards to the relationship between the burning of bodies, directly linked to the wrath of God, it was most probably the same wrath of God which had the burning of Saul's body as a subsequence to his sinful actions. More importantly though, the bones of Saul were buried after his body was burnt and not ground to a pulp! Again, even after all Saul's atrocities, his bones are buried according to the statutes of scripture together with the bones of his sons. (Another reason for burning the body's may have been to prevent the philistines to again take the bodies and reattach them to the wall, like they had previously done)

> ***1Sam 31:13 And they took their bones, and buried them under a tree at Jabesh, and fasted seven days.***

As I have mentioned earlier, I am not immune to deceit and especially since one must always discover new truths in scripture, one must also be prepared to revise previous convictions when God reveals (opens) the scriptures more and more. I now need to share such a revision of my own. In my previous book I made the statement that Saul committed suicide and keeping in mind what we have read so far, it does not seem like I made the statement in error. I have never heard of any person or teacher, not supporting the fact that Saul committed suicide. In my studies for this book, however I came across new scriptural facts.

Let's have a look…
After Saul fell into his sword, in other words appeared to have committed suicide, he asked the Amalekite for assistance…

> *2Sam 1:8 And he said unto me, Who art thou? And I answered him, I am an Amalekite.*
> *2Sam 1:9 He said unto me again, <u>Stand, I pray thee, upon me, and slay me: for anguish is come upon me, because my life is yet whole in me.</u>*
> *2Sam 1:10 <u>So I stood upon him, and slew him, because I was sure that he could not live after that he was fallen:</u> and I took the crown that was upon his head, and the bracelet that was on his arm, and have brought them hither unto my lord.*

We learn from this that Saul was very weak from his suicide attempt, but he did in fact not die. His life was still "whole" in him. He instructed the Amalekite to finish him off, so to speak. The Amalekite obeys Saul's instruction and kills him. He then takes the crown and bracelet to David as proof that Saul had in fact died.

What follows is yet again a wonderfully significant life lesson from Gods Word!

> *2Sam 1:13 And David said unto the young man that told him, Whence art thou? And he answered, I am the son of a stranger, an Amalekite.*
> *2Sam 1:14 And David said unto him, <u>How wast thou not afraid to stretch forth thine hand to destroy the LORD'S anointed?</u>*
> *2Sam 1:15 And David called one of the young men, and said, <u>Go near, and fall upon him. And he smote him that he died.</u>*
> *2Sam 1:16 And David said unto him, <u>Thy blood be upon thy head; for thy mouth hath testified against thee, saying, I have slain the LORD'S anointed.</u>*

Even though the sins of Saul were inconceivably bad, David still honours Saul as an anointed of God. If we consider the testimony by the Amalekite in today's day and age, we would probably acquit him of any retribution for his act, but what does David do? He has the Amalekite killed, on the spot! Why, because the Amalekite took a life of an anointed of God, even though Saul's sins were terrible, to put it mildly.

On a different subject which is not part of this book, we learn something very valuable from these events. Saul was probably weak and dizzy due to blood loss, to such an extent where he did not have enough strength or energy to stab himself again, in order to complete the suicide. However, the person who took him out of his misery so to speak got killed for assisting

Saul. What do we learn from this? The practice of assisting someone to die, i.e. mercy death, assisted suicide, euthanasia is totally against scripture!

(In the month of July 2014, the Anglican Archbishop Emeritus Desmond Tutu, stated 'in his personal capacity', that he supports euthanasia and that South African laws must be changed. This is in addition to same-sex marriages and abortion that he also supports amongst other atrocities which are directly in opposition the scriptures – why am I not surprised?)

You will remember that one of the methods of God's anger or punishment manifest itself in burning of bodies and crushing of bones. Saul's sins were so bad that God used the same method here. Some may argue that there were no other option but to burn the bodies of Saul and his sons. God is not bound to circumstances which He cannot control my friend! There is no way God will go totally against His own Word, (scriptures) just because He cannot control the physical circumstances.

You may think I am making this up, but I recently read a book where the author answers questions related to, what we may call "collateral damage". For example, a plane crashes and everyone on board dies. Why did everyone die, is the question? There must have been some of Gods children on the plane, we automatically assume. The answer given by the author? He states that Gods children were simply at the wrong place at the wrong time. Excuse my French, but this is nothing but bullshit! An event occurs where death and dismay is going to take place and God says: "oops, sorry I wasn't aware that you were going to be there my child, well bad luck I guess, wrong place at the wrong time. I am sorry; this is not the God I worship! I may very well be dyslexic, but I can assure you…

My God is not dyslexic!

One more extremely important note from these events we have to consider is, after all that have happened to Saul, his bones were still buried according to the statutes of scripture! I am not sure whether Saul's skull was buried with his bones. The events would indicate that it wasn't, but I can't support this with scripture. (If you perhaps know the answer to this question dear reader, I would appreciate an email from you)

Burial – Old Fashioned Technology

Let's be honest with each other and make the statement which the majority of people will make namely:

"The traditional burial or funeral is old fashioned, old technology and outdated in our "modern era".

This argument is given momentum by the following statement:
"If the technology for cremation was available in biblical times, the Israelites would have surely used it."

Let me remind you that we have already listed a multitude of verses in scripture where the following is clearly comprehensible:
Burning of bodies
Bones burnt to lime (ashes)
Bones crushed and broken to pieces
Bones removed from graves to be burned and crushed.

We may want to argue that the above does not explicitly indicate cremation, but let's do like God instructs us…Jesus says:

> **Mat 22:29 _Jesus answered and said unto them, Ye do err, not knowing the scriptures, nor the power of God._**

"ye do err" means "you stray" because we do not know the scriptures.

Let's Search scriptures then.

> **Act 17:11 _These were more noble than those in Thessalonica, in that they received the word with all readiness of mind, and searched the scriptures daily, whether those things were so._**

The god Molech

Again, in my other book we delve deeply into the details regarding the god Molech, who he was, which practices were dedicated to him and how he was worshipped, even by the Israelites amongst others. In a nut shell, he was the god of fire and especially small children and babies were sacrificed in the most brutal and disgusting ways to please Molech.

Tophet – Valley of Slaughter

Tophet is a place where archaeologists unearthed thousands of children's bones. These children, from young children to babies, were burnt alive as a sacrifice to Molech. God later changed the name of Tophet to: "The valley of Slaughter", because of the brutal, barbaric slaughter of children which served as sacrifices in idol worship.

> *Jer 19:5 They have built also the high places of Baal, to burn their sons with fire for burnt offerings unto Baal,* which I commanded not, nor spake it, neither came it into my mind:
> *Jer 19:6 Therefore, behold, the days come, saith the LORD, that this place shall no more be called Tophet, nor The valley of the son of Hinnom, but The valley of slaughter.*

Note what God says: this barbaric practise did not even enter His mind. He never commanded nor spoke of it!
(Baal, Molech and Milcom are different names, amongst others, for the same god)

Let's look at the meaning of **"Tophet"**.
Strong's Hebrew and Greek Dictionaries[13]
Tophet – Word Number H8613

תָּפְתֶּה

tophteh
tof-teh'
***Tophteh*, a place of cremation: Tophet.**

Did you get that dear reader?

A Place of Cremation!

Despicable Abomination

Scripture contains a multitude of passages related to this despicable abomination, but we will only look at a few, just so we get the picture.

> *Eze 16:20 Moreover* thou hast taken thy sons and thy daughters, whom thou hast borne unto me, and these hast thou sacrificed unto them to be devoured. Is this of thy whoredoms a small matter,
> *Eze 16:21 That thou hast slain my children, and delivered them to cause them to pass through the fire for them?*

Did you get that? God calls this:

"WHOREDOM"

> *2Chr 28:3 Moreover he burnt incense in the valley of the son of Hinnom, <u>and burnt his children in the fire, after the abominations of the heathen</u> whom the LORD had cast out before the children of Israel.*

God declares it an **ABOMINATION OF THE HEATHEN** to burn bodies with fire. This is the reason why God only uses this abomination on the condemned in His anger and wrath!

Again…

THOU SHALT NOT DO SO!
THIS IS AN ABOMINATION!

> *Deu 12:31 <u>Thou shalt not do so unto the LORD thy God: for every abomination to the LORD, which he hateth, have they done unto their gods; for even their sons and their daughters they have burnt in the fire to their gods.</u>*

God says: "Thou shalt not", but the church says: "Thou shalt!"
Now look at the verse that follows directly after the one above:

> *Deu 12:32 <u>What thing soever I command you, observe to do it: thou shalt not add thereto, nor diminish from it.</u>*

If God calls this practice an abomination, a whoredom, and God explicitly commands us not to do it and even tells us not to add or diminish anything from it, ask yourself the following questions:

- *Can we add to it what the church and preachers of today tells us and accept cremation as not condemned by the Bible, by God even?*
- *Can we diminish from it and state that we are not cremating to Molech, therefore cremation is not condemned by the Bible?*

Let me remind you of the following very significant event and God's feeling towards this abomination which drew God's wrath in a frightening manner!

> *Amo 2:1 Thus saith the LORD; For three transgressions of Moab, and for four, I will not turn away the punishment thereof;* <u>*because he burned the bones of the king of Edom into lime:-*</u> *(ashes)*
> *Amo 2:2 But* <u>*I will send a fire upon Moab, and it shall devour the palaces of Kerioth: and Moab shall die with tumult, with shouting,*</u> *and with the sound of the trumpet:*

Cremation existed long before Jesus Christ Price!

Can you see that cremation was in existence from the earliest times? Can you see that it is a whoredom in Gods eyes? Can you see that it draws God's wrath? Can you see that God uses this abomination only as severe punishment for his enemies, the condemned, who gravely sinned against Him?

Can you really sit back and still declare that there is absolutely nothing wrong with cremation? In the absurd event that you do, I don't have a problem with it, except for one small technical issue. If you would just agree that you don't believe in God's Word, we can be good friends. You are welcome to try and prove me wrong in this regard, but you may find it to be a little difficult. You however remain most welcome; I am always open to new convictions in light of scripture, so long as you quote scripture.

The Body – Not simply Remains!

What does scripture teach us regarding the body?

> *1Cor 6:14 And God hath both raised up the Lord, and will also raise up us by his own power.*
> *1Cor 6:15 <u>Know ye not that your bodies are the members of Christ? shall I then take the members of Christ, and make them the members of an harlot? God forbid.</u>*
> *1Cor 6:16 What? <u>know ye not that he which is joined to an harlot is one body? for two, saith he, shall be one flesh.</u>*
> *1Cor 6:17 <u>But he that is joined unto the Lord is one spirit.</u>*
> *1Cor 6:18 Flee fornication. Every sin that a man doeth is without the body; but he that committeth fornication sinneth against his own body.*

> *1Cor 6:19 What? know ye not that your body is the temple of the Holy Ghost which is in you, which ye have of God, and ye are not your own?*
> *1Cor 6:20 For ye are bought with a price: therefore glorify God in your body, and in your spirit, which are God's.*

So far we have learned that to burn bodies is an abomination and whoredom. A huge misconception has manifested itself in Christianity where the Word of God refers to whoredom. Immediately we all assume that this term, "whoredom", is not applicable to us, we are churchgoing folk, for Pete sake, we shout! The truth is that whoredom; most of the time refers to idolatrous acts. Again we say: We don't practice any form of idolatry, we have absolutely nothing to do with it! If you reason like this, a rude awakening awaits you. I guarantee - if you are a main stream church member, you are practicing idolatrous acts without even realising it. I discuss many of these so-called Christian rituals which are as pagan as can be in my previous book.

Anyhow, to have yourself or your loved ones cremated is whoredom against God, period! What's more, you desecrate the body, a creation of God which is not your own and does not even belong to you!

We look at few more verses concerning the importance of the body. You may think that it's only applicable to the living body, but we will see later that the remains are also very important.

> *Ecc 5:6 Suffer not thy mouth to cause thy flesh to sin; neither say thou before the angel, that it was an error: wherefore should God be angry at thy voice, and destroy the work of thine hands?*

Don't by means of a decision to cremate, cause your body to sin, with your mouth and later say that it was an error, because God will be angry!

Even the beast's body will be destroyed by fire! (This beast is not a goat or a dog)

> *Dan 7:11 I beheld then because of the voice of the great words which the horn spake: I beheld even till the beast was slain, and his body destroyed, and given to the burning flame.*

Our bodies will also burn, if we continue to make a mockery of God's Word!

> *Mat 5:30 And if thy right hand offend thee, cut it off, and cast it from thee: for it is profitable for thee that one of thy members should perish, and not that thy whole body should be cast into hell.*

> *Mat 10:28 And fear not them which kill the body, but are not able to kill the soul: but rather fear him which is able to destroy both soul and body in hell.*

You will remember that after Jesus's resurrection, He had flesh, bones and even ate food.

> *Mat 26:12 For in that she hath poured this ointment on my body, she did it for my burial.*

If the dead body is simply "remains" which can be thrown to the dogs, or worse, thrown into the fire like a piece of wood, why do we read he following in scripture? Ask yourself why? Is it because there were no cremation technology, or has it been written and recorded as an example and guide for us to follow, a statute even?

> *Mat 27:58 He went to Pilate, and begged the body of Jesus. Then Pilate commanded the body to be delivered.*
> *Mat 27:59 And when Joseph had taken the body, he wrapped it in a clean linen cloth,*
> *Mat 27:60 And laid it in his own new tomb, which he had hewn out in the rock: and he rolled a great stone to the door of the sepulchre, and departed.*

> *Mar 14:8 She hath done what she could: she is come aforehand to anoint my body to the burying.*

> *Luk 24:2 And they found the stone rolled away from the sepulchre.*
> *Luk 24:3 And they entered in, and found not the body of the Lord Jesus.*

If Jesus was cremated, would He have been resurrected? I don't know, but what I do know is: how can one possibly associate cremation with what we just read?

> *Joh 2:21 But he spake of the temple of his body.*

Once again, if this woman was cremated, this miracle would not have been in the Bible!

> *Act 9:38 And forasmuch as Lydda was nigh to Joppa, and the disciples had heard that Peter was there, they sent unto him two men, desiring him that he would not delay to come to them.*
> *Act 9:39 Then Peter arose and went with them. When he was come, they brought him into the upper chamber: and all the widows stood by him weeping, and shewing the coats and garments which Dorcas made, while she was with them.*
> *Act 9:40 But Peter put them all forth, and kneeled down, and prayed; and turning him to the body said, Tabitha, arise. And she opened her eyes: and when she saw Peter, she sat up.*
> *Act 9:41 And he gave her his hand, and lifted her up, and when he had called the saints and widows, presented her alive.*
> *Act 9:42 And it was known throughout all Joppa; and many believed in the Lord.*

Redemption of our body

> *Rom 8:23 And not only they, but ourselves also, which have the firstfruits of the Spirit, even we ourselves groan within ourselves, waiting for the adoption, to wit, the redemption of our body.*

> *1Cor 6:19 What? know ye not that your body is the temple of the Holy Ghost which is in you, which ye have of God, and ye are not your own?*
> *1Cor 6:20 For ye are bought with a price: therefore glorify God in your body, and in your spirit, which are God's.*

It says here that our bodies do not belong to us. This is what God's Word says. Do you believe what God's Word says? If so, does it not tell you that we do not have a say in terms of the disposal of our bodies as far as cremation is concerned, because it does not belong to us? We have been bought with a very high price; therefore glorify God also with your body by not committing it to the pagan practise of burning it to whoredom!

We are familiar with the good old 1 Corinthians 13 which is often quoted at weddings.

> *1Cor 13:2 And though I have the gift of prophecy, and understand all mysteries, and all knowledge; and though I have all faith, so that I could remove mountains, and have not charity, I am nothing.*
>
> *1Cor 13:3 And though I bestow all my goods to feed the poor, and though I give my body to be burned, and have not charity, it profiteth me nothing.*
>
> *1Cor 13:4 Charity suffereth long, and is kind; charity envieth not; charity vaunteth not itself, is not puffed up,*

Paul is not talking about cremation here. He is implying that even if he is so humble that he is willing to burn his own body i.e. desecrating it, and he has no love, it will profit nothing. If you however have any love for God, you will never commit this abomination, not against your own body, nor against a loved one's body. I hear people say: "I love the Lord", but do we really know what it means to love God?

To love God is to keep his statutes and to gain knowledge of Him, getting to know Him. Will you marry someone of whom you know nothing about? Their preferences, what they love, what they hate, their dreams, passions and goals? If not, how can we declare that we love God if we don't know what He loves, what He hates, what His plans are etc. Worst of all, how can we love God if we have no knowledge of Him? You may think that you know God from all your years of attending church, but I put it to you that the God of the Bible and the god of the church, is not the same god, not by a long shot my friend! Ask yourself how on earth a spiritual leader can teach "the flock" that they have the right to choose between cremation and a traditional burial. They can teach this, but on one condition, they must then admit the following:

> ## Job 21:14
> *Therefore they say unto God, Depart from us; for we desire not the knowledge of thy ways.*

We will now have a closer look at 1 Corinthians 15. It is quite a lengthy passage related to the body, but take head of the first verse we quote, which coincidently is synonym with the verse quoted above.

> ### 1Cor 15:34
> ### *Awake to righteousness, and sin not; for some have not the knowledge of God: I speak this to your shame.*

Paul says:

"Some of you don't have knowledge of God and this is to your shame". Paul is not talking to some undiscovered pigmy tribe in the Amazon; Paul is speaking to Gods people here! Most of the time, these people who have no knowledge of God is the well-respected congregation member, the doctor and professor of theology. They think they know everything due to their theological qualifications, and they teach people thus, but in reality they have no knowledge of God, most commonly these people are the GREAT CHRISTIAN'S of this world! It seems to me, the higher up in theology you are, the less your knowledge of God is!

> *1Cor 15:35 But some man will say, How are the dead raised up? and with what body do they come?*
> *1Cor 15:36 Thou fool, that which thou sowest is not quickened, except it die:*
> *1Cor 15:37 And that which thou sowest, thou sowest not that body that shall be, but bare grain, it may chance of wheat, or of some other grain:*
> *1Cor 15:38 But God giveth it a body as it hath pleased him, and to every seed his own body.*

Paul says:

If you were to enquire about the resurrected body you will be a fool. Does this then contradict what we have learned about the body of Jesus and the bones of the dead which will be covered with sinews, flesh and spirit? No, not in the slightest! Jesus's resurrected body had flesh and bones and He even ate food after his resurrection, but it was not the same flesh as we have on our bodies now. Jesus's body was (and still is) the "glorified" body. In short, Paul is saying that if we think that we will be resurrected with the same (vile) body we have now, we will be fools. We have to die in order to be resurrected (although there would be some in the last day whom will not have to die in order to receive their "glorified" body). "Dying" in this passage is synonymous with the dead body inside a grave. Why? Because the current body is sown, like a grain of wheat in the soil, which will (symbolically) grow into the resurrected glorified body!

(How about a quick experiment? Take a grain of wheat, burn it to ashes in an oven until there is nothing but a speck of dust left, then bury it in the garden. Count exactly how many days it takes for a wheat plant to grow from this "grain". Please let me know of your finding – If I am still alive :-)

Then only will God give the seed (the buried body or remains) a glorified body as it pleases him (To whom He wants to give)

Question: Did we in any way, shape or form read that cremation is being taught, validated or approved? **NO!**

1Cor 15:39 All flesh is not the same flesh: but there is one kind of flesh of men, another flesh of beasts, another of fishes, and another of birds.
1Cor 15:40 There are also celestial bodies, and bodies terrestrial: but the glory of the celestial is one, and the glory of the terrestrial is another.
1Cor 15:41 There is one glory of the sun, and another glory of the moon, and another glory of the stars: for one star differeth from another star in glory.
1Cor 15:42 So also is the resurrection of the dead. It is sown in corruption; it is raised in incorruption:
1Cor 15:43 It is sown in dishonour; it is raised in glory: it is sown in weakness; it is raised in power:

Paul says:
All flesh is not the same just as we have learned from the previous section. He teaches us that the flesh of men and the flesh of animals are different.
The celestial (heavenly) body is different from the terrestrial (earthly) body and even the glory of these bodies is different, i.e. heavenly and earthly. The flesh and bones of Jesus, after His resurrection is not the same flesh and bone with which He died and our bodies will be the same, before and after, as was that of Jesus. The body is sown in dishonour, but raised in glory! Never again will the resurrected flesh and bone age, decay, get sick or die, ever again!

Question: Did we in any way, shape or form read that cremation is being taught, validated or approved? **NO!**

1Cor 15:44 It is sown a natural body; it is raised a spiritual body. There is a natural body, and there is a spiritual body.
1Cor 15:45 And so it is written, The first man Adam was made a living soul; the last Adam was made a quickening spirit.
1Cor 15:46 Howbeit that was not first which is spiritual, but that which is natural; and afterward that which is spiritual.

> *1Cor 15:47* *The first man is of the earth, earthy: the second man is the Lord from heaven.*
> *1Cor 15:48* *As is the earthy, such are they also that are earthy: and as is the heavenly, such are they also that are heavenly.*

We have to take special note to what Paul says here: "a Spiritual body is raised". For some or other reason I always thought that we were going to be spirits, like ghosts when we receive our "spiritual" bodies". The proverbial ghost, sitting on a cloud and playing the harp. I suspect there are people who still have this misconception about the heavenly, resurrected body. So, when we read of the spiritual body, we automatically think of a ghostlike, smoke like "thong" that floats in the air. It is also because of this misconception that people think there is nothing wrong with cremation i.e. we will be a ghost floating in the wind with no flesh or bones!

To justify cremation on this bases, I trust you can see, is an enormous blunder!

Question: Did we in any way, shape or form read that cremation is being taught, validated or approved? **NO!**

We continue.

> *1Cor 15:49* *And as we have borne the image of the earthy, we shall also bear the image of the heavenly.*
> *1Cor 15:50* *Now this I say, brethren, that flesh and blood cannot inherit the kingdom of God; neither doth corruption inherit incorruption.*
> *1Cor 15:51* *Behold, I shew you a mystery; We shall not all sleep, but we shall all be changed,*
> *1Cor 15:52* *In a moment, in the twinkling of an eye, at the last trump: for the trumpet shall sound, and the dead shall be raised incorruptible, and we shall be changed.*

Paul says:

We will look exactly the same in heaven as we look on earth at the moment. We will bear the same image.

Ask yourself, do you even have the right to completely destroy your image (including your bones) by cremation if we will "borne", in other words have the same likeness in heaven? Would this blatant desecration of the same image on earth as in heaven be acceptable to God, even when the Bible tells you that your body does not belong to you? In the words of Paul: "GOD FORBID!"

The flesh and blood which cannot inherit heaven is explained by Paul when he tells us that:

All flesh is not the same. There are earthly bodies and heavenly bodies.

The corruptible is sown (buried) and the incorruptible (heavily body) is resurrected.

The earthly body is not the same corruptible flesh and blood of the incorruptible body of the glorified body. We can never enter heaven with the same flesh and blood we have here on earth.

Some people will still be alive during the resurrection. These people will receive a heavenly body in the twinkling of an eye, without having to die first, because they cannot inherit heaven with the same corruptible flesh and blood we have on earth. This is also testimony to the fact that we will have exactly the same image as we have now, after the resurrection!

All considered thus far, the dead are referred to as have been sown, buried and not those whom have been scattered as fine bone powder!

It sort of brings new meaning to the following well known verse, doesn't it?

Gal 6:7 Be not deceived; God is not mocked: for whatsoever a man soweth, that shall he also reap.

What will you "reap" when you "soweth" cremation…..?

Question: Did we in any way, shape or form read that cremation is being taught, validated or approved? **NO!**

1Cor 15:53 For this corruptible must put on incorruption, and this mortal must put on immortality.
1Cor 15:54 So when this corruptible shall have put on incorruption, and this mortal shall have put on immortality, then shall be brought to pass the saying that is written, Death is swallowed up in victory.
1Cor 15:55 O death, where is thy sting? O grave, where is thy victory?
1Cor 15:56 The sting of death is sin; and the strength of sin is the law.

Paul says:
The sting of death is sin and the strength of sin is the law.
What have we learned so far? That it would be a sin to have yourself or anyone else cremated and this **IS A SIN!**

Question: Did we in any way, shape or form read that cremation is being taught, validated or approved? **NO!**

More about the Body

Paul says he carries the marks of Jesus in his body, meaning the scars of when Paul was beaten and tortured.

> *Gal 6:17 From henceforth let no man trouble me: <u>for I bear in my body the marks of the Lord Jesus.</u>*

Jesus carries the same scars of the crucifixion, even after his resurrection. In other words, His glorified body is such an identical image or replica to His previous earthly body, that it even has the identical scars! How on earth could one, knowing this, justify cremation in any way or form whatsoever?

> *Joh 20:25 The other disciples therefore said unto him, We have seen the Lord. But he said unto them, <u>Except I shall see in his hands the print of the nails, and put my finger into the print of the nails, and thrust my hand into his side, I will not believe.</u>*
> *Joh 20:26 And after eight days again his disciples were within, and Thomas with them: then came Jesus, the doors being shut, and stood in the midst, and said, Peace be unto you.*
> *Joh 20:27 <u>Then saith he to Thomas, Reach hither thy finger, and behold my hands; and reach hither thy hand, and thrust it into my side: and be not faithless, but believing.</u>*
> *Joh 20:28 And Thomas answered and said unto him, My Lord and my God.*

Would Jesus have had these scars if He was cremated? I don't know. You will have to decide on your own.

Here we are taught that Jesus is the saviour of the body. Not scattered bone fragments!

> *Eph 5:23 For the husband is the head of the wife, even as Christ is the head of the church: and <u>he is the saviour of the body.</u>*

Just a couple more statutes regarding the importance of the body:

> *Lev 21:5 They shall not make baldness upon their head, neither shall they shave off the corner of their beard, <u>nor make any cuttings in their flesh.</u>*

> ***Lev 19:28*** ***Ye shall not make any cuttings in your flesh for the dead, nor print any marks upon you:*** *I am the LORD.*

Now ask yourself: If you now know that we will look the same in heaven as we do on earth, even with scars, what gives you the right, if you declare that you believe the Word of God, to take this image and burn it to oblivion with fire and grind the most valuable of all, the bones to a fine powder in the earthly hell of cremation?

(For the young people of today – It would appear that in today's day and age, if a person is not covered in tattoos they need to be admitted to a psychiatric ward because they are totally antisocial. Now, my books are not written for the non-believer, nor the self-professed believer who doesn't give a rats behind about the Word of God. My books are written for Gods elected, those who truly know what it means to know God, to seek knowledge of Him. For the rest, I don't give a rats behind either. I am not asking you to believe me, nor am I a soul winner for God, like the churches. My task is to share Biblical truths with the person who desires to follow Gods Word only. For those people I say, from scriptures, please have nothing to do with tattoos and piercings, believe me, I know what I am talking about! For the rest, go wild, follow the majority and tattoo even your toenails!

> *"nor print any marks upon you: I am the LORD."*

Chapter 6

Thou Shalt not Judge!

Awake to righteousness, and sin not; for some have not the knowledge of God: I speak this to your shame.

1Cor 15:34

THE UDT Preachers

I have baptised my UDT preachers as such, due to the following, let's see if you can spot it.

> *2Tim 4:3 For the time will come when they will not endure sound doctrine; but after their own lusts shall they heap to themselves teachers, having itching ears;*

Can you see it? Not?
Let me explain:

> *2Tim 4:3 For the time will come when they <u>will not endure sound doctrine</u>; but after their own lusts shall they <u>heap to themselves teachers</u>, having itching ears;*

God specifically tells us in His Word that there will be a time when people will heap (appoint) for themselves, teachers (preacher's) because they have itchy ears. Another way of putting it will be: They appoint for themselves teachers who can soothe their ears with what they like to hear, regardless of what the bible says. These people are appointed and paid by the people who they need to soothe in their hearing of what they prefer to hear. This scenario has the subsequent result that if the preacher so much as dares to preach biblical truths, where these truths differs from what the employers (congregation members) wants to hear, he gets fired or loses paying congregation members!

These preachers are:

Unsound

Doctrine

Teachers

They are all the same. I make the following statement:
Theological colleges, theological universities and theological cemeteries, sorry – "seminaries" do not teach people to find nor learn the truth, but their goal is in fact to teach how to conceal and disguise the truth. In my other book I discuss works of some of the highest South African theological professors and it is shocking when you compare their teachings with scriptures. People would contact me and ask me in disbelief: "Did the professor really say that?"

You see dear reader, in my 25 years plus of Bible study (which means absolutely nothing anyway) I have witnessed time and time again, the golden truth of the following Words of Jesus:

> **_Mat 11:25_ At that time Jesus answered and said, _I thank thee, O Father, Lord of heaven and earth, because thou hast hid these things from the wise and prudent, and hast revealed them unto babes._**
> **_Mat 11:26_ Even so, Father: for so it seemed good in thy sight.**

I guarantee you, backed by God Himself, the Bible is not locked for ordinary people like us and only understood by the church and its so-called wise men, like they try and convince us.

I can never say it enough:

ALWAYS BEWARE OF THE CHURCH AND HER TEACHERS!!!

> **_Jer 2:8_ The priests said not, Where is the LORD? and they that handle the law knew me not: the pastors also transgressed**

> *against me, and the prophets prophesied by Baal, and walked*
> *after things that do not profit.*
> *Jer 10:21 For the pastors are become brutish, and have not*
> *sought the LORD: therefore they shall not prosper, and all their*
> *flocks shall be scattered.*
> *Jer 23:11 For both prophet and priest are profane; yea, in my*
> *house have I found their wickedness, saith the LORD.*
> *Eze 34:1 And the word of the LORD came unto me, saying,*
> *Eze 34:2 Son of man, prophesy against the shepherds of Israel,*
> *prophesy, and say unto them, Thus saith the Lord GOD unto*
> *the shepherds; Woe be to the shepherds of Israel that do feed*
> *themselves! should not the shepherds feed the flocks?*
> *Eze 34:3 Ye eat the fat, and ye clothe you with the wool, ye kill*
> *them that are fed: but ye feed not the flock.*

Even though I am a South African citizen and we will look at one of the highest South African church presidents, most churches and most preachers and ministers around the entire globe are no different in their teachings regarding cremation.

Church Leaders and Cremation

Doctor Isak Burger is the president of the Apostolic Faith Mission in South Africa.

I call him the Pope of the AFM, merely to indicate his absolute authority over the AFM.

(For those who are not aware, the name "Isak" is Afrikaans for the Biblical name "Isaac".

Apology:

In the Afrikaans version of my book, I also quoted the Afrikaans version of Burger's book. Although his book was translated in English, I was unable to obtain a copy of the English version. Therefore, when I quote passages from Burger's book, it will be my own translation into English. In this regard, please do not take my translation of the text in quotations marks as literally accurate, word for word and letter for letter, but rather concentrate on the message the quotations portray, as every effort has been made to accurately reflect the core message of every quoted passage, from his book, in Afrikaans: **"5 Minute voor en na die dood"**. It is for this reason that I will refrain from using quotation marks, but still display my translation in bold and italic text.

On page 1, the reader is informed that Burger's book has been translated into English, Arabic, Indian dialect and soon it will also be available in Portuguese and Russian. Burger's book is actually a combination of 2 previous books he had written and combined and we are told on page 7 that 180 000 books have been printed. On the book cover it states: "More than 130 000 sold".

Why do I deem it important to share this information? If, God forbid, the good doctor is in fact a UDT (Unsound Doctrine Teacher) we have at the very least, a potential number of 180 000 people who may be corrupted in terms of cremation and the Bible. Although we will not be looking at the main subject of the book, we look briefly at his teachings regarding cremation contained in his book.

On page 192, we read the following:

> *Is it wrong to have myself cremated?*
> *Thought the Bible does not leave us in the dark regarding what happens to one's spirit/soul, the question regarding what should or needs to happen with the body is being asked more and more. The bible is clear about what will happen with the body during the resurrection. Regardless of the condition of the body, whether it is in a grave, in a state of decomposition, returned to dust or burnt to ash, devoured by a beast, or in the ocean, whatever the condition of the believers body, no matter what and where, on the day of resurrection, the Lord Jesus Christ will resurrect and revive that which is left, where after the believer will be in heaven, with Christ for ever.*

He then quotes in brackets the following verses:
(1 Cor. 15:51-54 and 1 Ths. 4:15-17).

He then states:

> *The question however is whether it is wrong or sinful if the remains of a believer are cremated.*

Please note: The doctor says that the body (remains) of the believer will be resurrected, even if it was cremated (burnt to ash). He then quotes two sections from scripture in brackets)

A phenomenon I have seen in all my years of reading so-called Christian books is that when the highly educated theologian makes a statement, they usually supply a quotation from scripture in brackets and then continue with their teaching. Ask yourself why this seems to be the norm? Is it to save time? Or perhaps to save a tree?

Allow me to explain, in my first book I quote almost 2000 verses from scripture and display it word for word in the book. The book you are reading now quotes more than 800 verses! Why? Because I hate trees and want to use as much paper as possible? No! It is so that you, the reader can see what the scripture actually says, on the same page as my commentary to equip you with the means to decide, on the same page, if you agree or disagree with me and to see if what I claim is actually written in scripture, is true or not. I noticed a few people who read my first book extremely slowly. When asked why they are reading so slowly, they answer: "Because we check just about every bible verse you quote in your book, to see if it is actually written in my Bible". (Even though the entire verse is quoted in my books)

I then ask them: "Don't you trust me? Do you think I would quote verses if it is not in the Bible? They answer: "No it's not that we do not trust you, it's just that we can hardly believe these verses are actually written in the Bible as we have never heard of nor read these verses in many years in church and never came across it any other books.

The question you must constantly ask yourself is: "Do I disagree with the author, or do I disagree with the Bible?" This is the primary reason why I quote so many scriptures.

The reason for this lengthy explanation is, usually when we read a book, written by some or other top notch theologian, we find a few scriptures quoted in brackets and that's it! He is the highly educated and if he says it's like that, then it is like that. What on earth would compel me to actually look up the verses in scripture and see for myself if the quoted scriptures in fact do support the statement of the "Christian author"? Why should I do like scriptures instruct me and search for myself, if the highly qualified professor in theology make the statement, he is indeed much higher qualified than I am. My friend, this is the root of the demise of Gods people, right there! We are too lazy to search the scriptures, like we are commanded to do, and too eager to eat and swallow every piece of deceit, motivated by our false belief that it's only the puppet behind the pulpit or the professor of theology who can understand scripture! We must make every possible effort to get away from this "mother of all misconceptions", which eats away at our religion like an aggressive cancer!

Now, let's look at the verses in brackets.

Remember the good doctor's statement:

> **_Regardless of the condition of the body -whether it is burnt to ash, the Lord Jesus Christ will resurrect it_**

> **_1Cor 15:51_** **_Behold, I shew you a mystery; We shall not all sleep, but we shall all be changed,_**
> **_1Cor 15:52_** **_In a moment, in the twinkling of an eye, at the last trump: for the trumpet shall sound, and the dead shall be raised incorruptible, and we shall be changed._**
> **_1Cor 15:53_** **_For this corruptible must put on incorruption, and this mortal must put on immortality._**
> **_1Cor 15:54_** **_So when this corruptible shall have put on incorruption, and this mortal shall have put on immortality, then shall be brought to pass the saying that is written, Death is swallowed up in victory._**

Do you see written here that people whom were cremated shall be resurrected? Me neither!

The next quotation of the doctor in brackets:

> **_1The 4:15_** **_For this we say unto you by the word of the Lord, that we which are alive and remain unto the coming of the Lord shall not prevent them which are asleep._**
> **_1The 4:16_** **_For the Lord himself shall descend from heaven with a shout, with the voice of the archangel, and with the trump of God: and the dead in Christ shall rise first:_**
> **_1The 4:17_** **_Then we which are alive and remain shall be caught up together with them in the clouds, to meet the Lord in the air: and so shall we ever be with the Lord._**

Do you see written here that people whom were cremated shall be resurrected? Me neither!

TAKE NOTE:

I am not implying in any way that God will not resurrect a cremated body; we will get to that later. What I am saying is the doctor does not prove his statement with the verses he quotes i.e. these verses do not state that God will resurrect the cremated, the good doctor ASSUMES this. The Bible does not say this!

The doctor continues by listing a few arguments in favour of cremation (just as I do in this book) and then makes a few statements regarding scripture. A very interesting fact is, whether the doctor is aware of it or not, he does not quote Amos 2:1-2 at all. I wonder why not? Maybe it's just an oversight or maybe he just never crossed paths with the verse in all his years of theological studies.

Just in case you forgot about this verse, here it is again:

> _Amo 2:1_ _Thus saith the LORD; For three transgressions of Moab, and for four, I will not turn away the punishment thereof;_ **because he burned the bones of the king of Edom into lime:** _Amo 2:2_ But **I will send a fire upon Moab,** and it shall devour the palaces of Kerioth: and Moab shall die with tumult, with shouting, and with the sound of the trumpet:

On page 196 we read the following:

> **The fact is however that Christians today feels different regarding this issue, possibly due to the practical reason given earlier. What conclusion can then be reached? Is it really wrong? The biblical practice is clear. One could ask if the biblical practice is dogmatic and prescribed or if it must be regarded a mere Jewish culture, something like the head-covering during the time of Paul which is not an issue today. There is definitely a case to be made for this.**

My Comments:
Number One:
Either you believe in scripture or you don't. Period! If it is in scripture, it is in scripture. If you choose to cancel what is written is scripture by labelling it as "Jewish culture" then you don't believe scripture!

Number Two:
The head covering for a woman is not an issue today, the good doctor proclaims. This is true, but who decided this? Not God or scripture, but the church decided it is old fashioned and so the preachers are paid to what? To ….. **UDT** (To Teach Unsound Doctrine! To soothe the ears and get well paid for it!)

Scripture is extremely clear regarding the head covering of a woman, and note that this is in the New Testament!

> *1Cor 11:4* *Every man praying or prophesying, having his head covered, dishonoureth his head.*
> *1Cor 11:5* *But every woman that prayeth or prophesieth with her head uncovered dishonoureth her head: for that is even all one as if she were shaven.*
> *1Cor 11:6* *For if the woman be not covered, let her also be shorn: but if it be a shame for a woman to be shorn or shaven, let her be covered.*
> *1Cor 11:7* *For a man indeed ought not to cover his head, forasmuch as he is the image and glory of God: but the woman is the glory of the man.*
> *1Cor 11:8* *For the man is not of the woman; but the woman of the man.*
> *1Cor 11:9* *Neither was the man created for the woman; but the woman for the man.*

And more:

> *1Cor 11:13* *Judge in yourselves: is it comely that a woman pray unto God uncovered?*
> *1Cor 11:14* *Doth not even nature itself teach you, that, if a man have long hair, it is a shame unto him?*
> *1Cor 11:15* *But if a woman have long hair, it is a glory to her: for her hair is given her for a covering.*

It is a pity we cannot make contact with Paul, I would have liked very much to inform him that the good theological doctor has in fact judged according to verse 13 and found that it is perfectly acceptable for a woman to pray to God without a head covering. Sorry Paul, the doctor has spoken and you should listen! We don't want anything to do with your (Paul's) so-called Jewish cultures.

What did Jesus teach?

> *Mat 5:17* *Think not that I am come to destroy the law, or the prophets: I am not come to destroy, but to fulfil.*
> *Mat 5:18* *For verily I say unto you, Till heaven and earth pass, one jot or one tittle shall in no wise pass from the law, till all be fulfilled.*
> *Mat 5:19* *Whosoever therefore shall break one of these least commandments, and shall teach men so, he shall be called the least in the kingdom of heaven: but whosoever shall do and*

> *teach them, the same shall be called great in the kingdom of heaven.*

Number Three:
Why is tithing and offering to fund churches not a Jewish culture, but the highest...

DOCTRINE in ANY CHURCH?

> *Jud 1:3 Beloved, when I gave all diligence to write unto you of the common salvation, it was needful for me to write unto you, and exhort you that ye should earnestly contend for the faith which was once delivered unto the saints.*
> *Jud 1:4 For there are certain men crept in unawares, who were before of old ordained to this condemnation, ungodly men, turning the grace of our God into lasciviousness, and denying the only Lord God, and our Lord Jesus Christ.*

We read on page 196:

> *Ultimately, it is every believer's personal choice in light of the above information. We should respect each other's conviction in this regard and not judge one another*

This is not just UDT, but the ultimate Unsound Doctrine Teaching! Let me translate from the Wilsenach translation:

> *To hell with the Bible, you can decide for yourself!*
> *If your fellow believers choose to cremate themselves or their loved ones, give him love and respect, but never ever offend them!*

Don't pollute my religion with the bible!

This reminds me, I was working with a staunch Christian many years ago and we were discussing the bible every so often, but every time I told the person what the bible says and that it opposes what he believes, he did not accept it. I then offered to bring my bible to work and show him that the bible actually says what I am telling him. What was his response? I kid you not! His response was: "I am comfortable and happy with my current church religion and I am not interested in polluting my belief system with the bible". Needless to say, I was never so dumbfounded by anything in my life before. This was a sad day indeed as I realised then, biblical truths are being vigorously opposed, not by Satanists and atheists, but by the very people who claim to believe the bible and claim to serve God, churchgoing folk. What a dismal heartbroken event for me to accept... I literally spent years grappling with this reaction. I also heard this more and more over time.

There was this Afrikaans TV pastor who basically stated the following: "If a church brother of yours wants to dispute what you believe by using the bible as evidence, he is not from God, but from Satan" I actually ordered the DVD just to have his statement on record. It was devastating for me to hear theologians make statements like this, but I also realised where my colleague learned to say the things he said - from the leaders of God's flock, nonetheless! Well, in time I got to deal with this, accept it if you will and again it was Jesus who came to my rescue by saying the following after He **"offended"** the Pharisees (the preachers of those days)...

> **Mat 15:14** *Let them alone: they be blind leaders of the blind. And if the blind lead the blind, both shall fall into the ditch.*

Who is going to judge us?

The church and her clergymen, priests and pastors will have it that we must not judge anyone, but what does scripture say?

> **Eph 5:10** *Proving what is acceptable unto the Lord.*
> **Eph 5:11** *And have no fellowship with the unfruitful works of darkness, but rather reprove them.*

So, who or what is going to judge us then?

> **Joh 12:48** *He that rejecteth me, and receiveth not my words, hath one that judgeth him: the word that I have spoken, the same shall judge him in the last day.*

Yes dear reader, the same Word of God, the Scriptures will be what judges us. We need to ask ourselves if we are prepared to stand before Jesus and state that the "traditional burial" was merely a biblical "Jewish" culture and therefore we have the option to choose, individually what we prefer. I for one do not want to find myself in that situation.

We are taught by the highest theologian professors that the Bible is not to be understood literally. We must regard it on the same level as Little Red Riding Hood, by implication. Further to this, we are taught that especially the Old Testament is out-dated, a bygone that serves very little purpose (if anything at all) in today's day and age. The majority of scripture we looked at so far originates from the Old Testament, but what does the bible say, in the NEW TESTAMENT?

> **1Ths 5:20** *Despise not prophesyings.*

> *1Ths 5:21 Prove all things; hold fast that which is good.*
> *1Ths 5:22 Abstain from all appearance of evil.*
> *1Ths 5:23 And the very God of peace sanctify you wholly; and I pray God your whole spirit and soul and body be preserved blameless unto the coming of our Lord Jesus Christ.*

What does scripture mean with: "***Despise not prophesyings***"? What "prophesyings"? This refers to the Old Testament. The Old Testament is described as the "law" and the "prophets" by Jesus himself:

> *Mat 5:17 Think not that I am come to destroy the law, or the prophets: I am not come to destroy, but to fulfil.*

By the way, not many people are aware of it, but the Old Testament actually runs up to John. Yes, I am aware that our Bible states the New Testament starts with Matthew; however this is not what Jesus says:

> *Luk 16:16 The law and the prophets were until John: since that time the kingdom of God is preached...*

We continue:

Scripture further states we should prove all things and hold fast that which is good. Just as we cannot sleep with a prostitute to "prove all things" to know whether this is good or bad, you cannot cremate yourself to "prove" whether it is good or bad. In the same passage it continues and states that we must abstain from all evil. There are certain things which we just know is evil, nobody has to teach you that its evil, you know it is, therefore abstain from it, just like cremation is evil. And then we are specifically told to preserve not only our soul, but also our bodies, blameless unto the coming of Jesus. This does not only coincide with the Old Testament, but with the entire Word of God! How much more reprimanding do we need?

> *1Ths 5:22 Abstain from all appearance of evil.*
> *1Ths 5:23 And the very God of peace sanctify you wholly; and I pray God your whole spirit and soul and body be preserved blameless unto the coming of our Lord Jesus Christ.*

How do we preserve our bodies, blamelessly, when we decide to – against the total statutes of the scriptures – have it cremated and have our bones crushed to powder? Then we are told not to rebuke anyone doing this, but scripture once again says something different. Note in the following passages we find the instruction to rebuke, reprove and also the clear warning that the time will come that people will not take to sound doctrine, but shall employ preachers and church leaders who will soothe their itchy ears so that they can turn their ears away from the truth and cling to fables!

> *2Tim 4:1* *I charge thee therefore before God, and the Lord Jesus Christ, who shall judge the quick and the dead at his appearing and his kingdom;*
> *2Tim 4:2* *Preach the word; be instant in season, out of season; reprove, rebuke, exhort with all longsuffering and doctrine.*
> *2Tim 4:3* *For the time will come when they will not endure sound doctrine; but after their own lusts shall they heap to themselves teachers, having itching ears;*
> *2Tim 4:4* *And they shall turn away their ears from the truth, and shall be turned unto fables.*

We are instructed to distinguish good from evil.

> *Heb 5:14* *But strong meat belongeth to them that are of full age, even those who by reason of use have their senses exercised to discern both good and evil.*

What would you say if someone, regardless of his high theological qualifications, teaches us that it does not matter, we can decide if we want to cremate and no one must rebuke us? The Bible tells us to distinguish the good from the evil and distinguish we have to!

Even Paul tells us to admonish (rebuke, reprimand, scold) one another!

> *Rom 15:14* *And I myself also am persuaded of you, my brethren, that ye also are full of goodness, filled with all knowledge, able also to admonish one another.*

If we then come to understand that to say we may choose what we find to suit ourselves and no one may "rebuke" us is against everything scripture teaches, what are we to do? Yet again, scripture has the answer!

> *Gal 1:8* *But though we, or an angel from heaven, preach any other gospel unto you than that which we have preached unto you, let him be accursed.*

The church and her teachers, teach that we must love everyone, but God's Word teaches me if anyone, this includes the church and her teachers of false doctrine, preached another gospel other than that of the Bible, **LET HIM BE ACCURSED!**

Why do we search and also find answers from Gods Word?

> *2Tim 3:16 All scripture is given by inspiration of God, and is profitable for doctrine, for reproof, for correction, for instruction in righteousness:*
> *2Tim 3:17 That the man of God may be perfect, throughly furnished unto all good works.*

Because ALL SCRIPTURE, not parts of it, is given by the inspiration of God and is profitable for a lot of things, but also for, wait for it.... REPROOF! Say what? Yes you heard right!

A last warning from scripture is the following very important instruction:

> *Eze 3:18 When I say unto the wicked, Thou shalt surely die; and thou givest him not warning, nor speakest to warn the wicked from his wicked way, to save his life; the same wicked man shall die in his iniquity; but his blood will I require at thine hand.*
> *Eze 3:19 Yet if thou warn the wicked, and he turn not from his wickedness, nor from his wicked way, he shall die in his iniquity; but thou hast delivered thy soul.*

Why am I then trying to warn you against cremation, at all costs? The church teaches that all sins are the same, but that is also a false teaching. There are different levels of sin. The church teaches that we will all be subjected to the same punishment, but that yet again is not true.

> *Jas 3:1 My brethren, be not many masters, knowing that we shall receive the greater condemnation.*

The "masters" referred to in the above passage are the teachers, teachers of God's Word for example. This includes everyone preaching or teaching from Gods Word. These teachers will receive a greater condemnation, and that is why I attempt to bring you the truth from scripture as best I can, because this greater condemnation includes me, the author of this book! But I have to take head – If I don't warn you, your blood is on my hands! If I warned you and you don't listen and decide to follow the teachings of the ravenous wolves in sheep's clothing, then I am set free, your blood is on your hands.

My apologies dear reader, I forgot a very important aspect. I am not paid by any religious organisation or church; therefore I can call a spade a spade. The church's teachers on the other hand must be very careful what they say as they can lose their jobs in an instant if they start preaching the truth from scripture which differs from the church's false doctrine or when it is politically or socially incorrect. Many men of the cloth were fired already, yes FIRED for committing this cardinal sin against the church; for teaching biblical truths!

Can you understand why I agree with Jesus when he states that they take the key of knowledge away from us? Not only don't they enter, but they also hinder us from entering. (Note that "lawyers" referred to in this passage are the teachers of biblical law, in other words the teachers, preachers and pastors of the churches of today)

> *Luk 11:52 Woe unto you, lawyers! for ye have taken away the key of knowledge: ye entered not in yourselves, and them that were entering in ye hindered.*

My statement obviously does not depict a good Christian who is supposed to love all, never reprimand etc. etc. Well, I am not a Christian and I never want to be a Christian. I am a child of the God of Abraham, Isaac and Jacob, a believer and a follower as best I can, but never a Christian my friend! I put it to you that Jesus was not a Christian. You may think that I have taken leave of my senses.

Well, then I have a formal challenge for you:

1. *Prove from scriptures that Yahshua (Jesus) was a Christian, compared to the churches definition of Christianity and religions beliefs, creeds and dogmas of today.*
2. *Prove that all Yahshua's (Jesus's) teachings as per the scriptures, matches what the churches teach today.*

You see dear reader, the scriptures tells me the following very valuable truth:

> *1Tim 2:3 For this is good and acceptable in the sight of God our Saviour;*
> *1Tim 2:4 Who will have all men to be saved, and to come unto the knowledge of the truth.*
> *1Tim 2:5 For there is one God, and one mediator between God and men, the man Christ Jesus;*

I read not of a preacher or church clergyman who is the mediator between God and me…

What 'saith' the Scriptures?

My books are written to do just this. My books cause disagreements and division between father and son, mother and daughter and yes, even amongst a household. Why is this? Simply because one will choose to accept the truth and others will remain clinging to false doctrine! One will choose scripture which is God's Word and the other will choose the good pastors teachings. What does Jesus say? He says, if you choose mother or father or mother or son or daughter over Him, you are not worthy of Him. At this point you may feel that I have completely lost it, but dear reader, these are not my words. Read what Jesus says in His Word, the Holy Bible:

Mat 10:33 *But whosoever shall deny me before men, him will I also deny before my Father which is in heaven.*
Mat 10:34 <u>*Think not that I am come to send peace on earth: I came not to send peace, but a sword.*</u>
Mat 10:35 <u>*For I am come to set a man at variance against his father, and the daughter against her mother, and the daughter in law against her mother in law.*</u>
Mat 10:36 <u>*And a man's foes shall be they of his own household.*</u>
Mat 10:37 <u>*He that loveth father or mother more than me is not worthy of me: and he that loveth son or daughter more than me is not worthy of me.*</u>

Luk 12:51 *Suppose ye that I am come to give peace on earth?* <u>*I tell you, Nay; but rather division:*</u>
Luk 12:52 *For from* <u>*henceforth there shall be five in one house divided, three against two, and two against three.*</u>
Luk 12:53 *The* <u>*father shall be divided against the son,*</u> *and the son against the father; the* <u>*mother against the daughter,*</u> *and the daughter against the mother;* <u>*the mother in law against her daughter in law,*</u> *and the daughter in law against her mother in law.*

This is why the Word of God tells us that these men or teachers whom do not teach pure scripture, are trying to enter the gospel violently (*presseth*) and the violent wants to take the kingdom of heaven by force!

> *Luk 16:15 And he said unto them, Ye are they which justify yourselves before men; but God knoweth your hearts: for that which is highly esteemed among men is abomination in the sight of God.*
> *Luk 16:16 The law and the prophets were until John: since that time the kingdom of God is preached, and every man presseth into it.*

> *Mat 11:12 And from the days of John the Baptist until now the kingdom of heaven suffereth violence, and the violent take it by force.*

A last thought on this subject as follows:

The Scribes, Pharisees, etc. the highly educated theologians of today, locks the kingdom of God, not only do they not enter themselves, but they also prevent us from entering. Please note that it is Jesus talking here, and in the New Testament.

> *Mat 23:13 But woe unto you, scribes and Pharisees, hypocrites! for ye shut up the kingdom of heaven against men: for ye neither go in yourselves, neither suffer ye them that are entering to go in.*

These so-called spiritual leaders cross oceans and land to make one convert and then they make that convert a child of hell!! Twofold more than they are themselves. And you think that this author has absolutely gone mad, but hold on, these are not my words, these are the words of Jesus Himself!!!

> *Mat 23:15 Woe unto you, scribes and Pharisees, hypocrites! for ye compass sea and land to make one proselyte, and when he is made, ye make him twofold more the child of hell than yourselves.*

If you are stunned it is not because this is new and shocking information, it is because you will never hear these words from the puppet behind the pulpit. This however does not in any way cancels the words of our Messiah. Why is this? Well, simply because the truth of the church is nothing, but the gold (money) is everything.

> *Mat 23:16 Woe unto you, ye blind guides, which say, Whosoever shall swear by the temple, it is nothing; but whosoever shall swear by the gold of the temple, he is a debtor!*

Please allow me to state that I am not against any person, but I am most definitely against the false teaching and the system of false doctrine. If only a single person can unshackle themselves from this system and follow God in truth, all my efforts will not be in vain.

The Judgement of cremation

In the verses which follow, please take note of the direct link between fire, burning and judgement.

> *Rev 18:7 How much she hath glorified herself, and lived deliciously, so much torment and sorrow give her: for she saith in her heart, I sit a queen, and am no widow, and shall see no sorrow.*
> *Rev 18:8 Therefore shall her plagues come in one day, death, and mourning, and famine; and she shall be utterly burned with fire: for strong is the Lord God who judgeth her.*
> *Rev 18:9 And the kings of the earth, who have committed fornication and lived deliciously with her, shall bewail her, and lament for her, when they shall see the smoke of her burning,*
> *Rev 18:10 Standing afar off for the fear of her torment, saying, Alas, alas, that great city Babylon, that mighty city! for in one hour is thy judgment come.*

> *Lev 10:1 And Nadab and Abihu, the sons of Aaron, took either of them his censer, and put fire therein, and put incense thereon, and offered strange fire before the LORD, which he commanded them not.*
> *Lev 10:2 And there went out fire from the LORD, and devoured them, and they died before the LORD.*

Note the verse above; they performed something which God had not commanded them to do and they were devoured by fire. Then consider very seriously that God never ever commanded cremation for his children, but used it only in dire punishment in His wrath as the passages below prove! Together with punishment of fire, also note the destruction of bones, as is the case with any cremation!

> *Lev 20:14 And if a man take a wife and her mother, it is wickedness: they shall be burnt with fire, both he and they; that there be no wickedness among you.*

~ 124 ~

Lev 21:9 And the daughter of any priest, *if she profane herself by playing the whore, she profaneth her father: she shall be burnt with fire.*

Num 16:35 And there *came out a fire from the LORD, and consumed the two hundred and fifty men* that offered incense.

Num 24:8 God brought him forth out of Egypt; he hath as it were the strength of an unicorn: *he shall eat up the nations his enemies, and shall break their bones,* and pierce them through with his arrows.

Num 26:10 And the earth opened her mouth, and swallowed them up together with Korah, when that company died, *what time the fire devoured two hundred and fifty men:* and they became a sign.

Deu 5:25 Now therefore why should we die? *for this great fire will consume us: if we hear the voice of the LORD our God any more,* then we shall die.

Jdg 9:20 But if not, *let fire come out from Abimelech, and devour the men of Shechem,* and the house of Millo; *and let fire come out from the men of Shechem, and from the house of Millo, and devour Abimelech.*

Zec 9:4 Behold, the Lord will cast her out, *and he will smite her power in the sea; and she shall be devoured with fire.*

2Sam 22:8 Then the earth shook and trembled; *the foundations of heaven moved and shook, because he was wroth.*
2Sam 22:9 There went up a smoke out of his nostrils, *and fire out of his mouth devoured: coals were kindled by it.*

2Kin 1:10 And Elijah answered and said to the captain of fifty, If I be a man of God, *then let fire come down from heaven, and consume thee and thy fifty. And there came down fire from heaven, and consumed him and his fifty.*

2Kin 1:14 Behold, *there came fire down from heaven, and burnt up the two captains of the former fifties with their fifties:* therefore let my life now be precious in thy sight.

Job 1:16 While he was yet speaking, there came also another, and said, <u>The fire of God is fallen from heaven, and hath burned up the sheep, and the servants, and consumed them; and I only am escaped alone to tell thee.</u>

Psa 21:9 Thou shalt make them <u>as a fiery oven in the time of thine anger: the LORD shall swallow them up in his wrath, and the fire shall devour them.</u>
Psa 21:10 Their fruit shalt thou destroy from the earth, and their seed from among the children of men.
Psa 21:11 For they intended evil against thee: they imagined a mischievous device, which they are not able to perform.

Psa 78:62 He gave his people over also unto the sword; and was wroth with his inheritance.
Psa 78:63 <u>The fire consumed their young men;</u> and their maidens were not given to marriage.

Pro 5:7 Hear me now therefore, O ye children, and depart not from the words of my mouth.
Pro 5:8 Remove thy way far from her, and come not nigh the door of her house:
Pro 5:9 Lest thou give thine honour unto others, and thy years unto the cruel:
Pro 5:10 Lest strangers be filled with thy wealth; and thy labours be in the house of a stranger;
Pro 5:11 <u>And thou mourn at the last, when thy flesh and thy body are consumed,</u>
Pro 5:12 And say, How have I hated instruction, and my heart despised reproof;
Pro 5:13 And have not obeyed the voice of my teachers, nor inclined mine ear to them that instructed me!
Pro 5:14 <u>I was almost in all evil in the midst of the congregation and assembly.</u>

Isa 24:6 Therefore hath the curse devoured the earth, and they that dwell therein are desolate: therefore <u>the inhabitants of the earth are burned, and few men left.</u>

Jer 48:45 They that fled stood under the shadow of Heshbon because of the force: <u>but a fire shall come forth out of Heshbon, and a flame from the midst of Sihon, and shall</u>

> *devour the corner of Moab, and the crown of the head of the tumultuous ones.*

> ## *Eze 22:31 Therefore have I poured out mine indignation upon them; I have consumed them with the fire of my wrath: their own way have I recompensed upon their heads, saith the Lord GOD.*

Why do I quote so many passages from scripture, because I hate trees? No! I do it so that you can be assured if someone teaches you that God does not condemn the burning of bodies in the form of cremation, for His children, they are outright lying! Scripture reveals scripture. How many verses will one have to find to cancel out all the scriptures we have quoted thus far and even then the Bible will collapse in its entirety as scripture can never contradict itself.

Let's just throw in a few more passages for good measure:

> *Heb 6:7 For the earth which drinketh in the rain that cometh oft upon it, and bringeth forth herbs meet for them by whom it is dressed, receiveth blessing from God:*
> *Heb 6:8 But that which beareth thorns and briers is rejected, and is nigh unto cursing; whose end is to be burned.*

Again, note the wrath, judgement and condemnation of God, manifesting in fire and ashes!

> *Eze 28:18 Thou hast defiled thy sanctuaries by the multitude of thine iniquities, by the iniquity of thy traffick; therefore will I bring forth a fire from the midst of thee, it shall devour thee, and I will bring thee to ashes upon the earth in the sight of all them that behold thee.*
> *Eze 28:19 All they that know thee among the people shall be astonished at thee: thou shalt be a terror, and never shalt thou be any more.*

Our vile body will be transformed to become identical to the glorious body of Jesus.

> *Php 3:20 For our conversation is in heaven; from whence also we look for the Saviour, the Lord Jesus Christ:*

> *Php 3:21 Who shall change our vile body, that it may be fashioned like unto his glorious body, according to the working whereby he is able even to subdue all things unto himself.*

Did you read that "ashes" shall be transformed to the glorious body? Neither did I. The body will be transformed. We are all aware that in this day, many bodies will be nothing but dust due to decomposition over thousands of years, but not the bones my friend. Later we look more in depth at the bones, but can you remember what Jesus's body looked like after His resurrection? He had flesh and bones. He even had the scars where the sword entered His side and yes, He even ate food! How on earth I ask, could anyone link this to cremation?

The following passages teach us yet again not to despise (disregard) the prophesies. What is the prophesies? It is the Old Testament! But coupled to the same passage we receive the instruction to blamelessly preserve our bodies unto the coming of Jesus. Now I ask:

"HOW IN SEVEN BLUE BLAZING HELLS, CAN THIS BE ASSOCIATED WITH CREMATION?"

This can never ever be reasoned away, even with the highest, most complicated theological bull-twang!! Dear reader, you have to choose. Sometime you have to decide if you are a follower of God and His Word (instructions), or the word of the church and her false teachers whom teaches that there is absolutely nothing wrong with cremation.

> *1The 5:20 Despise not prophesyings.*
> *1The 5:21 Prove all things; hold fast that which is good.*
> *1The 5:22 Abstain from all appearance of evil.*
> *1The 5:23 And the very God of peace sanctify you wholly; and I pray God your whole spirit and soul and body be preserved blameless unto the coming of our Lord Jesus Christ.*

Our bodies belong to God. Who are we to, against His statutes, do with our bodies as we see fit. Who are we to demand a self-decision? Because the spiritual leaders tell us that we have the right to? Please remember dear reader, the church and her leaders are not going to judge you, God's Word is going to judge you and once this judgement is passed you cannot file an appeal!

> *Col 2:17 Which are a shadow of things to come; but the body is of Christ.*

~ 128 ~

People will however argue that scripture refers to the living body and when the person dies, this verse is not applicable. This will be sad as you should, by now, have a very clear view of scripture regarding the importance of the body, the "disposal" of the remains and the utmost importance of especially the bones. Let's have a look:

> **Php 1:20** *According to my earnest expectation and my hope, that in nothing I shall be ashamed, but that with all boldness, as always, so now also Christ shall be magnified in my body, whether it be by life, or by death.*

Can you see this? That Christ be magnified by the body, even in death? This can also signify the method of death, but we have learned so much from scripture in this regard that it may very well be referring to the body in the state of death. For example: the difference between the scriptural burial and the ungodly act of cremation. We may further this argument with the following question:

If burning to ashes is clearly the undeniable wrath and punishment of God, from scripture, and we turn our bodies over to the crematorium, knowing full well that our bodies do not belong to us, then we hate our flesh, not so?

> **Eph 5:29** *For no man ever yet hated his own flesh; but nourisheth and cherisheth it, even as the Lord the church:*

How can we ever justify this barbaric act, knowing that we are flesh of His flesh and bone of His bone?

> **Eph 5:30** *For we are members of his body, of his flesh, and of his bones.*

It may be that bitter enders still argue that the remains are totally insignificant and worthless…

Are you aware that even Satan had a dispute with the angel Michael regarding a dead body?

Just before we look at this, let's look at another passage where people went after strange flesh and what their punishment was.

> **Jud 1:7** *Even as Sodom and Gomorrha, and the cities about them in like manner, giving themselves over to fornication, and going after strange flesh, are set forth for an example, suffering the vengeance of eternal fire.*

If it is true that a dead body is simply remains, worthless and may be dealt with however we choose, how can it be that Satan and the angel Michael were in a dispute regarding a dead body, the body of Moses?

> *Jud 1:9* *Yet Michael the archangel, when contending with the devil he disputed about the body of Moses, durst not bring against him a railing accusation, but said, The Lord rebuke thee.*

How much more scripture, dear reader, do you need?

Allow me to share my view; if after all the scriptures we studied up to this point, you still remain unconvinced that cremation is an abomination, then I say to you:

No problem, please just don't tell me you believe in Gods Word. Just remember, if you don't believe His Word, it is impossible to believe in Him and also to follow Him. Admit the latter and move on, good luck...

If you are chosen by Him and you go ahead with the cremation of yourself or your loved ones bodies, then maybe the following is applicable: Even if you had lots of children, lived many years, had a good life and you have no burial, a miscarriage is better than you.

You may be furious with me for saying this; I hope you are, as these are not my words.

> *Ecc 6:3* *If a man beget an hundred children, and live many years, so that the days of his years be many, and his soul be not filled with good, and also that he have no burial; I say, that an untimely birth is better than he.*

Arguments under magnification

We look at the arguments promoting cremation again in relation to what we have learned from scripture thus far. I give my opinion, but you must decide for yourself. The most important thing to remember when you decide for yourself is, are you disagreeing with me, the author, or are you disagreeing with scripture, God's Word. Disagreeing with me is perfectly fine and acceptable, in fact I welcome it, the other is not...

Economical: *Cremation is cheaper.*

When we are "herded" in a certain direction by the invisible powers of this world, there will always be a superficial benefit in the form of a carrot, a false carrot like a cost saving or perceived cost saving in this case.

I am not entirely convinced that a scriptural burial, in the ground, necessarily has to be more expensive than cremation, however:

- It is much cheaper to go to hell than to heaven.
- It is much cheaper not to educate your children.
- It is much cheaper to listen to the preacher than search the scriptures yourself.
- It is also much cheaper to hand over your tithing and offerings to church as opposed to fighting for God -no matter what!

Hygienic: *Decomposition is hazardous.*

When we have decomposing bodies lying around, yes it is dangerous, but not when they are buried according to the burial practices of scripture. In fact, not to bury is to make the land unclean!

> *Eze 39:12 And seven months shall <u>the house of Israel be</u> <u>burying of them, that they may cleanse the land.</u>*
> *Eze 39:13 <u>Yea, all the people of the land shall bury them; and it</u> <u>shall be to them a renown the day that I shall be glorified, saith</u> <u>the Lord GOD.</u>*
> *Eze 39:14 And they shall sever out men of continual employment, <u>passing through the land to bury with the</u> <u>passengers those that remain upon the face of the earth, to</u> <u>cleanse it:</u> after the end of seven months shall they search.*
> *Eze 39:15 And the passengers that pass through the land, <u>when</u> <u>any seeth a man's bone, then shall he set up a sign by it, till the</u> <u>buriers have buried it</u> in the valley of Hamongog.*
> *Eze 39:16 And also the name of the city shall be Hamonah. <u>Thus shall they cleanse the land.</u>*

Do you really think that God would prescribe a burial that would cause sickness and epidemics? No, not if we follow his statutes.

Aesthetical Value:

Cremation is not associated with decomposing bodies; therefore it is clean and more acceptable.

If you believe this false statement you are seriously misled – please see Chapter 7 and re-evaluate this argument.

The Time Factor:

The cremation service may be held long after grandma's cremation and her ashes may be stored or scattered anywhere.

When scripture teaches that to bury is to cleanse the land, I will argue from a scriptural perspective to scatter or store ashes is to make the land or house unclean! Why do we have to get the body in the ground as fast as possible? Because God has designed it to be dealt with this way to prevent any hygienic issues arising. The time factor then is also void of any validity from a scriptural point of view.

Cold character:

The graveyard always brings forth a sombre feeling in those attending the funeral.

This may be so, but the act of cremation is no less sombre. In fact, with cremation it is a case of where the eye does not see the heart does not grieve. Reconsider this argument after you read the following chapter. Even this is a very poor attempt with its sole intension to discredit the scriptural burial.

Grave Pillaging

People even dig up steel coffins and cart it off to the nearest recycling depot!

Was it also pillaging when Moses carted the bones of joseph through the desert for more than 40 years?

Was it also pillaging when Josiah dug up the bones and burnt it by order of God?

I put it to you that even grave pillaging may very well have to do with God's wrath and that the chosen, true child of God, will never have their grave pillaged. Bones however may be exhumed and moved to another resting place.

To take everything scripture teaches regarding this subject and nullify it on the basis that some graves have been pillaged is the same as saying: "My child stole a cookie, therefore I amputated his hands".

ABSOLUTELY ABSURD!!!

Property:

The space problem.

Some countries may very well have a space problem, but there are plans to be made and solutions to be had. There are very small countries with a very dense, even over population, who manages the dead and never runs out of space. Some countries recycle graves. The body is buried according to scripture and after a period, depending obviously on temperature, soil etc. the bones are exhumed and laid to rest in an ossuary. This is sometimes called "Secondary burial" and it is perfectly acceptable according to scripture. Just recall the story of Joseph's bones. In fact, in the book of Jasher it states that it was not only the bones of Joseph, but the bones of all twelve the patriarchs bones which accompanied Moses through the desert.

I am sorry, but the "no space" argument is full of holes.

<u>Technology:</u>
There were no crematoriums in biblical times; therefore the only logical disposal method was the ground burial.
Now we have advanced, computerised crematoriums and we have to utilise this technology.

The problem is we have already seen from scriptures that many thousands, maybe millions of people, children and babies have been burned, cremated so to speak. If it was due to God's wrath or simply the result of barbaric paganism religion, these people were very well accustomed to the burning of bodies. To argue that we now have advance crematoriums and therefore we must be grateful to commit these barbaric acts by computer control is nothing short of insanity.

<u>The Majority:</u>
Cremation numbers are soaring amongst Christians as it becomes more acceptable in Christianity.

IT MAY SHOCK YOU, BUT I AM NO "CHRISTIAN"!

I am a believer, a child of God with the Bible as my fundamental foundation, God's Word whom became flesh and dwelt among us. A Christian is a product of the church, not of scripture.

> *<u>Joh 1:12</u> But as many as received him, to them gave he power to become the sons of God, even to <u>them that believe on his name:</u>*

If you claim to believe in His Name, you will also believe in what He teaches us in His Word and leave cremation to the churches, the Christians, the heathens and the none believer's!

> *<u>Joh 1:13</u> Which were born, not of blood, nor of the will of the flesh, nor of the will of man, but of God.*

Not born of a church, but of God! You cannot join God like you do a church! You are either born of God or you aren't. If you are not born of God, you can join a hundred churches, but you will never be "born" of God.

> *<u>Joh 1:14</u> And the Word was made flesh, and dwelt among us, (and we beheld his glory, the glory as of the only begotten of the Father,) full of grace and truth.*

The Word became flesh, in Jesus. Should you betray his Word, you will betray Him as your Creator: Yahshua!

Let's talk **MAJORITY:**

You may not follow the majority in wrong doing. You can not dilute and nullify the Word of God with silly and stupid, but politically and socially correct arguments to nullify his statutes, laws and the perfect examples He gave us!

> _Exo 23:2_ _**Thou shalt not follow a multitude to do evil; neither shalt thou speak in a cause to decline after many to wrest judgment:**_

Everybody is under the impression that the majority is always, yes always correct. As long as I am part of the crowd and follow the mainstream, I must be doing something right, right? Wrong! This argument totally blows my mind and I will tell you why. We have senses, feelings and hopefully logic, but regardless of what the latter directs us to do, even if we vividly realise what we are doing is wrong, we acquire a false sense of "everything will be okay", as long as I am part of the group which guarantees that I will fit in, socially, politically and yes, spiritually as well. The truth is, from a biblical perspective, when you are part of the large group, you should really, and I mean really, be concerned. You should listen for the siren and look for the flashing red lights. This may sound like an absurd logic, but the Bible is filled with passages that state just this. Let's observe just a few examples:

> _Mat 7:14_ _**Because strait is the gate, and narrow is the way, which leadeth unto life, and few there be that find it.**_

> _Rom 11:4_ _**But what saith the answer of God unto him? I have reserved to myself seven thousand men, who have not bowed the knee to the image of Baal**_

> _Jer 3:14_ _**Turn, O backsliding children, saith the LORD; for I am married unto you: and I will take you one of a city, and two of a family, and I will bring you to Zion:**_

Worldwide, "Christianity" consists of an estimated 30,000+ denominations [14], yes – more than thirty thousand! This is not 30,000 church buildings, this is 30,000 different versions and interpretations of the same bible you and I have and read! Just the other day I read an article where the writer stated the following:

"If you want to make money, start a religion"

How true that declaration is, I totally agree!

This begs the question, how on earth do 30,000 different interpretations, from the same bible, relate to the following verse in that same bible?

> *Eph 4:4 There is <u>one body</u>, and <u>one Spirit</u>, even as ye are called in <u>one hope</u> of your calling;*
> *Eph 4:5 <u>One Lord, one faith, one baptism</u>,*
> *Eph 4:6 <u>One God and Father</u> of all, who is above all, and through all, and in you all.*

Oh and please don't forget, every single on of the 30,000 denominations are correct and the other 29,999 are most probably going to hell because they have a different conviction, even if it is a small difference, but each of these reads and studies the same bible! How is this possible? How could all this come from ONE SPIRIT of ONE GOD? The only possible answer I can derive is that the bible is reduced to a mere piece of clay or putty which I can shape how, when and where I want, to suit myself, to create a "god" that serves me and nobody dares judge me! The problem of course when one does this is that you are busy with your own religion, which you cannot support, nor substantiate from scriptures. This is all fine with me, just don't tell me this horse dropping is a fig and then expect me to eat it as well!

Chapter 7

The Cover Up

Her priests have violated my law, and
have profaned mine holy things: they
have put no difference between the
holy and profane, neither have they
shewed difference between the
unclean and the clean, and have hid
their eyes from my sabbaths, and I am
profaned among them.

Eze 22:26

Dust to dust

It's possible dear reader that you, with millions of other people regard the "ash" as the product of a cremation. This is of course the "ash" which remains after the body was burnt, almost the same ash we get form having had a barbeque after the wood or charcoal was burnt away.

Well, this unfortunately is one of the biggest lies in the cremation story!

I translate from page 201 of Dr Isak's book:

> *The body returns to the basic elements of the earth – dust. It makes no difference whether the body was buried and decomposes in a natural way or if it was cremated, digested by wild animals or fish. The end result is basically the same – dust.*

Please permit me to translate from the Wilsenach Translation:
When you are buried, eventually only dust remains.
When you are cremated, eventually only dust remains.
This "dust" is the same basic elements which remain.
Dust by decomposition and dust by cremation – is the same dust.

This is what the most honourable theologian doctor tells us. Please remember this as we continue with our study…

Let's observe the bone

I do not wish to bore you with the composition of the bone, but you may find the following information interesting:[15]

At birth, a baby has 270 bones in its small body. As the infant grows, some of the bones "fuses" together to eventually form only 206 bones in the adult. The largest bone, as you may know is the "femur" (thigh bone) and the smallest bone is of course the tiny bones in the ear.

For the Engineers, some stats related to our bones:
Compressive Strength: **170 Mpa**
Tensile Strength: **104-121 Mpa**
Shear Strength: **51.6 Mpa**

All this really means is that our bones are designed to support a huge load. One needs only to observe people with "metabolism problems" to realise the amount of weight our bones can carry. (Please note that did not use the term "fat" or "overweight"… My wife is very allergic to chocolates and cake – when she consumes the latter, her hips, thighs and buttocks swells terribly : -)

Fact remains, our bones can carry 3 to 4 and perhaps 5 times the weight for which it was designed, however the bone breaks relatively easy when a horizontal force is applied.

How long does a bone last?

Our source [16] provides an example of a dinosaur skeleton which was discovered in the desert area of Utah (USA). The smart people say that a sand dune collapsed onto – and buried a live dinosaur. The age of the skeleton of the dinosaur is estimated at 185 million years old.

(In my opinion though, we do not have the ability to correctly age any item of more than a couple of hundred years. Even the most advanced dating technologies have to assume a great deal of factors for the calculation to work, which then influences the age, depending on the assumptions made. I regard this as scientific pornography, but then again, who am I to make such statements) However, lets just for argument sake accept that this dinosaurs bones were extremely old.

The oldest funeral

Our source provides the following heading:
"Red Lady of Paviland"[17]

"She" is apparently the first, almost complete human skeleton ever discovered. There is also a human skeleton which was discovered in Europe, which was buried the "traditional" way, in other words in the ground. She was discovered between 15 and 18 January 1823 by Rev. William Buckland in South Wales. The smart people later discovered it was a "he" and not a "she" in fact it was the skeleton of a young man. They have dated the bones as being 33,000 (thirty three thousand) years old. Again, I don't attach any significant value to the said age, but again let's just accept that these bones were very old. The point is: This person was buried the traditional way and the bones are very, very old.

There is another source[18] which alleges a skeleton of an estimated 110 pounds, 4 foot long woman which is estimated at 4.4 million years old that was excavated in Ethiopia.

Foto: Pedroserafin

Really we don't even need to reference these sources. Take for example a nice juicy T-bone steak and bury it in your garden. Go and exhume it after 50 years and see if the meat is still attached to the bone. You will find that the meat decomposed and was taken up by the soil, returned to dust if that term suits you better. I am willing though to bet that the bone will still be there and has not "returned to dust". This we know from a phenomenon called "common sense". Let's allow the benefit of the doubt and just agree that it takes a long, long time for bones to return to dust or rather decompose to nothing.

The Bone house

"Ossuary"[19] - A better description is probably a "bone house" or "house of bones". This "Ossuary" is actually a chest, building, well or place that serves as the final resting place of the deceased's bones or skeleton. It is generally used where space is limited. A body is buried in a temporary grave and after a period of time, approximately a year or so, the bones are exhumed from the grave and placed in the ossuary. (We need to note that the rate of decomposition varies, depending on a number of factors.)

The bones are placed in boxes of numerous interesting designs, even manufactured from different materials and called, "bone boxes".

Decomposition

We need to observe a few images depicting the decomposition process. It may be, as they say on television, "not meant for sensitive viewers", but we must keep in mind that it is part of God's creation (design) and whether we like it or not, it's how He designed the process! We will be looking at the pig (one of the unclean animals)
Photos By: JenCom

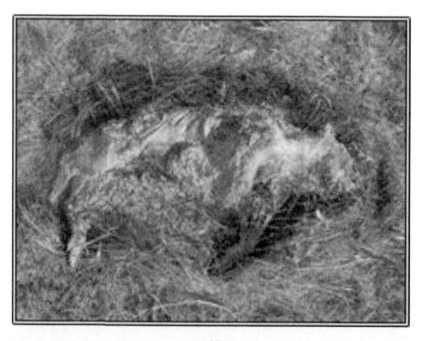

What do we learn from observing this process?

The entire body, every part of flesh and other soft material is stripped from the bones; absorbed by the soil (earth), back to dust, but the bones do not disappear like the rest of the body. After the entire decomposition process has been completed, the bones remain.

How much heat can a bone withstand?

Bones do not melt, but calcifies. It seems to be an impossible task to find the precise temperature at which the bone will be reduced to a powder by applying heat. There is a wealth of resources and all of them disagree with each other in terms of the numbers. Thus we will work with a hypothetical figure from somewhat accurate sources when we do some comparisons.

We know that the bone mainly, but not entirely, consists of calcium. Calcium Oxide has a melting point of 2572 °C, however calcium oxide is not a true composition of the human bone, but we need to consider the temperature of the crematorium oven, operating between 870 °C and 980 °C, and in some cases heated to 1150 °C

Now let us observe some melting temperatures of metals:

Zinc:	419 °C
Aluminium:	660 °C
Sterling silver:	893 °C
Silver (Mint):	897 °C
Brass:	905 °C
Silver (Pure):	961 °C
Gold (24 carat):	1063 °C
Copper:	1084 °C
Titanium:	1670 °C

Considering the temperature of the cremation oven, in extreme cases of 1150 °C, we note that all the metals above melted, from Zinc to Copper. The term "mild steel" is a bit misleading. Someone who is not familiar with the steel may assume that it is soft steel and can be moulded by hand, but this steel is very hard. This is the type of steel used in and around our homes in items such as gates, burglar proofing etc. The point is, mild steel is anything but soft, but even mild steel's melting point is 1350-1530 °C (The variation in the melting point temperatures varies due to the different compositions of the different types of mild steel). What does this have in common with the human bone? To be honest, not much, but of interest is the following: Note the melting point of Titanium at 1670 °C, well above that of mild steel. Remember this fact, when we observe a few other interesting, but related issues.

Bones don't turn to dust

One of the greatest misconceptions which are commonly accepted is as follows:

When people talk about or consider cremation, they believe that only "ash" remains after the cremation process has been completed. Nothing could be further from the truth. Let's consider our research thus far – what happens to the body? The body is VAPORISED by applying enormous amounts of heat. You will recall there is a second burner which incinerates any and all tiny body parts or organic material which enters the second chamber. This effectively means that almost nothing is left; everything disintegrates and is incinerated to vapour.

When there is nothing left of the body, all the matter that is left in the cremation oven is collected, after it cooled down of course, and stored in a container. This remains then is, wait for it – BONES! The bones are not reduced to ash; let me say that again – **The bones are not reduced to ash, lime or dust!** The bones are dried out, some have split open due the enormous heat, but it does not turn into "ash". In fact, there is practically no ash after the cremation. The bones are then placed in a machine, after items like jewellery; teeth-fillings etc. have been removed. This machine is called a "cremulator". My latest English dictionary does not even list this word yet. Even the so-called "ash" is not called "RE-mains", but "CRE-mains". The cremulator is basically just a very strong blender on steroids which is scared of nothing, except...

TITANIUM!

The bones are then unceremoniously thrown into this machine and ground and crushed to a fine substance with a rough texture. This substance is then called "ash" which is handed to the loved ones as their dearly departed loved one's "ashes". The harsh reality is, this so-called "ash", is nothing but your loved ones bones which have been liquidised in an industrial blender like fruit juice! We then go ahead and scatter grandma's "ashes" on the farm or her beloved holiday venue or in the ocean, or we even put it on the mantle place. This is however grandmas bones which have broken, blended and desecrated and not her ashes!

Below is a close-up photograph I have personally taken of a dog's "ashes" after the dog was cremated. The ash is in a plastic bag, taken straight out of the beautiful wooden box it came in but one can clearly see that this not ash, but crushed bone. Please also note that the colour is mainly white with just a darker patch here and there.

I trust you can see that these are bones and not "ash". The only possibility for real ash to look this would be to magnify it about a 1000 times I would guess.

Besides possible jewellery and teeth fillings, there are still a few items remaining after the cremation. Of course there are metal plates and screws if the person had operations to reattach broken bones etc. What is more important in our study is the hip-replacement operation. The prostheses is made from, you guessed it...TITANIUM. The titanium hip replacement remains unblemished. It may have a few carbon stains from the burning process, but that's it, and even this could easily be wiped off with a cloth. Now for the big question: If the melting point of titanium is 1670°C, why are the bones still present and not burned to ash? Could it be that the melting point of bone is so high that even the cremation oven will not be able to withstand such high temperatures? I think the evidence speaks for itself.

The Tooth!

I will not bore you with regards to the teeth. You've often seen, read or heard of someone who died in a car or home -inferno which was so charred that the only means of identification was to use the person's dental records. I "rest" my "case" as far as the teeth are concerned. In my research I was unable to find out whether the teeth are ground up together with the bones, or if it is being thrown away with some of the un-ground bones. (Some sources states the melting point of teeth to be somewhere between 1760°C and 2300°C.)

Dust to ash or ash to dust?

What does God say?

> **Gen 3:19** *In the sweat of thy face shalt thou eat bread, till thou return unto the ground; for out of it wast thou taken: for dust thou art, and unto dust shalt thou return.*

"From dust you are made, and to dust you shall return"

Next we read about the "ash" (powder) which was cast (scattered) on the graves. Initially it sounds fine, but wait…

> **2Kin 23:6** *And he brought out the grove from the house of the LORD, without Jerusalem, unto the brook Kidron, and burned it at the brook Kidron, and stamped it small to powder, and cast the powder thereof upon the graves of the children of the people.*

Before we adopt the churches methodology of "soothing the ears" of the majority, lets also read a few verses before and after the verse we quoted above to understand the full context of what is being described here…

> **2Kin 23:4** *And the king commanded Hilkiah the high priest, and the priests of the second order, and the keepers of the door, to bring forth out of the temple of the LORD all the vessels that were made for Baal, and for the grove, and for all the host of heaven: and he burned them without Jerusalem in the fields of Kidron, and carried the ashes of them unto Bethel.*
> **2Kin 23:5** *And he put down the idolatrous priests, whom the kings of Judah had ordained to burn incense in the high places in the cities of Judah, and in the places round about Jerusalem; them also that burned incense unto Baal, to the sun, and to the moon, and to the planets, and to all the host of heaven.*
> **2Kin 23:6** *And he brought out the grove from the house of the LORD, without Jerusalem, unto the brook Kidron, and burned it at the brook Kidron, and stamped it small to powder, and cast the powder thereof upon the graves of the children of the people.*

> *2Kin 23:7 And he brake down the houses of the sodomites, that were by the house of the LORD, where the women wove hangings for the grove.*

Once again we see that this judgment has yet again, kindled the wrath of God and this is not a "cremation service" but yet again a form of punishment!

Let's observe a few more verses with regards to dust, linked to ash or powder.

> *2Kin 23:15 Moreover the altar that was at Bethel, and the high place which Jeroboam the son of Nebat, who made Israel to sin, had made, both that altar and the high place he brake down, and burned the high place, and stamped it small to powder, and burned the grove.*

Again a judgment of God!

> *2Chr 34:6 And so did he in the cities of Manasseh, and Ephraim, and Simeon, even unto Naphtali, with their mattocks round about.*
> *2Chr 34:7 And when he had broken down the altars and the groves, and had beaten the graven images into powder, and cut down all the idols throughout all the land of Israel, he returned to Jerusalem.*

Again, the reduction of these graven images to powder (dust) as a result of God's wrath!

How should we return to dust?

How should we return to dust after we die, what do scriptures say?

> *Job 10:9 Remember, I beseech thee, that thou hast made me as the clay; and wilt thou bring me into dust again?*

Just as God ordained, as we read in the Holy Scriptures, in this way must we return to dust.

> *Gen 3:19 In the sweat of thy face shalt thou eat bread, till thou return unto the ground; for out of it wast thou taken: for dust thou art, and unto dust shalt thou return.*

Let me remind you of our good theologians doctors statements: (my summary)

When you are buried, eventually only dust remains.
When you are cremated, eventually only dust remains.
This "dust" is the same basic elements which remain.
Dust by decomposition and dust by cremation – is the same dust.

Dear reader, you should by now be aware that this "dust" is most definitely not the same, as the good doctor would have us believe, but who am I to say… I am not a theologian.

> *Job 34:14 If he set his heart upon man, if he gather unto himself his spirit and his breath;*
> *Job 34:15 All flesh shall perish together, and man shall turn again unto dust.*
> *Job 34:16 If now thou hast understanding, hear this: hearken to the voice of my words.*

May I be as bold as to request of you, dear reader, never to accept what I say, but please accept what God says and realise that "cremation" is a pagan ritual that is not from God, in fact God only approves this paganism in punishment, when His wrath is ignited!

When God says in His Word:

> *Psa 90:3 Thou turnest man to destruction; and sayest, Return, ye children of men.*

It does not mean CREMATION!

Are you aware of what scripture says about rebuking someone? And do you know what scripture says about people (preachers and the like) that flatter the flock with the tongue?

> *Pro 28:23 He that rebuketh a man afterwards shall find more favour than he that flattereth with the tongue.*

Beware of the bootlicker… the one that says: You may decide, the choice is yours, the substance – ash – is the same and it does not matter, God will resurrect you and you will go to heaven, its not necessary to act according to God's Word, for it is old-fashioned and obsolete, we are modern people etc. etc. etc.

Next, we will look at some real events surrounding the practice of cremation which the honourable Christian leaders promote so vigorously in our day and age.

The "Tri-State" Crematorium incident

The Tri-State Crematorium is (was) located in the northwest of the state of Georgia in the U.S.A. During 2002, the crematoriums affairs were investigated, which led to the liquidation of the crematorium as well as criminal charges against the owner(s). Tommy Marsh established the business in the mid-1970s, to fill a gap in the cremation market. During 1996, Tommy's son, Ray Brent Marsh, became the operational manager, due to ill health of his father.

A truck driver whom delivered gas at the crematorium became suspicious and called the police. He claimed that he saw dead bodies on the premises of the crematorium. The Walker County Sheriff's Department was informed twice of these allegations. They did pay a visit to the estate, but they did not report anything out of the ordinary.

On 15 February 2002, the "Environmental Protection Agency" investigated the allegations, with the following initial findings as follows:
(Again, maybe not for sensitive "readers", but if you intend to indulge in this pagan practice, you must also be aware of the irregularities and atrocities associated with it.)
With the initial inspection, the research team found a human skull and some human bones on the premises. After further inspection, the inspectors found a multitude of dead bodies lying literally stacked one on top of the other, rotting in warehouses, scattered in vault-like rooms and everywhere on the site of the crematorium.

Between 1996 and 2002 more than 2000 bodies were sent to the crematorium for cremation. The research team detected a total of 339 dead bodies on the premises which were not cremated. A Federal Disaster Unit was called in. They were equipped with a mobile mortuary to come and "clean" the site. The bodies had to be identified, but it proved to be a daunting task because of the advanced state of decomposition of many of the bodies. Some of the bodies were reduced to nothing more than mere skeletons. This resulted in only 226 bodies which were positively identified, from the original 339 cadavers. DNA tests were employed where the dead still had living relatives, but the rest could not be identified.

On the charge of 339 bodies from 2000 that were not cremated, Ray Brent Marsh argued that the "retort" (furnace or oven) was not fully operational. The furnace was tested and although there were some technical problems, the inspectors found that it was still in working order. In spite of this finding, 339 bodies were half buried, stacked in storage rooms, rotting or simply discarded in the bushes on the premises.

The million dollar question is: What did the relatives receive in their urns, supposedly containing the "ash" of their loved ones?

Wait for it…. A mixture of wood and cement!

Ray Brent Marsh was arrested and 787 charges were laid against him, he faced a possible imprisonment of 1000 (One Thousand) years.

Here is the big SURPRISE! You've read in this book just how important the remains are and how to deal with the remains, you read how terribly important the bones of the dead are and how to treat the bones and you even read that the **archangel Michael was in a battle of words with Satan over the body of Moses.**

> ***Jud 1:9 Yet Michael the archangel, when contending with the devil he disputed about the body of Moses, durst not bring against him a railing accusation, but said, The Lord rebuke thee.***

When Ray Brent Marsh's defence team asked the following question in court:

*"**Whether a human corpse had any pecuniary value.**"*

In other words "Does the dead body have any monetary value?"

The answer…?

*"**The traditional common law holding is that a corpse does not have pecuniary value**"*

"Pecuniary" means "monetary" or "financial" value. So the ruling was:

*"**a corpse has no monetary value**"*

(Later in the book you will however see just how valuable a body is, in monetary value no less!)

Marsh received a prison sentence of 12 years, obviously with time off for when he was in custody. Interestingly Marsh's answer to the question: "wouldn't it have been easier to just cremate the bodies?" his answer:

> *"To those of you who may have come here today looking for answers, I cannot give you."*

Five years after the incident, Marsh's lawyers reported that both Marsh and his father suffered from Mercury poisoning, apparently due to a faulty filter system at the crematorium. (Mercury is one of the side products of the cremation process).

Obviously a multitude of civil claims were brought against the crematorium, but the final result was that the site may never operate again as a business, in order to preserve the site as the final resting place of the dead due to the disgusting way in which these bodies were treated.

Well, we can be thankful that this type of atrocities does not happen in our wonderful rainbow nation of South Africa? Or does it...?

Middelburg – Transvaal – South Africa

While I was working on this book, and quite near completion, my brother came to visit and we briefly discussed the topic of my latest book (this one). I gave him a summary of the content of the book and he told me that he read something recently which I may find interesting.

I did some research and found the following information. We start with the source entitled:

> *"Mass grave shocker - Observer expose: Wheelbarrows full of human bones thrown into a hole by the crematorium every day" by Gerhard Rheeder*[20]

I translate some excerpts:

Wheelbarrows filled with human bones are thrown into a hole by Middelburg Crematorium employees on a daily basis. This macabre practice has been in existence since the inception of the Middelburg Crematorium 15 years ago. Truck loads full of cats and dogs carcasses, from as far as Krugersdorp are also cremated and these bones are also thrown into the same hole, together with discarded human bones.

The bones of hundreds of people from Secunda, Barberton, Nelspruit, Lydenburg, Ermelo, Belfast, Standerton and Brokhorstspruit can be found in a number of holes behind the crematorium. Many of these deceased's loved ones can be sure that their loved ones bones have been discarded with many other peoples, cat's and dog's remains, in one hole.

The article explains the problem started when some of the undertakers complained that the "ash" provided by the crematorium is not "white" enough. A decision was taken to discard all bones with tarnish marks on them, into the holes which belong to the crematorium.

(I truly hope dear reader that you are able to see what is happening here. This particular crematorium reportedly operates at temperatures between 800°C en 1000°C, although it could be increased to 1500°C and even after this intense heat – **THERE ARE BONES AS WHITE AS SNOW WITH NO SCORCH MARKS ON THEM!**)

The Observer reported that the vast majority of bones in the holes were; wait for it…**White and without blemish!** One of the crematoriums employees confirmed to the observer that only a small portion of the crushed bones are handed to the relatives, the rest gets thrown in the holes.

The article states that the holes are kept closed with a large plate with a little trapdoor, which is covered with dirt so that people would not detect the deceit. During the visit of the Observer, the plate was still hot from the 8 bodies which were cremated that day, of which the bones were dumped in the hole. It is not clear how many of the "mass graves" exists on the premises, but that almost the entire lawn at the back of the crematorium is one large mass-gravesite.

From the "Middelburg Observer" of Friday, 2 November 2012, with the heading, "Bones dumped in hole after cremation – A Mass Grave, by Gerhard Rheeder", I list some excerpts as follows:

We are already familiar with the process, but the Observer lists the following: (My translation)

> *Personnel open the oven to see if the flesh were reduced to ashes, after which the bones are placed on a cooling plate to cool down. Any metals are removed by using a magnet and then the bones are ground to bio-degradable granules so that the relatives may scatter the ashes if they so choose.*

Lets just take a few notes from the above – this article confirms that the bones are gathered after the cremation. You will recall there is nothing left of the body in the form of ash. Then the article confirms that the bones are ground. It then says that the "ashes" may be scattered, but it confirmed already that it is not ashes, but BONES WHICH ARE GROUND! I trust you see the deception here, not because I said it, but it is confirmed in a news paper hot of the press!

We continue:

> *According to Independent Crematoriums South-Africa's brochure, families are assured that they <u>only</u> receive their loved ones ashes as the cremation oven can only accept one adult at a time.*

This is like saying: "When this butcher makes your sausage, you can be assured that it is with the meat of one cow only, because we only slaughter one cow at a time"

We trust the butcher that he would at any and all costs only mince the meat of one cow, then clean the mince machine and then only proceed to mince the next cow, while he keeps the meat of the first cow separate, just before he continues to make the sausage, from only a single cow's meat, right? Yeah…right….

> *Before a cremation may proceed, an appointed medial arbitrator must approve the cremation, after- the identity of the deceased has been obtained and verified, the cause of death been established and that the cremation is not against the wishes of the deceased.*

Let's note the last remark:

> *that the cremation is not against the wishes of the deceased*

We will look more closely into this statement towards the end of the book. Another surprise:

> *Mr Danie Coetzee, regional manager of the Independent Crematoriums South-Africa declares that the throwing away of bones is not out of the ordinary, but rather unknown….we expect that the families will be made familiar with this practise by the undertakers that the relatives do not receive all the remains…*

Allow me to translate from the Wilsenach translation:

We have been throwing the bones of the cremated bodies into holes for a long time, but now that we have been caught red-handed, we blame the undertaker's for not sharing this information with the relatives!

Permit yourself to be in the shoes of the undertaker for awhile…

"Dear loved ones and relatives, here is your departed loved ones ashes, it is not all the remains though". You inform the relatives. "Well, why is this not all the remains?" the relative's ask. "Well…uh….if we grind the scorches bones with the white bones, the colour of the ash is not white enough…" you desperately try to explain. "What do you do with the remains you haven't given us?" the fuming relatives want to know. "Uhmm…uh… we throw it into a hole at the back of the crematorium together with other human bones, baboons, cats and dogs…etc."

Question:
As an undertaker, would you be able to do this, day in and day out, explain this vulgar despicable process over and over to all the grieving relatives, being interrogated by every relative every day?

Question:
Do you hear the Christian preachers who soothe our ears so skilfully and tell us that we can choose and nobody may tell us otherwise, and that nothing is wrong with cremation, share these gory details with us? Never!

Question:
Did you, who may have had a loved one cremated, know that the "ash" you received is not ash, but the ground and crushed pulverised bones of your loved one?

Question:
Did you, who may have had a loved one cremated, know that the majority of your loved ones remains have not been handed to you, but have been discarded, most probably in some vile, dreadful despicable manner?

Question:
Did you, who may have had a loved one cremated, know that in the same cremation oven, first a dog was cremated, then a cat, then your loved one and then a monkey?

Mr Danie Coetzee explains further:

> *I accept that some will have a problem with animal cremations, but they have to consider that human bodies are also cremated in the same ovens*

He goes on to say that families with pets may go to the crematorium and request that their pet be cremated individually with the remains to be returned to the family, but otherwise a number of animals will be cremated simultaneously in the same oven and their bones are also thrown in the same hole.

Mr Coetzee then states that he regards the hole as a grave which they purchase from the municipality for burial of the remaining bones.

The municipality however does not agree with this statement, they say:

> *Although we are aware of the holes in which bones are dumped and we even dig new holes when old holes are filled, we must state that the property belongs to the crematorium and is not municipality property; so says the head of Parks from the Steve Tshwete municipality, Dalene Lambrechts. She says she was not aware that animal bones are discarded together with human bones in these holes and also have no knowledge of how many holes have already been filled.*

If you are shocked by these facts, you must rather be grateful because me Lambrechts states that **people must be grateful that the bones of their loved ones don't end up in refuse bags at the municipal dumpsite** – reported the Observer.

Mr Coetzee begs the question: **"What is the alternative?"**
He explains that they can bury the bones in individual grave sites, but this will double the cost of the cremation.

(Oops – there goes the "cheap" cremation cost theory down the hole together with the bones…not so?)

Let's analyse these events:
The argument that a cremation is less expensive than a traditional burial evaporates like fog in sunshine when they have to bury the remains anyway! How many people are there who knows about the largest portion of the remains which needs to be buried anyway, when they receive the so-called

ashes? We've read already that the relatives are totally unaware of this and are definitely not notified by the crematorium related industry.

The shameful irony is: You think your loved one was cremated and you received "all" the "ashes" in the urn, but back at the ranch, or should I say "**at the back of the crematorium**", your loved ones bones have been buried already, in a mass grave, with a host of animals. Vile I tell you, absolutely revolting and disgusting…but nonetheless suitable for an abominable pagan barbaric practice like this!

Mr Coetzee states that they are doing research as to the availability of land as the government is considering procurement of crematorium ovens.

My comments?
Well, firstly as follows:
The church paves the way for the government and they, the church will always "prepare" the "flock" in this way, being it biblical or satanical, it does not matter. You will see in the near future how churches and Christian clergyman are going to preach and promote cremation at all costs. I will not be surprised if they declare the traditional burial a cardinal sin! They will tell you that cremation is "god's" will and it will be "god's" will, the god of this world, Satan! What's more is people will accept this as "god's" will because that same "god" will blind their minds!

> **2Co 4:4** *In whom the god of this world hath blinded the minds of them which believe not, lest the light of the glorious gospel of Christ, who is the image of God, should shine unto them.*

My second comment: If private companies are operating in this manner, can you imagine……
I wonder if the "muti" (black African medicine) is still potent when the sexual organs of a cadaver are harvested, just before cremation ensues….?

Still from the Observer under the heading "**Dogs do get cremated**":

> *The manager of the Middelburg Crematoria, Kezia Jacobz, confirmed Thursday that the bones of all who are cremated at the crematorium were thrown into a hole behind the crematorium. She says that the information is not passed on to families. Families are also unaware that animal bones along with human bones were thrown into the same holes. Jacobz apparently denied the majority of the remains were thrown into the holes. She says there remain virtually no bones after the cremation"*

(I wonder if this manager ever witnessed a cremation, hence her statement that there are virtually no bones left after the cremation. This procedure unfortunately does not operate in the same manner as barbecue charcoal or wood where only a little bit of grey powder remains after the fire died! Or is she totally oblivious of the fact that the regional manager of the *Independent Crematoriums South Africa, Mr Danie Coetzee,* has already "spilled the bones", I mean "spilled the beans"…)

Now I ask, how on earth may these pagan idolatrous processes that crush can and grind bones, along with animals bones discarded in the same hole, be reconciled with Scripture that says:

> **_Joh 19:36_** **_For these things were done, <u>that the scripture should be fulfilled, A bone of him shall not be broken.</u>_**

Why do you think these important aspects in Scripture are recorded for us by God himself? Is it not to serve as an example for us, so that we must follow in His footsteps or at the very least, do the best we possibly can?

> **_1Pet 2:21_** **_For even hereunto were ye called: because Christ also suffered for us, <u>leaving us an example, that ye should follow his steps:</u>_**

I recently spoke to a man considering cremation; he did not wish to be buried next to what he calls heathens in the same cemetery. Well uncle, how would you feel if your bones were cremated first and then buried with a few heathens, cats, dogs and donkey bones, altogether in the same hole? No, stick to the correct procedure! My own father is buried just a few graves away from one of the biggest communists South Africa has ever seen, but it is a thousand times more acceptable than cremation.

Furious relatives

On the web where the article appeared, (source listed already) a few very upset relatives shared their feelings towards the Middelburg Crematorium issues. I list some of their comments here without the names of the individuals to protect their identity, inclusive of spelling mistakes (sic).

> *"so dissapointed at middelburg crematorium - I have inharit a lo of money and I will use every sent I have to sue this people They are going to pay big time for misleading us as families I wil start riods if I have to this is so the end of this place even if I have to burrn them down!!!! Someone is going to pay !! With blood"*

"How can people do this to families didn't they think it would be discovered someday. How can the funeral homes like avbob lie to families like this and how can the people at the crematorium be so disrespectful about our loved ones remains to dump it into a whole with there remains of animals. Did we as the families not pay with tears and heart ache and now have to find out that our love one's remains is discarded in mass graves. How can the funeral homes the crematorium and even city council live with the fact. I pray that the families stand up against this practise. SOMEONE HAS TO PAY... I'm personally going to start action against avbob. Effected families let's stand up and contact carte Blanche!!!!!"

"My mother was also cremated at this place and it is very upsetting to realise that half of her remains are lying in a hole somewhere. The ash I collected from the crematorium was not even in a proper wooden box, but in a small cardboard box. This is really unacceptable, we may just as well have buried her. Shame on you!"

INHUMANE! – I wonder if their some of their family members were also as crudely dumped in hole with animal bones. Why could they not have informed right from the start that not all the remains could be cremated. My father in law was cremated there about three months ago, but if we knew the truth we would have given him a proper burial. Even though cemeteries also degrades over time, it is much better than to be dumped into a hole with other animal's bones! Someone HAS to take responsibility for this, we will not let this go!

My comments? There is only one of three scenarios up for discussion here:

You do not believe in God or His Word, and do this act without any moral or religious beliefs.
What are you complaining about?

You think you believe in God and His Word, but you exalt yourself above God and His Word, because you are a modern human and you can decide for yourself what is right and what is wrong, irrelevant of what the Scriptures teaches us.
What are you complaining about?

You believe in God and His Word and searched to find the right and the wrong regarding cremation. Your search however was limited to your preacher and he soothed your ears by saying you can decide and none may judge you. You were so happy because you heard what you wanted to hear. Well, now you know...

THESE PREACHERS ARE LYING TO YOU!

Bogus ash

From other sources with regard to cremation in general, there is a wealth of stories of people who did not receive their loved ones "real" ashes. There was the case of a relative whom scattered the ashes of their deceased at their favourite place as requested, but when the urn was emptied, a set of dentures fell out. The problem? Well, the deceased never had any dentures!

In another incident, the relatives scattered the deceased ashes in three different locations as directed by the departed. However, with the third scattering, a metal identification plate fell from the urn. The problem? The identification plate was not the identification plate of the deceased, but someone else's!

The body

One of the most difficult subjects I tried to research was: what happens to the body during the cremation process? There are very few sources containing information shedding more light on this subject. There is a book that was written regarding this information, but unfortunately it is unavailable and out of print. We will look at a single source, but I cannot confirm the accuracy of the information, but as with the rest of the content in this book as well as the application of logic and common sense, we have to keep some things in mind...

Whether this information which follows is true or not, we all know how the fat in a sausage heats up inside the skin when it is cooked or grilled. We also know just how far the hot, liquid fat or oil can eject from the sausage when the skin is pricked and we also know what happens to a piece of meat when left unattended on a fire. The meat shrinks, pulls, stretches, changes shape, changes colour to black and curls up. Disgusting as it may sound, the cremation process is not that different from what we observe with a piece of meat left on an unattended campfire. Consider what happens to an egg in a microwave oven if you forget to prick a hole in the shell. It explodes with pieces of egg all over the microwave surfaces.

Our body composition

We now know what the basic elements of the body is and what their percentages are, therefore we can look at what happens to the body when it is subjected to the furious flames and blazing heat of hell, sorry... I meant cremation.

First, the coffin, "burn box or container" burns away very quickly to ash which is collected in the crematoria filters. Steel components such as handles, screws, hinges etc. are later removed from the remains. The water content in the body, approximately 64%, evaporates quickly together with all the gasses trapped inside the body. After this, the flesh of the body starts to burn. At first, everything burns black, and then later, when the carbon binds with oxygen to form carbon dioxide, flames will remove all water and carbon from the bones, leaving snow white bones. Some bones will have dark carbon stains and this is normally caused by the use of cancer medication which is alleged to alter the bone composition.

The massive flames first consume the coffin from the top. Next is the cadaver's hair which is consumed in an instant. The skin is next with the fat and muscles being consumed by the fire shortly afterwards. It also happens from time to time that the body contacts and appears to sit in an upright position, arms and legs start to contract and makes the body appears to be alive. The reason for this is the blazing heat which contracts the muscles when gasses, water and fat evaporates. Remaining bodily fluids in the organs starts to cook and crackle and is ejected in all directions. At this stage the heart, lungs and other organs are visible against the sharp contrast of the white skeleton when the fat and skin has evaporated.

I think we should stop here, but you can use your imagination. This is so gruesome it is unthinkable, but if you find this shocking it is very good! You have to be aware what your body will be subjected to during a cremation and what's more, you must be aware what your dearly departed loved one's body will be going through during this pagan idolatrous practice. How else are you going to be able to make an informed decision, especially when you are being deceived by your church pastors and preachers?

Here is a rhetorical question – Does the body sit upright and come alive due to the burning process, contracting the muscles.... or .... Does it jump up with a: "Oh hell, what have I done!"
People whom are scared to awake in a coffin underground must consider these gruesome facts as well...

Please see the following image of a burning body inside a cremation oven during the cremation process, now see yourself in that same image and make a decision to follow the scriptures…

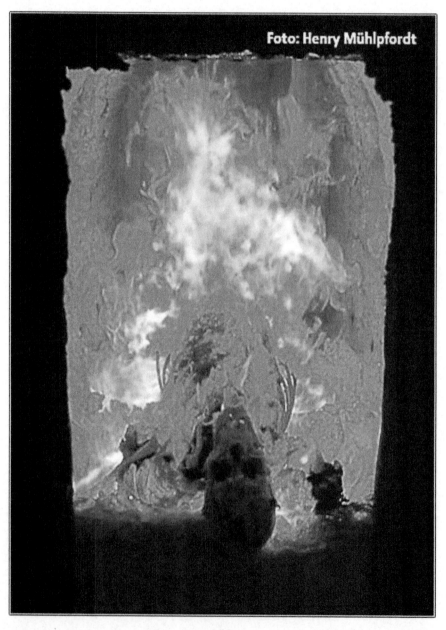

Foto: Henry Mühlpfordt

If this image shocks you it makes me really happy. You have to be aware of all the details regarding this practice. Grandma does not change with the snap of a finger from an adult body to a little bit of ashes inside a beautifully crafted ash-container. She goes through a pagan, unscriptural process which God Himself only reserves for His greatest enemies when He pours out His wrath! If you want to do this to your loved ones, at least do it having obtained all the gory details as well, gruesome or not, you will never be able to say: "I did not know"

> **Jas 4:17 Therefore <u>to him that knoweth to do good, and doeth it not, to him it is sin.</u>**

There will be people who say this description in terms of what happens to the body in the oven is not true, but I know one thing, do not tell me the body lies there in the oven, obedient and docile and evaporates from the chimney of the crematorium in a quiet little smoke trail. You are not going to tell me a donkey is a zebra without pyjamas.

Maybe you start to cry in the oven during your cremation. Not to worry, just request your idolatrous gods (companies) to deliver you…

> **Isa 57:13 <u>When thou criest, let thy companies deliver thee;</u> but the wind shall carry them all away; vanity shall take them: but he that putteth his trust in me shall possess the land, and shall inherit my holy mountain;**

When you are a-whoring with other gods, and believe you me, you are doing this unknowingly due to your church and your ministers smuggling pagan rituals into the church and calling it Christian, God says go and consult your gods for help!

I often wonder how many people feel that their prayers are unanswered, but they are unable to link the latter to the idolatrous worshipping of pagan practices…right there in their churches and homes!

Mercury Poisoning

Similarly, just a last word regarding the argument that cremation is "clean" and aesthetically more acceptable than a ground burial: This disgusting practice is far from clean; a more appropriate description for cremation would rather be a "fraudulent, deceitful, gruesome, disgusting, dreadful, revolting, sickening, spine-chilling, creepy, unclean, abominable mess!"

Do you remember the following argument in favour of cremation?

Hygienic:

A body which decomposes posts the following dangers:

- **Spreading of diseases and epidemics**
- **Polluting of underground water sources**

Of course, the dangers of decomposition are totally eliminated by the cremation process. Or so we are told...

Some excerpts from our source – my translation:

"Cremation costs to rise as tooth fillings poison the living"[21] by TOM KELLY

Relatives of the deceased must pay for new filters which need to ensure that mercury fumes are not released into the atmosphere. Costs are calculated to be an additional third of the current cost of a cremation. Environmentalists say that it is an absolute necessity to ensure the spiral fumes from the crematorium chimneys, caused by tooth fillings, do not pollute our air, waterways, soil, animals and food.

Mercury poisoning is linked to defects in new-born infants such as kidney illnesses and multiple sclerosis. Release of this metal through crematoriums is calculated at one sixth in England. If this situation is not curbed quickly, it is estimated that in 2020 the calculation will be two thirds, which will make crematoriums the largest mercury polluter in England.

Government forced the crematoriums to install at least half of the required filters by 2012. The cost of the filters is estimated at £300,000 each! This additional cost will be paid by relatives, regardless of whether the deceased had tooth fillings or not. Oops.... There goes the "cremation is cheaper" argument yet again!

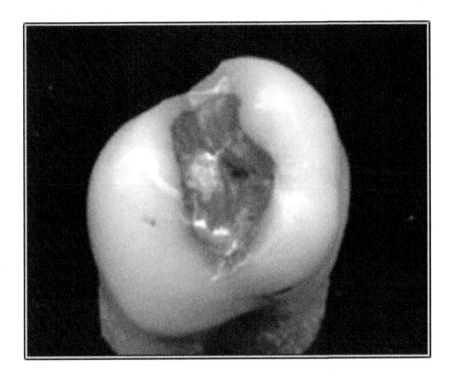

Millions of Brits have 2 to 4 grams of mercury in their mouths. Consider that a single gram of mercury can elevate poison to a dangerous level for fish in a 25 acre lake! Adults whom absorbed mercury or inhaled mercury fumes loose their appetite, becomes emotionally unstable, cannot sleep, develop abdominal problems as well as sore gums. Researcher's also found that higher levels of mercury raise the risk of heart ailments in men. High levels of mercury in food are very dangerous for pregnant woman as it attacks the central nervous system and brain of their unborn babies.

The alternative is to remove all tooth fillings from cadavers prior to cremation commencing, but due to the time involved, it would raise the cost of cremation considerably.

For those who are not aware, the undertaker must have documented proof that the cadaver is free from a pacemaker prior to the cremation process as the pacemaker explodes during the process. The cadaver must be cut open to ensure no pacemaker is present.

Our next source is entitled:

"Cremation pollution? Neighbours nervous as practice grows, some question mercury emissions from burning fillings" [22] **by Terence Chea.**

The residents of San Francisco, USA are resisting the erection of crematoriums close to neighbourhoods. Some scientists allege that crematoriums are safe and mercury poisoning is minimal to none. The Environmental Protection Agency however supply figures of up to 320 pounds of mercury released into the atmosphere by crematoriums, while activists are quoting figures of up to 3 tons.

The Neptune Society of North Carolina drew protestors from Richmond when they erected a crematorium only 2 blocks away from a day-care centre for children. Some of the protesters were displaying boards which read: "Over my dead body!"

The source also states the following important information:

> *"We don't want to be guinea pigs," said Henry Clark, who heads the West County Toxic Coalition in Richmond. "These things are not properly regulated. There's a scarcity of information on what chemicals they use in the process, and what is actually released."*

There are a few sources which discusses the mercury danger at length and with a lot of detail. Personally I think we barely even scratched the dangers of mercury poisoning in this book. Please feel free to research the mercury issue yourself:
"Crematory Emissions Data" [23]
"Crematory outcry has Minnesota cities weighing risks" [24]

I am not fond of scaring people, but some of my sources mentions Mercury and Mascara in the same sentence. Without painting myself into a corner, I would like to extend a friendly warning to the ladies to thoroughly check the ingredients of their mascara and make-up in general. Mercury is not a poison to be treated lightly. Just Google: "mercury in mascara". Normally where there is smoke there is fire as well… be aware that mercury on mommy's body has far reaching effects for the unborn baby.

Ash applications

I will be referring to "grandma's ashes" purely as a figure of speech. If I come across as mocking some of the things people do with the ashes of the deceased I am sorry, but these practices, from a biblical perspective is nothing less than utterly ridiculous. It simply confirms yet again that man has now become his own "god", works out his own salvation and decides for himself what is acceptable and what is not and stuff the bible. Remember that I am not judging cultures where cremations and associated rituals are practiced. I respect their religion and convictions and nobody should even attempt to change them. This book however is written for the following people only:

> **_Joh 17:9_ _I pray for them: I pray not for the world, but for them which thou hast given me; for they are thine._**
> **_Joh 17:10_ _And all mine are thine, and thine are mine; and I am glorified in them._**

I translate from our source[25]

If ash could paint

Take grandmas ash urn and a bit of acrylic paint, mix the two ingredients together and voilà, you have "ash paint". Now you (or an artist of your choice) may proceed to paint grandmas favourite landscape on a canvas and hey presto, grandma is permanently preserved in a painting you can hang on the living room wall. Just be careful what you do in the living room, grandma may be watching!

Sparkling ash

A certain company provides a service where they take human ash and use it make diamonds. The process roughly works as follows: The ash "supposedly" contains carbon which when subjected to intense heat and pressure will turn into a gem. The gem or diamond can then be set in a pendant or earrings and voila, grandma is always with you. You can even select the carat, cut and colour of the gem. You can even have it set in your engagement ring. Wouldn't that be wonderful? You can point to your ring on a sunny day and proclaim; "Isn't grandma sparkling in this wonderful sunshine!"

My problem with this is: What "ash" are they using? There is no ash, just crushed bone! People are gullible enough to believe anything aren't they?

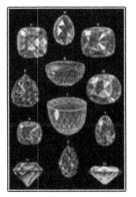

Ash moon-landing

Another service is where grandma's ashes are put in a tiny container which is ejected into outer space. Shortly they say, they will be able to propel or shoot this tiny container so it lands on the surface of the moon. There is also another option of a memorial voyage into outer space, which returns to earth again. This way, you can tell the story of grandma, finally achieving her dreams of becoming an astronaut in her old age.

Reef ash

Are you fond of oceanic life? Do you love diving in the ocean? Well, then there is a special option just for you. Grandma's ashes are cast into an artificial corral reef. This is then sunk on a special location out in the ocean where divers frequents the area. Beautiful fish and ocean organisms start to accumulate in and around the reef, and the best of all? Grandma does not even have to wear diving gear!

Tree ash

You send grandmas ashes to this organisation; they mix the ashes with potting soil and plant a bonsai tree in the soil-mix. They even attach a metal plate on the pot, so you don't get confused between grandma and granddads trees. If everything goes according to plan, they mail it to you via airmail, but not before they monitored it for 30 days to ensure that tree does not develop "ASHma".

Flying ash

An aviation company is prepared to "scatter" grandma's ashes from a distance of between 500 and 2000 feet. They say there is more "dignity" in this practice as opposed to just scattering the ashes on the ground. Well, if grandma always wanted to fly and perhaps skydive as well, this is just what the doctor ordered!

Off the topic a bit – did you know you don't have to have a parachute when you go skydiving? It's true! You only need a parachute when you want to skydive more than once…

Ash-busting balloon

A very creative company will put grandma's ash in a 5 foot, bio-degradable air balloon, fill it with helium and send it skyward up to a height of approximately 30,000 feet. This is of course if grandma had flown already, but she wants to achieve greater heights in life, or is that death..? The balloon is set to burst, (pop) at the nominal height and then the wind takes grandmas ashes to the four corners of the earth. Oh my…where her final resting place would be, no one knows.

Ash goes Guy

These guys are just the thing if grandma had a crush on Guy Fox. They have two models to choose from. The first is where they incorporate grandma's ashes into their fireworks. They shoot the fireworks out over the ocean and grandma's ash neatly floats down into the sea. The second option is fireworks; containing grandma's ashes which you can fire yourself at home. This way, grandma can scare the dog mindless for one last time, before she finally rests. Personally I think this is value for money, think about it…. Grandma flies, sky-dives and goes out with bang, before she falls in the ocean, and all of this with a single shot…

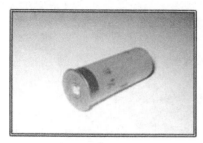

Thunder ash

There is no company providing this service. There are companies providing the service only using animal ash, but not human ash. The source however does supply a do-it-yourself guide for anyone who is interested. This is for the grandma's who loved western movies and such. Granma's ash is mixed with gunpowder and then used to load shotgun shells.

How and when you would "fire" these shells I am not sure.... Perhaps it

would come I handy when you have to defend yourself when there is a burglar or mugger.... Maybe you can shout something like: "Freeze or grandma will shoot!"

Nope, I have no idea…

Pencil ash

This is what I call an absolutely brilliant idea. Grandma can last years with this creative idea, an ingenious invention I tell you. Granma's ashes are fused together with graphite to form the lead you get in pencils. They claim to make approximately 240 pencils with grandma's ash. The pencils are sharpened with a special device which collects the shavings and so even the shavings are kept in memory of grandma. Now – lets assume the teacher suspects that Johnny did not do his homework himself and she confronts Johnny: "Johnny, don't lie now, who wrote in your notebook…?" Would it be correct if Johnny answers that it was his grandma?

Autopilot ash

The same company that manufactures the "ash-pencils" also have another brilliant idea. Grandma also flies, but it doesn't cost anything. They take the

ashes and incorporate it into seed which is then placed in a bird-feeder. The birds consume the seeds and carries grandma to who knows where. The "ejection" at the final resting place may not be that nice though.

Ash-in-one

This is for the golfers. There is a golf course with an "ossuary" under the putting green. Two of the practice holes are connected to the ossuary and grandpa's ashes may be thrown in these holes, where it comes to rest underneath the golf course. The question remains – does this mean grandpa finally achieved that hole-in-one?

Furthermore, ashes can be worked into glass, concrete stones or slabs for decorating the garden, necklaces and even time capsules. This is enough for now, but there is one last practice I have to share with you…

A very simple recipe:[26]
Take a bowl, wash well and dry.
Add one cup of ingredient "A" into the bowl.
Add one teaspoon of vodka into the bowl.
Mix well for about one hour.
If the mixture is too thin add more of ingredient A; if the mixture is too thick, add another teaspoon of vodka.
Once the mixture is ready, place in an airtight container and seal. Store it in a dark place.

What is this substance used for?

Tattoo Ink! – I kid you not!

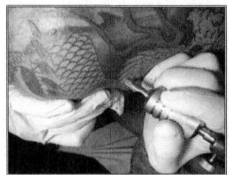

Would you like to guess what ingredient "A" is? Yes you guessed it, granny's ashes!
(Please do not try this at home, I have absolutely no idea if this recipe is true or not, I do know however that they really do tattoo with ink made from human ashes)

Yip, there you have granny, right on your shoulder. This is of course only until you are cremated yourself, but be positive; you can always point to the dragon on your shoulder and tell your friend that it's actually your grandma.

Your friend may be shocked and say something like: "Damn, was your grandma really that ugly?" Then you can explain how the system works and that the dragon it is not really your granny, it's just her ashes under your skin. Maybe you can even sing that song …. I've got you….under my skin… grandma.

The human Liquidiser

Alkaline hydrolysis is a process used in the disposal of human cadavers. The inventor is of the opinion that this process is ecologically more acceptable than cremation. The process is being marketed worldwide as an alternative to cremation as well as the traditional burial. Approximately 1000 people have chosen this process for their disposal since August 2007 (the source was quoted November 2012) in the USA. The majority of sources indicate the company "*Resolution Limited*" to be the main driving force behind this process.

My translation from our source:
"Alkaline Hydrolysis"[27]

The process

The body is placed in a cloth (bag) made if silk and then placed into a metal cage. This cage, containing the body is placed in a device called the "Resomator". The device, or machine is filled with water and "ley" (Potassium hydroxide), and heated to 160^0 C (320 ^{0} F). This "mixture" is regulated by a high pressure system to prevent over-cooking inside the vessel.

The body is then broken down over an approximate three hour period to basic elements. The end result is a green-brown tinted fluid which contains "*amino acids, peptides, sugars and salts*", with white porous bone "calcium phosphate" which can easily be broken by hand, but normally a "*cremulator*" is used to produce the white dust which is crushed bone, alias "ashes".

From the 50 states of the USA, 7 states have been granted permission to utilise this process. In some states this technology still needs to be studied and verified before public application will be granted. Subsequently this process has been legalised in 7 of the 50 states of the USA.

> *"In resomation, a body is placed in a steel chamber along with a mixture of water and potassium hydroxide. Air pressure inside the vessel is increased to about 145 pounds per square inch, and the temperature is raised to about 356 degrees Fahrenheit. After three or more hours, the corpse is reduced to bones that are then crushed into a fine, white powder. That dust can be scattered by families or placed in an urn. Dental fillings are separated out for safe disposal"*

A more fitting description for this mess would probably be "a human pressure cooker". What do you think happens to this green-brown soup? The answer is from our next source:[28]

> *"The most recent of these to land on American shores is a process that uses heat, pressure and chemicals to liquefy a body in just a few hours, leaving behind <u>sterile remains that can be poured into the wastewater system</u>"*

And there you have it! You are flushed like a child's dead goldfish "**DOWN THE TOILET**".

In case you have missed it, this is extremely important and crucial information you should take note of:
The white substance which remains can be broken by hand, but they use the same cremulator (industrial blender) to crush the bones which serves as ash for the relatives. Do you see the pattern again? Even this steam cooker which reduces an entire human body to a soup, cannot reduce the bones to powder, the bones remain!

The following website[29] lists the "advantages" of this process of liquefying human bodies.

> *"Resomation is an alternative to cremation and burial which offers a number of environmental benefits including:*
> * **A significantly lower carbon footprint**
> * **Significantly less energy required in the form of electricity and gas**
> * **No airborne mercury emissions**
> * **The sterile liquid effluent is safely returned to the water cycle free from any traces of DNA"**

Global Warming

Let us observe these four advantages more closely:

"The process lowers the carbon footprint"
By now you should know that the "carbon footprint" issue is being driven by "Global Warming". When I share the following, you may think that I must have smoked some of grandma's ashes, but to the contrary, this is absolutely true. You may just have never heard this before, hence your reaction:

> *Global Warming is one of the biggest political scams that ever existed!*

I have a mountain of information related to this subject which I have been studying for many years. This information, believe it or not, comes from highly recognised and respected scientists, stating with facts, figures and **GOOD** science that **Global Warming is a HOAX**. Speaking about HOAXES, one of the books written on this subject is titled:

The Greatest Hoax – How the global warming conspiracy threatens our future".

Documented evidence exposing global warming as a lie and a hoax are plentiful and endless if you care to do some research, however I am referring to this book due to the author, he is an American senator: James Inhope. He describes in detail how the entire scam operates, how it presently affects us, and how this scam is going to detrimentally affect our future to such levels we never even thought to be possible!

There is no such thing as Global Warming, caused, driven or influenced by mankind. There are many motives and agendas behind this scam and money is only one of them. Here is just a small example of exactly how money is sucked and scammed from the public.

From our source:[30]
"How South Africa's carbon tax may affect businesses"
The South African government is proposing to impose *carbon tax* estimated at ZAR 8,76 Billion on 40 companies. These companies are labelled as releasing the highest emissions of carbon dioxide. The amount of R75 per ton of CO^2 will gradually be increased to R200, estimated to generate a worldwide carbon tax of US $2.5 Billion. This is approximately R25 Billion South-African Rand, (using an exchange rate of 9). Please allow me to jot this down with all the zeros:

R 25 000 000 000

Well, we should be lucky that we as normal citizens won't pay, it will just be the corporations, or is it…? Companies do not lower their profits to cover these costs. They lower salary increases and bonuses, increase their product prices, and last on the list, lay workers off. On our salaries we are affected at three different levels:

Lower salary increases, increased expenses and the third aspect is interesting, since you have to pay for something else with your shrinking salary.......

I quote an extract from a source titled:

> ***"How much will you be forking out for the latest government tax when you buy a new car?"***

(By Fiona Zerbst, Aug 2010)

> *"The already struggling motor industry will be dealt a blow on September 1 when the new CO^2 vehicle emissions tax comes into effect. And the bad news is that the consumer will be absorbing the costs.*
>
> *In effect, the tax will be charged on all new cars and light commercial vehicles. Buyers will pay R75 for each g/km of CO^2 emissions above a threshold of 120g/km, the lowest threshold in the world. The price hike? About 2,5%.*
>
> *In the case of higher fuel consumption vehicles, the tax and the price effect could be as high as 6%. So the tax burden amounts to about R1,6-billion a year, in respect of new cars. A further R800-million taxes in respect of light commercial vehicles is also anticipated.*
>
> *To put that in real terms, it will theoretically add:*
>
> *R525 to a Yaris T1 1.0 3-dr MY 08—(CO^2 emission is 127, so you calculate the cost in terms of however many grams over 120 x R75).*
>
> *R3,675 to a Corolla 1.8 Advanced MY09 (CO^2 emission is 169).*
>
> *R5,250 to a Mercedes Benz B200 Turbo MPV MY08 (CO^2 emission is 190)"*

For example, here is a document with the heading:

"CARBON TAX FOR MOTOR VEHICLES"[31]

The first line of the article starts with:

"Climate change is caused by carbon emissions"

Here is my problem – you should be aware of all of these issues, but have you ever seen, heard or read the following with regards, to global warming? If you calculate the volume of all the gasses (CO_2) released by animals, the ocean, and nature, plants etc. and compare that to all the manmade gasses put together then the manmade gasses amounts to 0.3%.

I realise that I have digressed a bit with the global warming hoax, but what I am trying to get across is what is happening between the lines. This green-brown liquid human remains soup is going to be mandatory in future and I will tell you why – you guessed it – cremation is going to be blacklisted as releasing too much carbon gasses and it will be accepted in churches worldwide to save mother-earth and the climate! You know, the bible tells us to "search" and then it also tells us the following:

__Pro 22:3 A prudent man foreseeth the evil, and hideth himself:__
__but the simple pass on, and are punished.__

The people ruling the planet, and please don't think for one moment I am talking about governments and heads of states and countries, operates as follows: They create a crisis where no crises exists, then they draw public reaction to the crises with media brainwashing and when they achieved that, they storm in with their pre-manufactured "solution" to save whatever needs saving, but we are too blind to see the evil and therefore we are unable to hide. This so-called solution to the self-made crisis, enriches them and tears us to pieces, piece by piece en route to the new world order where there is but one religion and also one "god" and believe you me, this is not the God of the bible! If you think I am crazy its fine, I don't want the reader to believe a word I say, but do yourself a favour and do some research on your own…

We recently had a bit of snow during the winter at a certain area in South Africa. Although this is not a common occurrence which happens every year, it is normal every 7 to 10 years or so, since the beginning of time. However, when it snowed that day, the radio host was talking about the snow and said: "Just shows you what global warming can do". I did not know whether to laugh, cry or just crack myself! I was absolutely speechless…!

Let me summarise: if are not reading this book outside, please get up and go look at the sky, if it is not overcast. If it is dark, try again tomorrow morning. You should be able to see, without spectacles even, a huge fireball in the sky, much, much bigger than our little planet earth. We call it the sun. We as humans can do absolutely nothing to make that thing warmer or colder. We cannot WARM the GLOBE even if we tried our best…We are merely going through cycles. Cycles, occurring from Noah's days already, but this generation did not experience some of these cycles yet, that's all. The rulers of the world however are, super smart and they exactly know how to and when to…. Need I say more?

Enough with the digression – back to the so-called advantages of the human pressure cooker:

"The system uses less gas and electricity"
Maybe……I wouldn't know, but quite frankly my dear I don't give a …..

"No Mercury emissions in the atmosphere"
Of course not!

"The sterile fluid (remains) is dumped in the water system"

YUK!!!!!!!! Did I read correctly, this is an advantage? To drink grandmothers recycled soup from a faucet tomorrow morning in my drinking water…. An advantage……?

Liquid bone-ash

Even the manufacturers website[32] is misleading regarding the truth, just as with the cremation process. They declare that only *sterile liquid* and *bone ash* remains. Ask yourself how it is possible to have both liquid as well as ash from the same process. There are a few good photos on the web and you can also view a short animation of the process here.[33.]

The footage shows the body going into the pot or vessel, 94% water and 4% acid is pumped into the vessel, heat is increased and pressure added. Once the process is completed the door is opened, (obviously after the human soup has been dumped down the water drain). Here is the surprise again, guess what remains! ALMOST THE COMPLETE SKELETON, the scull, neck, spine, ribs, arms and legs! You can confirm this for yourself by having a look at the photos on their website.

Obviously the pacemaker, titanium hip replacement and tooth fillings also remain. These bones are sent to the *cremulator*, where the bones are crushed in the industrial blender and the so-called "ashes" are then given to the relatives. (I am not sure if they also discard some of the bones behind the "*resomater*" in a hole)

The best is, forget about getting tattooed with grandma's ashes, next week you can make a toast with friends and family, not ON grandma but WITH grandma, INSIDE YOUR GLASS OF SPARKLING WATER. The human-sauce is released in our water system, goes through the waterworks and then we consume it once again from our faucets! Should the water taste well, then you could say:"Mmmm… grandma really tastes great this morning!"

Who says humans can't be recycled…..?
Viva!
Liquidise the dead and feed them to the living!
Viva!

Plastination

I do not wish to dwell on this subject as much, but let's have a brief overview of the following process, from our source: The body is dehydrated with chemicals, all water and fats are decomposed this way. Inside a vacuum filled vessel, all muscles and remaining "anatomy" is filled with a special plastic compound similar to silicon. The body is then meticulously placed in a certain position or posture, and then placed on display in what they call "an educational pose". A few illustrations to follow:

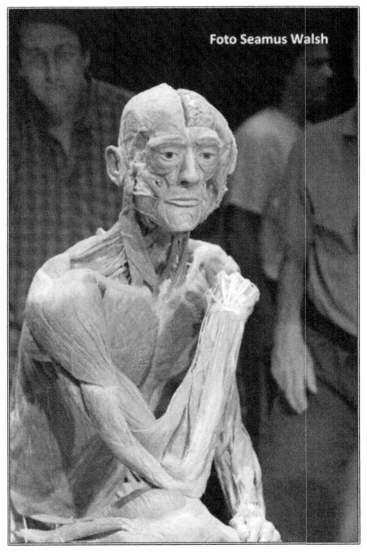

Foto Seamus Walsh

Foto: Paul Stevenson

This process works so well that I had to cover up a part of the human anatomy, almost like the church and the preachers covers the truth from us...

Is this not the ultimate? Now you can have grandma sitting next to you in real life, watching sitcoms with you, amazing technology! Wonderful

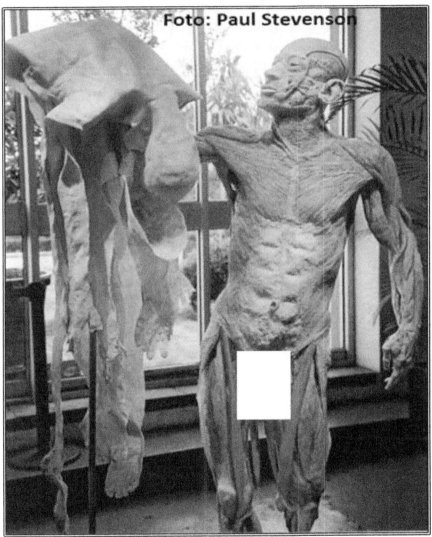

Foto: Paul Stevenson

technology indeed, but if you believe in the GOD of Abraham, Isaac and Jacob and believe in His scriptures and statutes, then this is technology straight from hell, straight from the god of this world.

If I may be as bold as to give my opinion as to how God probably feel about this....

Chapter 8

For whosoever shall be
ashamed of me and of my
words, of him shall the Son of
man be ashamed, when he shall
come in his own glory, and *in*
his Father's, and of the holy
angels.

Luk 9:26

Even elephants bury humans

"Kenya elephant buries its victims"[34]

A Kenyan Elephant buried a mother and child after it had killed them.

Lokalo Ekitela was on her way to the market when an elephant stormed her and her child and killed them. This event took place in Laikipia, a district in Kenya. Before the elephant returned to the jungle, it covered the two bodies with leaves and branches.

Elephants are renowned for burying their dead under leaves and branches. They also remain with their dead for extended periods of time, which one may describe as a period of mourning. When an elephant cow looses a baby elephant, she remains with the dead carcase for days on end.

It is however not that common for elephants to 'bury" humans. Normally they leave the bodies in the open when they kill a person, but there are many witnesses such as big game hunters who say that they have seen and also experienced themselves how elephants would attempt to "cover" humans with branches and leaves, who are merely sleeping in the veldt.

Elephant carcases, particularly the remains of the skeleton is usually carted to and stored in a single location, away from the herd, by the elephants. There are many theories related to this phenomenon which makes it difficult to understand the reasons why elephants do this. The Kenya Wildlife Organisation states that elephants will most of the time only threaten or kill humans to defend their territory. The reaction or attack is then rooted in self-defence towards its territory.

My reason for sharing this in the chapter where we will deal with scripture once gain? I am not sure, maybe just for useless information or maybe just to note that even animals have an instinct to bury their dead...

Follow the majority

If you were not previously familiar with the god Molech, you should by now know who and what he is, namely (amongst others) the GOD of FIRE. Small children were burnt alive as a sacrifice to this god; even Israelites practiced this ungodly ritual. Let us take note of what God's

feeling is related this abomination.

God orders us unequivocally not to let our children pass through the fire to Molech!

> *Lev 18:21 And <u>thou shalt not let any of thy seed pass through the fire to Molech</u>, neither shalt thou profane the name of thy God: I am the LORD.*

You desecrate the Name of your Creator when you partake in these rituals. Would you still willingly choose to provoke God…

> *Jer 25:6 And <u>go not after other gods to serve them</u>, and to worship them, and provoke me not to anger with the works of your hands; and I will do you no hurt.*
> *Jer 25:7 Yet <u>ye have not hearkened unto me</u>, saith the LORD; <u>that ye might provoke me to anger with the works of your hands to your own hurt.</u>*

…then comes the judgement which is so bad that even if you don't indulge in this whoredom, but know of someone who does and you don't do anything about it, God will cut you off!

> *Lev 20:1 And the LORD spake unto Moses, saying,*
> *Lev 20:2 Again, thou shalt say to the children of Israel, Whosoever he be of the children of Israel, or of the strangers that sojourn in Israel, <u>that giveth any of his seed unto Molech; he shall surely be put to death</u>: the people of the land shall stone him with stones.*
> *Lev 20:3 And I will set my face against that man, <u>and will cut him off from among his people; because he hath given of his seed unto Molech, to defile my sanctuary, and to profane my holy name.</u>*
> *Lev 20:4 And if the people of the land do any ways hide their eyes from the man, when he giveth of his seed unto Molech, and kill him not:*
> *Lev 20:5 <u>Then I will set my face against that man, and against his family, and will cut him off, and all that go a whoring after him, to commit whoredom with Molech, from among their people.</u>*

The Israelites committed whoredom against God, so much so that Solomon even built a high place (almost like a temple or shrine) for

Molech. This was such a despicable act that God took away Solomon's kingship. Note that the main cause for this was Solomon's strange (pagan) wife's who mislead him and caused him to worship these false idolatrous god's. You may say we don't live in that time, but I beg to differ, we are in that time with our Christian churches telling us everything and all is well, preachers tell us we may choose and no one may judge us. And all this is happening when God's scriptures are so abundantly clear.

(Note that Molech and Milcom and Baal is the same god)

> *1Kin 11:4 For it came to pass, when Solomon was old, that his wives turned away his heart after other gods: and his heart was not perfect with the LORD his God, as was the heart of David his father.*
> *1Kin 11:5 For Solomon went after Ashtoreth the goddess of the Zidonians, and after Milcom the abomination of the Ammonites.*
> *1Kin 11:6 And Solomon did evil in the sight of the LORD, and went not fully after the LORD, as did David his father.*
> *1Kin 11:7 Then did Solomon build an high place for Chemosh, the abomination of Moab, in the hill that is before Jerusalem, and for Molech, the abomination of the children of Ammon.*
> *1Kin 11:8 And likewise did he for all his strange wives, which burnt incense and sacrificed unto their gods.*
> *1Kin 11:9 And the LORD was angry with Solomon, because his heart was turned from the LORD God of Israel, which had appeared unto him twice,*
> *1Kin 11:10 And had commanded him concerning this thing, that he should not go after other gods: but he kept not that which the LORD commanded.*
> *1Kin 11:11 Wherefore the LORD said unto Solomon, Forasmuch as this is done of thee, and thou hast not kept my covenant and my statutes, which I have commanded thee, I will surely rend the kingdom from thee, and will give it to thy servant*

You may say: "I will never do anything like this". Well, look at verse 5 and note the god "**Ashtoreth**" which is another name for "**Ishtar**", now ask yourself the following question: "**Do I celebrate "Easter?**" If the answer is yes, then I'm afraid you are doing today, exactly as Solomon did then! Go and ask your pastor – he will tell you that I (the author of this book) don't know what I am talking about, that Easter is a Christian holiday and that you should probably burn this book as it does not belong in a Christian home. My comments? Your pastor is right – my books don't belong in

Christian homes; they only belong in the homes of Gods true children, followers of His Word, statutes and commandments to the best of their ability. (I am not kidding – I know churchgoing Christian folk who physically burnt my books!)

Keep one thing in mind though; there is a huge difference between Easter and Passover!

Then there is Christmas – another pagan event, through and through. Yes I also celebrated Christmas for many years until I started doing what God demands us to do, search the scriptures! I don't want to elaborate but to be very blunt I will give you the ingredients of Christmas and Easter, similar to a label containing the ingredient's you get on food items:

Ingredients per 100 Christians		
	Christmas	*Easter*
God	0%	0%
Satan	100%	100%

(Keep a lookout for my book discussing Christmas and Easter)

Dedicated worshippers of these pagan god's were the Moabites, Ammonites and Canaanites. Are you aware of the **ever lasting** judgement God has cast onto these nations? Amongst their offences was their affiliation with the god of fire, Molech?

> *Zec 14:21 Yea, every pot in Jerusalem and in Judah shall be holiness unto the LORD of hosts: and all they that sacrifice shall come and take of them, and seethe therein: <u>and in that day there shall be no more the Canaanite in the house of the LORD of hosts.</u>*

> *Deu 23:3 <u>An Ammonite or Moabite shall not enter into the congregation of the LORD; even to their tenth generation shall they not enter into the congregation of the LORD for ever:</u>*

> *Neh 13:1 On that day they read in the book of Moses in the audience of the people; <u>and therein was found written, that the Ammonite and the Moabite should not come into the congregation of God for ever;</u>*

(Yes, I am fully aware that the churches and preachers tell us that all this changes in the New Testament and everybody can now be saved, all you have to do is believe. This just proves yet again how theology covered-up the truth!)

The point is: This is a mighty and everlasting judgement.
Here is another artist impression of the god Molech or Milcom. Note the "oven" where the children were burnt (cremated) to these gods.

Here is a last portrayal of an artist impression. Once again take note of the "fire oven" and the small children.

You will have to decide for yourself when you are familiar with what the scriptures tells us if there is still nothing wrong with cremation. You will have to decide how true the statement is which says: "The bible does not explicitly prohibit cremation". I can also say like the good doctor: you may decide who you want to follow or serve, God or Milcom. That is truly your own decision, but there is also truly no way in hell you can choose God and cremation together! Cremation is part and parcel of Molech, Milcom and Baal and not part of God YAHWEH (I AM). Did you know that the word or rather name - **"yeshu'ah"**, which means salvation, occurs 78 time in the Old Testament. If you put YAHWEH in front of YAHSHUA it reads –

I AM SALVATION.

Back to the subject at hand:

> *1Kin 18:21 And Elijah came unto all the people, and said, <u>How long halt ye between two opinions? if the LORD be God, follow him: but if Baal, then follow him.</u> And the people answered him not a word.*

> *Zep 1:4 I will also stretch out mine hand upon Judah, and upon all the inhabitants of Jerusalem; and I will cut off the remnant of Baal from this place, and the name of the Chemarims with the priests;*
> *Zep 1:5 And <u>them that worship the host of heaven upon the housetops; and them that worship and that swear by the LORD, and that swear by Malcham;</u>*
> *Zep 1:6 And them that are turned back from the LORD; <u>and those that have not sought the LORD, nor enquired for him.</u>*

Please listen to my advice dear reader. Don't believe one word I have written in this book, but consult with God. How does one consult God? With your knees on the floor and your bible in your hand. What you should never do is consult your preacher because he is going to tell you what you want to hear, what is politically and socially acceptable at the time. He will be "soothing" your ears very skilfully! If you would just realise that the scriptures God gave us is the only measure and if it does not fit into scripture, it is not from God.

When you are sure that you have found the correct answer? Check if that answer agrees or disagrees with the following words of God.

> *Amo 2:1 Thus saith the LORD; For three transgressions of Moab, and for four, <u>I will not turn away the punishment thereof; because he burned the bones of the king of Edom into lime:</u>*
> *Amo 2:2 <u>But I will send a fire upon Moab, and it shall devour the palaces of Kerioth:</u> and Moab shall die with tumult, with shouting, and with the sound of the trumpet:*

> **Amo 2:3** *And I will cut off the judge from the midst thereof, and will slay all the princes thereof with him, saith the LORD.*

And please dear reader, if there is one thing you can believe it is this:
One of my uncles refused to even read my book about infant baptism vs. adult baptism, why? He simply stated that, wait for it... THE MAJORITY cannot be wrong!

> *"Majority is not a magic potion which corrects a wrong"*
> *- Piet Wilsenach*

> **Exo 23:2** **Thou shalt not follow a multitude to do evil**; *neither shalt thou speak in a cause to decline after many to wrest judgment:*

You achieve absolutely nothing when you take that which is wrong and try and force it to be correct, because the majority says it is.
This is exactly the reason why God warns us with the following words:

> **Hos 4:6** *My people are destroyed for lack of knowledge:*

Or follow scripture

You have read in this book what scriptures teach about the practices regarding the dead. "Go ye forth and do the same!" Have yourself and your loved ones buried according to what scripture demands. Please, intensely guard against having yourself or your loved ones bones crushed in and industrial blender and the rest thrown away in a hole with cats and dogs and other animals behind the crematorium.

> **Joh 19:36** *For these things were done, that the scripture should be fulfilled, A bone of him shall not be broken.*

> **1Pet 2:21** *For even hereunto were ye called: because Christ also suffered for us, leaving us an example, that ye should follow his steps:*

And should we choose not to follow his example, he has given us another example:

> **2Pet 2:6** *And turning the cities of Sodom and Gomorrha into ashes condemned them with an overthrow, making them an ensample unto those that after should live ungodly;*

Do not defile the land, make it unclean, by scattering the crushed bones of god's people, but rather respect the land, cleanse it by burying the dead according to scriptures statutes and examples!

> **_Eze 39:12_** **_And seven months shall the house of Israel be burying of them, that they may cleanse the land._**

And if all else have failed and I haven't made a dent yet, all I have to say then is, please do not choose the same fate for yourself as God had chosen for Satan:

> **_Eze 28:18_**
> **_...therefore will I bring forth a fire from the midst of thee,_**
> **_it shall devour thee, and I will bring thee to ashes..._**

Can you really,... no really,... can you choose the same fate for yourself which God has preserved for SATAN and be totally okay with that?

How to - bury

In my previous book I sort of hinted towards how I would like to be buried. I have to confess here that I referred to my dead body as mere dead flesh with very little respect, but after my research for this book, I realise very vividly that although the cadaver is literally mere dead flesh, we must be very careful how we deal with our dead bodies and our loved ones for that matter. Now I understand that there are ordinances, statutes and examples and yes, also punishment should we disregard what scriptures directs us to do in terms of our remains. This is after all our very last say, or decision before we, "leave earth" so to speak...

I have to however make the following abundantly clear:
Please don't attach any mystical value to the dead body like some cultures do. Please don't make an idol of the grave or gravesite. There are numerous people who visit the grave and then talk to the deceased; this is often portrayed in movies as well. Some even request assistance from the deceased in the form of advice, protection etc. This is so ungodly and

unscriptural it's not funny! We are told time and time again in the scriptures not to have anything to do with the dead. In addition, I have not yet read about any person in the bible to frequently visit another's grave, except of course when a new person is buried. Remember, I am not saying it did not happen, I am merely saying I have not read this as of yet in the scriptures. I don't visit graves myself, but I guess it could have a therapeutic effect to some and I am not against this, nor am I saying it is wrong to visit the grave.

The message here is very clear:
We must deal with the dead like the scriptures demand, nothing more and nothing less!

First: Don't have your funeral conducted by a church or a preacher affiliated with church.
I was talking to a person in regards to his mother in law who is not a member of a church. However, we can bow our heads in shame when we compare ourselves to her in terms of seeking the truth, her relationship with God and her utmost courage for her dedication to- and living the truth of scriptures as best she can. Now, this old lady was previously part of a church, but for many years now has not been in any church. This man then told me that he was trying to get his mother in law back in church. I asked him what she is supposed to do in church. He said that she must urgently get het act together with God, fix her relationship with God, so to speak. I told him that her relationship with God is in far better condition than any of us. He then defended with: "She may not have that long to live and who is going bury her if she does not belong to a church?"

Can I blame the gentlemen for his conviction and subsequent logic? Of course not! For this is the way we grew up, the church, the church and the church is everything. For him, the link between church and the act of burial is unbreakable, it goes hand in hand. This dear reader is another child, born of the mother "majority is always right". This view promotes the concept that if one's funeral is conducted from a church, there is some form of "holiness" induced into the event. To be buried by a person with a theological qualification proposes that all your earthly sins are suddenly forgiven and you are set on your path to heaven. Nothing can be further from the truth!

Let me explain by means of a formal challenge to any theologian out there:

> a) *Prove, from scriptures by quoting the appropriate passages that a child of God, must have his or her funeral conducted by a church.*

b) Prove, from scriptures by quoting the appropriate passages that a minister, priest, preacher, reverend, pastor or any other type of clergymen must conduct the funeral of a child of God.

My personal E-mail address appears at the beginning as well as in the back of this book, please let me know, I am always open to new convictions and willing to learn, provided you can quote scripture!

The author and the church?

I have studied the doctrines of many churches, and I can assure you, there is a bit of truth in all of them. Even the worst of the worst have some scriptural truth in their dogmas. They have to cover their lies and deceit with at least a bit of truth. A cat will never take a pill from you and swallow it, but if you cover it with food, so that the cat is oblivious to the hidden "lie" within, it will swallow the food and the lie very time. We are the same – we will not swallow the lie if it is not hidden or disguised in some form of truth or another. So, what does the author of this book have against the churches?

In a nutshell, I don't have much against the church, except for the following little technical detail:
I propose the church must obtain her own bible and let the bible of the God of Abraham, Isaac and Jacob be. The church must formulate a new bible, comprised of her own liturgy, faith confessions and convictions, written by her preachers and prophets, politically and socially correct with its fundamental base vested in the protection of human rights, choices and free will. A bible which contains all of what is acceptable to Christianity today. Then they can quote the following passage from their bible:

New World Order Bible
Book – "Free Will", Chapter 6 verse 66:
"And you are the lord god of yourself, you may decide on a ground burial, a cremation or a *"liquefication"*, and any man who judges you will immediately be beamed up to hell".

As easy as that, no questions and no arguments – even I promise to respect this bible and its church conviction. However, please don't tell me that the latter passage is written in my bible, the holy scriptures of my God!
(The only problem is, once the new world order is fully functional, we will not have one shred of "free will")

Almost every sermon is dedicated to people who must repent. Repent from what and to what. Not repent to the truth of scriptures, but to the falsehood of the churches! 30,000 different Christian denominations with 30,000 different Christian gods!

Which God are you praying to my friend?

What do I have against this type of repentance? Not much, just the following – They raise funds from God's flock to finance their missions over sea and land to make one **proselyte** and then once the person repented, they make him child a child of hell, twofold more than they themselves! This is what I have against the churches of today.

And you think: "A mad man wrote this book! If you do I am happy, it just goes to show just how deep you have been sucked into this deceiving theological quicksand...

Further more I declare that the church is not going to heaven and we who are trying to go to heaven is prevented from doing so, by the very same church!

And again you say: "A mad man definitely wrote this book!"

Let me explain: Ask yourself why on earth would I make such an irregular, unsubstantiated accusation against the church? Am I really a madman...? Or am I maybe, just maybe on the right side of truth? Well, I can assure you that I will not make accusations like this without substance, in fact the substance I refer to is of the highest possible degree, in this world and the next. No defence can be brought against refuting these allegations. Why? Because dear reader, those are not my words, I am merely quoting someone else. Who is this someone else you may ask. Let me introduce you to Him. His Name is Yahshua, the Christians call him Jesus Christ...and these are His own words, red letter in the KJV:

(Who is the church of today - other than the Pharisees, the doctors of law and the scribes?)

> _Mat 23:13_ *But woe unto you, scribes and Pharisees, hypocrites! for ye shut up the kingdom of heaven against men: for ye neither go in yourselves, neither suffer ye them that are entering to go in.*
> _Mat 23:14_ *Woe unto you, scribes and Pharisees, hypocrites! for ye devour widows' houses, and for a pretence make long prayer: therefore ye shall receive the greater damnation.*
> _Mat 23:15_ *Woe unto you, scribes and Pharisees, hypocrites! for ye compass sea and land to make one*

proselyte, and when he is made, ye make him twofold more the child of hell than yourselves.

Surely there could be a thousand reasons why Jesus Himself spoke these words. One of these reason may very well also be because scriptures are so abundantly clear about the difference between a ground burial and cremation, but our Pharisees, doctors of law and our scribes insist on convincing us that it does not matter, we are our own god's and we may decide and come hell or high water, no man is allowed to convince us otherwise or dare tell us we are not acting as scripture ordains, whether this is totally against scriptures doesn't matter one iota, in short:

The churches cannot stand the truth!
They are embarrassed by the Bible!

Should you wish to erect a tombstone, (gravestone, grave marker) don't do it in the form of a cross. Don't even use the image of a cross on the stone and lastly, no images, whether of Jesus or angels or anything else. No emblems whatsoever. To follow are few examples of this practice.

Avoid symbols and emblems, even if it is simple, noble grave.

Foto: HeinzLW

There is also a tendency lately where the deceased's favourite pastime or hobby is depicted on the grave stone. From fishing to motorcars and bikes and everything in between. My own opinion? Avoid this!

Furthermore, have you noticed these colossal tombstones? Calling it a tombstone at all maybe an incorrect description, due to the size of it. It looks more like an apartment made from granite, enough room to house five homeless families.

What motivates this practice I am not sure. Is it to indicate for all of eternity just how rich the deceased was? Is it perhaps to show other people at the grave site, just how much money the family possess? Or is it perhaps to transfer the "high status" of this life, across to the next life?

Do they think they are transported or are somehow "beamed-up" with the tombstone, bells, whistle's and all to the afterlife in order that those waiting in the queue in the afterlife can see them coming and instantly make way for the "most high", so to speak? May be with a tombstone like this you don't have to "queue" in the afterlife….? I really have no idea.

Here is an example of a tombstone, requesting the living, to pray for the departed soul, and this dear reader is highly unscriptural.

Another practice to avoid like the plague is a new tendency to have a "party" at the gravesite of the dearly departed, inclusive of gifts, cakes, party hats and drinks. The theory is that the departed also partakes in the festivities and at the same time witnesses how the living still "loves" the departed by having a birthday party, at the grave. Stay far, far away from ungodly practises like this, leave it for other people, but don't associate yourself with this behaviour in any way.

> *Psa 106:28 They joined themselves also unto Baalpeor, and ate the sacrifices of the dead.*

> *Psa 115:17 The dead praise not the LORD, neither any that go down into silence.*

> *Psa 88:5 Free among the dead, like the slain that lie in the grave, whom thou rememberest no more: and they are cut off from thy hand*

> *Psa 88:10 Wilt thou shew wonders to the dead? shall the dead arise and praise thee? Selah.*

> *Ecc 9:5 For the living know that they shall die: but the dead know not any thing, neither have they any more a reward; for the memory of them is forgotten.*

Before I started my research for this book, I told my family that they must not erect a tombstone for me, since I am not there any more. Since then I have learned that scripture does tell us about a grave marker. Lets then look at the possibilities for a good grave marker or tombstone.

We briefly touched on "Bone Boxes", but on these boxes were very simple inscriptions like the persons name and perhaps surname.

(If you look at the inscription it appears that the picture may be upside-down, but keep in mind; Hebrew is read from right to left)

This is my opinion only – I suggest the simplest form of a gravestone with the following inscription: name, surname, birthdate and date of death. And perhaps if you so wish, a passage from the bible, but then from the KJV - and not any other politically correct bible. We all know who Vincent van Gog was right? I suppose he really qualifies for one of those "five family" tombstones, but below is an image of him and his wife's tombstones. In my opinion, totally acceptable and duly sufficient:

Sometimes a gravestone contains inscriptions as to the career or achievements of the deceased, which I don't agree with, however in the case of a slain soldier who died in another country or people whom were killed because they were fighting for truth, I think it may be acceptable.

Here is another example of an inexpensive, simple but acceptable tombstone which is the one below. Only the name and the two dates appear on the stone – (which I removed from the picture)

The method

How to conduct a church-less funeral? Very simple! Last respects and the viewing of the body can be arranged at the undertaker's premises. This needs not to be for every single person attending the funeral, but mostly for family and close friends. If required, an allowance can be made for other people to view the body by the hearse, at the cemetery, for just a few minutes. I would actually insist to view the body at the graveyard, just to make sure it is in fact my loved one in the coffin, stranger things have happened you know. My father always had very good advice:

Only trust the man you shave and nobody else!

The funeral procession will then make its way to the cemetery, from the undertaker's premises. Those whom are familiar with the location of the cemetery can proceed there directly and wait for the arrival of the hearse. A friend or family member who is a religious person, trusted by the family may speak a few words while the coffin is being lowered into the grave. No flowers or hands full of dirt are thrown onto the coffin. The family then takes the shovels and proceed to cover the coffin, right to the top of the grave. Other family or friends may also assist in this task as it is hard work, especially on a hot summer's day when people are dresses in suits.

I have often witnessed where the relatives, after the funeral proceedings ended, leave the cemetery with the grave still open. This is difficult for me to grasp as I was taught since childhood that the family (with close friends assisting) covers the grave, to the brim. Nobody else even dares touching a shovel. Some people leave the covering of the grave to municipal workers to complete, while they leave the cemetery. This is hard for me to understand. In some cases I agree, there may be no one capable of covering the grave, but then at least witness the complete covering of the grave by whomever before you leave the cemetery. Do not walk away from the uncovered grave!

The point is: NO CHURCH and most definitely NO SCRIBE OR PHARISEE!
What if I have a preacher in the family who wants to conduct the funeral from their church? We can't tell him that we do not want him to conduct the funeral of our loved one. Much less tell him that we will get a believer to say a few words at the grave site, this will cause an endless family feud!

What if I wish to be buried, but my children choose to cremate me? What if I want to be buried, but my parents choose cremation? What if I want to bury my departed brother, but the rest of my siblings wants to cremate? What do I do?

The answer to these questions is so clear and so simple, but unfortunately the answer is not politically correct, nor socially acceptable, however this is where you have to decide who you are going to listen to, who you are going to follow and who you are going to obey, because Jesus makes the answer abundantly clear:

> **Mat 10:37 He that loveth father or mother more than me is not worthy of me: and he that loveth son or daughter more than me is not worthy of me.**
> **Mat 10:38 And he that taketh not his cross, and followeth after me, is not worthy of me.**

This may be hard hitting, but the fact is – your mother, father, brother or sister doesn't count one iota, all that matters is your choice to follow HIM and if you choose them above HIM, you clearly have problems coming your way.

When you have done everything in your power to convince your family of your biblical convictions, but you are unable to influence their decision - walk away! Withdraw yourself and have no part of the funeral arrangement and don't even be present at the funeral proceedings. I know…. "But this will only bring disagreement and hardship in the family and I don't want to be responsible for that". Well, once again, Jesus has the answer for you my friend…

> *Mat 10:34 Think not that I am come to send peace on earth: I came not to send peace, but a sword.*
> *Mat 10:35 For I am come to set a man at variance against his father, and the daughter against her mother, and the daughter in law against her mother in law.*
> *Mat 10:36 And a man's foes shall be they of his own household.*

From the bottom of my heart dear reader, I know this is not easy, much easier said than done, but stay committed to His Word, come what may – I wish you all the best in this regard – the author.

> *Act 5:41 And they departed from the presence of the council, rejoicing that they were counted worthy to suffer shame for his name.*

> *Act 9:16 For I will shew him how great things he must suffer for my name's sake.*

Compulsory cremation

When they take our bones and dump it in a hole at the back of the crematorium with animal bones and then still has the audacity to tell us we should be happy they don't put it in refuse bags and dump it at the rubbish-dump, then surely we can bury these bones ourselves cant we? I hope someone is prepared to fight for this when they make cremation compulsory by law.

Should they attempt to declare a traditional ground burial illegal, making cremation compulsory – to save the planet or some such bull dust - use every and all channels available to fight this. If this fails, make sure we get the bones before they liquidise it in the industrial blender and properly bury it. You have to however mark the grave as scripture states. (Please keep in mind that you have to act within the parameters of the applicable laws in your country or area)

Remember, if we are forced to be cremated and we have exhausted all other avenues to obtain the scriptural burial without success, we will not be held accountable for this grievous sin of cremation - but they will!

Hell

It is not my intention to elaborate on hell, but I do want you to notice the similarity between how scriptures describe hell and what happens inside the cremation oven…

> *Rev 20:10 And the devil that deceived them was cast into <u>the</u> <u>lake of fire and brimstone</u>, where the beast <u>and the false</u> <u>prophet</u> are, and shall be tormented day and night for ever and ever.*

Take note that the **false prophet will also be cast into the fire**! Those who preach everything people like to hear, but so far removed from scriptures as heaven and hell itself.

> *Mat 25:41 Then shall he say also unto them on the left hand, Depart from me, ye cursed, <u>into everlasting fire,</u> prepared for the devil and his angels:*

> *Mat 18:8 Wherefore if thy hand or thy foot offend thee, cut them off, and cast them from thee: it is better for thee to enter into life halt or maimed, rather than having two hands or two feet to be cast into everlasting fire.*

What does hell look like? I have no idea and I don't want to speculate, but I have a feeling it's probably not very dissimilar to the inside of a cremation oven…?

Foto: Henry Mühlpfordt

I almost want to say that if you have yourself cremated, with full knowledge of the truth of scriptures, that you did not allow God to make anything of you when you were whole, how will He make something of you when you have been devoured by fire. (This is not blasphemy, but simply a metaphor, a figure of speech...) You may believe in God, but you do not CHOOSE God and there is a cosmic difference between believe and choose my friend.

> *Eze 15:5* *Behold, when it was whole, it was meet for no work: how much less shall it be meet yet for any work, when the fire hath devoured it, and it is burned?*

You will recall that Gods spoken words, in other words, scriptures will judge us. This is of the utmost importance dear reader. When you stand in the proverbial queue to receive your judgement, it will not be the pastor, the preacher or even the great Dr Isak Burger who will be judging you, but SCRIPTURES! You will also not be allowed to defend yourself by stating that the pastor told you it was okay. Your instruction was to study the scriptures, period!

> *Joh 12:48* *He that rejecteth me, and receiveth not my words, hath one that judgeth him: the word that I have spoken, the same shall judge him in the last day*

We will be judged by what we have done in our bodies, whether good or bad. We now know that our body does not belong to us, how can we then allow it to be sent through fire to worship the god Molech?

> *2Cor 5:10* *For we must all appear before the judgment seat of Christ; that every one may receive the things done in his body, according to that he hath done, whether it be good or bad.*

For whatever reason, since I was small, I always thought that we will be like ghosts in the afterlife. I thought Jesus was like a ghost when he was resurrected. What's more, I suspect a lot of people still believe this, which then makes it perfectly acceptable if we are cremated because you will not have any flesh or bones when you are resurrected, well...hold on for a minute there....

> *Luk 24:39 Behold my hands and my feet, that it is I myself:* <u>**handle me, and see; for a spirit hath not flesh and bones, as ye see me have.**</u>

Cleary, Jesus had flesh and bones after being resurrected. I hope this tells you something which I don't have to repeat.

On second thoughts, let me repeat…
Why do you think fire nor the acid in the human *liquefier* can not disintegrate our bones? Did God perhaps design our bones so that it may last? And now that we cannot find any process to destroy our bones, we go ahead and purposefully design an industrial machine that can obliterate our bones to a powdery substance and call it ashes? If this does not cause a stir in your senses then I don't know what will…

> *1Joh 3:2 Beloved, now are we the sons of God, and it doth not yet appear what we shall be:* <u>*but we know that, when he shall appear, we shall be like him; for we shall see him as he is.*</u>

> *Php 3:21 Who shall <u>change our vile body, that it may be fashioned like unto his glorious body, according to the working whereby he is able even to subdue all things unto himself.</u>*

> *1Cor 15:48 <u>As is the earthy, such are they also that are earthy:</u> and as is the heavenly, <u>such are they also that are heavenly.</u>*
> *1Cor 15:49 And as we have <u>borne the image of the earthy</u>, we shall <u>also bear the image of the heavenly.</u>*

> *Mat 13:49 So shall it be at the end of the world: <u>the angels shall come forth, and sever the wicked from among the just,</u>*
> *Mat 13:50 <u>And shall cast them into the furnace of fire:</u> there shall be wailing and gnashing of teeth.*
> *Mat 13:51 Jesus saith unto them, Have ye understood all these things? They say unto him, Yea, Lord.*

Can God resurrect humans that have been cremated? Absolutely! Will He do so? I think so. Why? Perhaps to give them new flesh and bone just before they enter eternity, the mother of all crematoriums, **THE HELL!** (Please note that this is a hypothetical figure of speech and not a "doctrine"! - It is not my intention to indicate what God will and will not do, neither to condemn people to hell)

> *Joh 5:28 Marvel not at this: for the hour is coming, in the which all that are in the graves shall hear his voice,*
> *Joh 5:29 And shall come forth; they that have done good, unto the resurrection of life; and they that have done evil, unto the resurrection of damnation.*

Firstly: Who will hear His voice? Those who are in the graves or those in the ditch behind the crematorium together with animal bones? Those who are in the graves or those whose ashes are scattered on the country side or in the ocean? You can trust me in this – nowhere in the bible does it say: "and those whose ashes have been used as tattoo ink will hear his voice and be resurrected".

Secondly: If you really stuffed up anyway, you will also be resurrected – for DAMNATION!

> *Mat 11:24 But I say unto you, That it shall be more tolerable for the land of Sodom in the day of judgment, than for thee.*

May I be so bold as to ask you, just as Jesus did: "have ye understood all these things?"
And I truly hope you answer: "Yea Lord"

> *Mat 13:51 Jesus saith unto them, Have ye understood all these things? They say unto him, Yea, Lord.*

Arguments revisited

As promised, we need to revisit the arguments in favour of cremation.

Economical:
After the mercury filters have been installed and they stop throwing our bones in a ditch, this argument is null an void.

Hygienic:
Did we not learn that it poisons humans, animals, fish, lakes and drinking water due to mercury emissions? No really….!

Aesthetical value:
Yes, it is truly esthetical to know that my loved ones bones have been dumped in a hole behind the crematorium with cats and dog –bones, cremated in the same oven, it makes me feel so proud, very esthetical indeed. And don't forget about the body that practically jumps up and

down in the oven with fat crackling and bodily fluids squirting from all directions out of the body from the flames and heat. Yes, very esthetical indeed don't you think? Much more esthetical than laying a body to rest in the ground…

The Time factor:
The whole purpose is to lay the deceased to rest as quickly as possible, and not to make festivity of the event three months later. Someone died; it's not a wedding for Pete sake!

Cold character:
Yes, the cemetery and the grave render a cold character, and grandmas bones in a mass grave behind the crematorium, together with animal bones renders a warm feeling? The only "warm" feeling you will get from a cremation is when you're standing next to the oven on a cold day!

Grave Pillaging:
The highest grade of pillaging is to take the bones of the deceased and throw it into a monster industrial blender with hardened steel balls which crushes and grinds it to a powder! This my friend is pillaging of the highest degree of a body that does not even belong to you.

Property:
If you want to sleep you need a bed. If you want to follow scripture, you need a grave. You cannot argue that you will get the same rest from sleeping in a chair because there is no room for a bed in the bedroom. There are plans to be made. Some of the smallest countries with the highest population never run out of burial space.

Technology:
Does technology gets preference above the Word of God? Even if Satan himself is the designer of it? Allow me to answer from the Word of God:

> *Jos 24:15 And if it seem evil unto you to serve the LORD, choose you this day whom ye will serve; whether the gods which your fathers served that were on the other side of the flood, or the gods of the Amorites, in whose land ye dwell: but as for me and my house, we will serve the LORD.*

The Majority:
Let me answer the same as before:

> *Exo 23:2 Thou shalt not follow a multitude to do evil…*

I am sorry dear reader, but not a single one of these arguments holds any water and the scriptural way of burial is not just the best, but for God's elect, the only way!

Satan's hirelings can accumulate six mountains worth of arguments, but it will for all eternity be totally against scriptures and therefore against our God, the One who created us!

The RESURRECTION

Our good doctor says in his book on page 193: (my translation)

> *The end result is the same. It may be argued that the "ash" which remains is chemically, basically the same as the end result of a conventional burial and the decomposition which follows, namely "dust". Cremation is then merely an acceleration of the process.*

After we searched, like scripture instructs to do, we can make the following statement:

To say that the "ash" which remains is chemically the same as with a traditional burial, is like saying – "The petrol with which I fill my motorcars gas tank, is chemically the same as the exhaust gasses emitted by the cars exhaust pipe, after it is has been through hell, I mean the combustion chambers of the engine, or is it the crematoriums gas chamber". Does this argument make any sense at all, I ask with tears in my eyes?

2Cor 4:4 *In whom the god of this world hath blinded the minds of them which believe not...*

I have an uncle who refuses to drink water unless it has been boiled and left to cool down, no matter how thirsty he is. This is quite a difficult choice of lifestyle, but what makes him choose it anyway? The answer is very simple – there was "something" in the water that is not there anymore after it has been boiled. Just the same, there was something in the petrol of the car that is not there anymore after is was turned to gas and burned inside the engine and the same principal applies to our body's and bones. There was something in our bones or bodies that is not there anymore after it was sent through hell, an analogy for the crematorium. Therefore: a loyal congregation member may believe that the "ash" is chemically the same, but I wont eat this fig which is really a horse dropping! (Maybe because I can prove scientifically that a horse dropping and a fig is chemically, basically not the same...)

Maybe this is not such a big deal, maybe it's not an issue at all, but when we decide we must have all the facts and when someone says there is no difference I say: THERE IS!

You will recall the good doctor's quotation from his book:

Is it wrong to have myself cremated?
Thought the Bible does not leave us in the dark regarding what happens to one's spirit/soul, the question regarding what should or needs to happen with the body is being asked more and more. The bible is clear about what will happen with the body during the resurrection. Regardless of the condition of the body, whether it is in a grave, in a state of decomposition, returned to dust or burnt to ash, devoured by a beast, or in the ocean, whatever the condition of the believers body, no matter what and where, on the day of resurrection, the Lord Jesus Christ will resurrect and revive that which is left, where after the believer will be in heaven, with Christ for ever.

He then quotes in brackets the following verses:
(1 Cor. 15:51-54 and 1 Ths. 4:15-17).

Let's just look at the quoted passages again:

> *1Cor 15:51 Behold, I shew you a mystery; We shall not all sleep, but we shall all be changed,*
> *1Cor 15:52 In a moment, in the twinkling of an eye, at the last trump: for the trumpet shall sound, and the dead shall be raised incorruptible, and we shall be changed.*
> *1Cor 15:53 For this corruptible must put on incorruption, and this mortal must put on immortality.*
> *1Cor 15:54 So when this corruptible shall have put on incorruption, and this mortal shall have put on immortality, then shall be brought to pass the saying that is written, Death is swallowed up in victory.*

> *1The 4:15 For this we say unto you by the word of the Lord, that we which are alive and remain unto the coming of the Lord shall not prevent them which are asleep.*
> *1The 4:16 For the Lord himself shall descend from heaven with a shout, with the voice of the archangel, and with the trump of God: and the dead in Christ shall rise first:*
> *1The 4:17 Then we which are alive and remain shall be caught up together with them in the clouds, to meet the Lord in the air: and so shall we ever be with the Lord.*

Please note again that none of the passages quoted by the good doctor even so much as hints at bodies which were burnt to ash, devoured by a beast, or in the ocean. It also does not say: "whatever the condition of the believer's body" The doctor assumes this. I also believe that all will be resurrected, but I just want to indicate that the doctor does not substantiate his claims with the passages he supplies in brackets. Be that as it may, I would like us to focus on the following line:

> **whatever the condition of the believers body, no matter what and where, on the day of resurrection, the Lord Jesus Christ will resurrect and revive that which is left, where after the believer will be in heaven, with Christ for ever**

But first I would like to introduce you to word – if you are not familiar with it already.
This word is – "Oxymoron"
It literally means "sharp-dull" or "keen-stupid" [35]

~ 214 ~

Two examples which describe this word are: "Clearly confused" and "True myth". A better description is something like "bitter-sweet", but I like the "**keen-stupid**" and the "**clearly confused**" more.

Now – I believe the scriptures and scriptures say we will all be resurrected, some to everlasting life and some to condemnation. I have no problem with this. How does the bible say we must deal with the dead? You should know that very well by now, but does the bible say how, which way or what method the body must return to dust? Let's have a look:

> *Isa 51:7 Hearken unto me, ye that know righteousness, the people in whose heart is my law; fear ye not the reproach of men, neither be ye afraid of their revilings.*
> *Isa 51:8 For the moth shall eat them up like a garment, and the worm shall eat them like wool: but my righteousness shall be for ever, and my salvation from generation to generation.*

> *Job 24:20 The womb shall forget him; the worm shall feed sweetly on him; he shall be no more remembered; and wickedness shall be broken as a tree.*

Even those who "revile" against God will be "eaten by the worm" and not consumed by fire.

What does the church say? Everybody can be saved, everybody's sins can be forgiven and everybody can go to heaven, right? In the first place, there are different levels of sin and in the second place, there are unforgivable sins (three of which I am familiar with) and in the third place, even forgiveness also has limits.

If you have read this book thus far you can disregard every word you have read, but you cannot disregard the scriptures you have read in this book. This means – you now know what the truth is. You can still decide for yourself, like the good doctor says, but because you know what the truth is; you are in a little bit of a tight spot. Let me explain:

> *Heb 10:26 For if we sin wilfully after that we have received the knowledge of the truth, there remaineth no more sacrifice for sins,*
> *Heb 10:27 But a certain fearful looking for of judgment and fiery indignation, which shall devour the adversaries.*

When you sin, after you have been introduced to the truth, there is no more sacrifice for the sin. Also note that a fiery indignation will devour these people who refuse to listen.

> **Jam 4:17** *Therefore to him that knoweth to do good, and doeth it not, to him it is sin.*

Right, back to my friend – Oxymoron.

"Bitter sweet" does not gel, just as "keen-stupid" does not gel, but "keen stupid" or "clearly confused" is a very good description for half of all the theologians, preachers, ministers, pastors, priests and theology doctors and professors. No, I should not say things like this – I apologise and recant my statement - half of all the theologians, preachers, ministers, pastors, priests and theology doctors and professors are not "keen stupid" or "clearly confused".

To say that a person who received the truth about cremation and still decides to have him/herself cremated, will be revived as a believer and will be in heaven with Christ for ever is …… you guessed it – an:

OXYMORON

Our Creator will judge. He will resurrect and He will judge, but if I look at the scriptures, I cannot tolerate cremation. I will say, just as the good doctor, you may decide if I am talking bull dust. You have every right to reject me, in fact I hope you do, but please, please never reject scripture, I beg you!

> **1Cor 3:16** *Know ye not that ye are the temple of God, and that the Spirit of God dwelleth in you?*
> **1Cor 3:17** *If any man defile the temple of God, him shall God destroy; for the temple of God is holy, which temple ye are.*
> **1Cor 3:18** *Let no man deceive himself. If any man among you seemeth to be wise in this world, let him become a fool, that he may be wise.*
> **1Cor 3:19** *For the wisdom of this world is foolishness with God. For it is written, He taketh the wise in their own craftiness.*
> **1Cor 3:20** *And again, The Lord knoweth the thoughts of the wise, that they are vain.*

Dear reader, please forgive me for I am not intending to beat a dead horse, but what strikes me is verses 19-20. Let's analyse this for a moment. God says the wisdom of this world is foolishness and he takes the wise in their own craftiness and that the thoughts of the wise are in vain. Now lets have a look once again at the good doctor, the wise doctor, the doctor whom studied for years on end to be as wise as he is: he says that no matter what the condition of the believers body, whether it is ash or anything else, Jesus will resurrect and revive that which is left and this believer will be in heaven, with Christ forever.

Let me translate in simple language:
If the believer has sinned by having themselves cremated (and you cannot deny that this is a grievous sin), God will forgive the sinner because he is a believer and he will be resurrected to everlasting life, no matter the sin.

There's a few oxymoron's in this statement. If the believer is in fact a believer and gained knowledge of the truth by the grace of God, that cremation is an abomination, and the believer still opts for cremation, the bible says that there is no sacrifice for this sin, but the good doctor says no problem, it doesn't matter, you will receive everlasting life anyway. This my friend sets a precedent with far reaching effects – what is the precedent?

The precedent is: It does not matter what sins we commit, nothing matters, we will not be judged for it and we can be assured that we will be with Jesus for ever. This effectively means that we can discard the bible today because it is not worth the paper it is written on; that we can commit any and all sins we like, but still be assured of everlasting life wit Jesus. And this my friend leads directly into the highly acceptable statement, even preached and promoted by certain Christian preachers, that all religions leads to "god", no matter what you call this "god" and no matter what road you take. If you are in fact a believer and you search the scriptures, you cannot but believe that this must come from an oxi – Moron!

2The 2:12 **_That they all might be damned who believed not the truth, but had pleasure in unrighteousness._**

Human steam cooker approved?

Do you remember the glass of water that contains grandmas liquefied remains, obtainable from the faucet?

The big question is, will Dr Burger and his theologically educated colleagues also promote this vulgar method of disposal of the dead when it starts to take off? They will have to, because they already declared it doesn't matter what the condition of the remains, you will be in heaven.

I am not a prophet, but mark my words, maybe not in our lifetime, but the time will come when the church will teach their congregation there is nothing wrong with liquefying the dead and feeding it to the living. They don't have a choice.

There is only one scriptural way to bury and that is a ground burial, the so-called "traditional funeral" but because they have already given cremation the Christian stamp of approval, they will have to find other reasons to promote the steam-cooker disposal method of remains. My guess would be one of two reasons or both. One is to demonise cremation by using some of the verses linking God's judgements to "fire", (which we have quoted in this book), to attach a negative, possibly sinful connotation to cremation and of course the second would be, in order to save the planet and the climate, liquefying the dead as opposed to cremation would be endorsed as the Christians high moral ground.

Against cremation

What exactly does the author have against cremation? I can assure you that I have absolutely nothing against cremation, nothing – nada! The religions dictating that their gods demand cremation in order for the deceased to be re-incarnated or to allow the soul to depart on its journey or for whatever other reasons are perfectly acceptable, leave them, that's their religion, respect it and let them be for so are they ordained to do. The people, who serve no god, let them be, if they choose cremation it is perfectly acceptable, respect their choice and let them be. Church members and Christians who chooses to have their loved ones and themselves cremated are not doing anything wrong. The people who claim to love "god", serve "god" and worship "god" who chooses cremation, let them be.

BUT – in seven blue blazing abominable devils, don't tell me you believe in Gods Word and then declare there is nothing wrong with cremation. You see, there are millions of people declaring that they "love" God, serve God and worship God, even believe in the bible they would say, but the truth is, they have no idea who God is, don't believe what Gods Word says and they absolutely have no idea what it means to "love God".

But then again, what do I know? I am an unlearned an ignorant man with no theological qualifications and don't even belong to a church, how would I know? The other side of that coin is – it is such a privilege for me to be unlearned and ignorant that I feel blessed because of it, for me it is the greatest honour in this world to be unlearned and ignorant. You want to know why? Well, what if I say that both John as well Peter was

> *Act 4:13 Now when they saw the boldness of <u>Peter and John,</u> and <u>perceived that they were unlearned and ignorant men,</u> they marvelled; and they took knowledge of them, that they had been with Jesus.*

I am so happy that I am "unlearned"…

> *Luk 10:21 In that hour Jesus rejoiced in spirit, and said, <u>I thank thee, O Father, Lord of heaven and earth, that thou hast hid these things from the wise and prudent, and hast revealed them unto babes:</u> even so, Father; for so it seemed good in thy sight.*

Perhaps I should apologise for my words, but unfortunately I am unable to do that, on account of the following:

> *Luk 9:26 <u>For whosoever shall be ashamed of me and of my words, of him shall the Son of man be ashamed…</u>*

> *Rom 1:16 <u>For I am not ashamed of the gospel of Christ:</u> for it is the power of God unto salvation to every one that believeth…*

Now I have questions

What about my loved ones?

Some of my loved ones were cremated, will they be in the kingdom of God or not? I had them cremated, but I was unaware that it was wrong.
Let us attempt to find answers for these questions, based purely on the sin of cremation. What does scripture say?

> *1Pet 2:25 For <u>ye were as sheep going astray; but are now returned unto the Shepherd</u> and Bishop of your souls.*

Perhaps we have gone astray before (possibly because of the false teachers in the churches), but now we have received the knowledge of truth. The burden is now on us to make decisions and believe me, those decisions carry huge repercussions and dire consequences if not made in conjunction with the truth we received, make no mistake!

> *Heb 10:26 For if we sin wilfully after that we have received the knowledge of the truth, there remaineth no more sacrifice for sins,*
> *Heb 10:27 But a certain fearful looking for of judgment and fiery indignation, which shall devour the adversaries.*

This tells me, by God's grace and His will only we may receive forgiveness when we were not aware that we sinned. (This is of course excluding the three unforgivable sins). However, this forgiveness has a shelf-life, so to speak and I say this with utmost respect. It expires as soon as God enlightened us with the truth, but we still choose to follow the broad path and follow the majority in wrong doing, then only a fiery indignation waits, because by doing this we are crucifying the Son of God all over again and putting Him to shame!

> *Heb 6:4 For it is impossible for those who were once enlightened, and have tasted of the heavenly gift, and were made partakers of the Holy Ghost,*
> *Heb 6:5 And have tasted the good word of God, and the powers of the world to come,*
> *Heb 6:6 If they shall fall away, to renew them again unto repentance; seeing they crucify to themselves the Son of God afresh, and put him to an open shame.*

We can never ever declare who goes to heaven and who goes to hell. It is God and only God who decides. (interestingly though, just observe when you attend a funeral in church, the pastor always say the deceased is now in heaven – where they get the authority to do this I am not sure, but then again it does sooth the ears of the relatives, doesn't it?). Nonetheless, when we search the scriptures we find numerous guidelines and if I consider what scriptures tell us, my opinion would be that if the person or the relative was not aware that cremation was such a grievous sin, they will be forgiven and like the doctor says, grandma's ashes will be resurrected.

It may very well be that you were in turmoil about the decision and then you decided to enquire as to what scriptures have to say about cremation by asking your good old church preacher, of course he said there was nothing wrong, you can decide and no one may judge you – in this case the sin will be on him, but be careful – you have a responsibility to search the scriptures as well, in prayer of course…

(I just want to say that for every one million preachers, there is one lonely preacher who bluntly refuses to perform a cremation service – hats of to you Mr Preacher – keep up the good work and stand fast! Don't let them bring you down…)

It may be possible that you consulted a preacher that looks like a sheep, but in fact is a ravenous wolf!

Isa 5:20 Woe unto them that call evil good, and good evil; that put darkness for light, and light for darkness; that put bitter for sweet, and sweet for bitter!
Isa 5:21 Woe unto them that are wise in their own eyes, and prudent in their own sight!

Mat 7:14 Because strait is the gate, and narrow is the way, which leadeth unto life, and few there be that find it.
Mat 7:15 Beware of false prophets, which come to you in sheep's clothing, but inwardly they are ravening wolves.

> **Mat 7:16** *Ye shall know them by their fruits. Do men gather grapes of thorns, or figs of thistles?*

> **Mat 23:14** *Woe unto you, scribes and Pharisees, hypocrites! for ye devour widows' houses, and for a pretence make long prayer: therefore ye shall receive the greater damnation*

With respect and utmost caution, I don't think I am in error when I say that you no longer have to chastise yourself in this issue. Ask for forgiveness and move on when you received it.

> **Joh 8:11** *... And Jesus said unto her, Neither do I condemn thee: go, and sin no more.*

Unfortunately though, unlike the preachers who sooths the ears with unsound doctrine, which they are paid for, we have to ask some other questions as well:

Will God allow one of His elect to be cremated by mistake? I know people who never read books and never studied the bible related to the subject of cremation, but they seem to instinctively know that cremation is ungodly and inhumane and they are repelled by it. What causes this instinct which is totally according to scripture? I would like to believe that it can only come from God.

If what I have stated here is incorrect, I ask God to forgive me and ask him to show me where I err so that I can correct my mistakes. Why do I say this? Because...

> **Rev 12:9** *And the great dragon was cast out, that old serpent, called the Devil, and Satan, which deceiveth the whole world: he was cast out into the earth, and his angels were cast out with him.*

Satan deceives the whole world and I, the author am in no means immune to this deceit.

What about disasters?

History holds many events where people have been mass-cremated. In this case, the hygienic argument came into effect which posed a real risk of epidemics if a speedily disposal of the bodies were not executed. What about those people, are they going to hell? I would argue that the same principal applies – the persons wishes were perhaps to be buried, but eventually he/she was cremated due to circumstances. I don't think the person will be accountable for acts like this. If an old lady wishes to be buried and the children decides, after she passed away to cremate her, then she will not be held accountable for this act, however the children will be, this I can promise you.

There is however something else I would like you to consider or at least ponder over.

Only good people are buried

Personally I am not aware of a single funeral where a bad person was ever buried. How many funerals have you attended where the preacher said: "Here lies John Doe, dead in his coffin, truly a wonderful day for his wife and children and society in general! He abused his wife, beat her senseless her from time to time, rented out his children and broke his children's bones when they were only two months old because they cried. He was a monster who terrorised not only his family, but the entire community!"

I never even heard of such a funeral. You only hear how wonderful, lovable, good model and well mannered the person was. We know its bull dust, but nobody dares speaks the truth about the atrocities of the person. If every person was truly the person as described at the persons own funeral, the world would be a much better place, not so? Why? Because no one is going to hell right...? Wrong! The bible is abundantly clear about the majority whom will end up in hell, but where are these people, the majority going to hell, when only good people are buried?

The point is this: The man who perished in a disaster of nature and was cremated, the woman who died in a plane crash with little to none of the body left, charred and burnt beyond belief, what about them? Surely they will be resurrected, yes God can resurrect them, but are we perhaps asking the wrong questions here?
Must our first question not be: Why did they die the way they did? What is the reason for these horrific deaths? A man is blown to smithereens in a bomb explosion. The first question should not be: "Will he be going to heaven?", but rather: "Why was he killed in the explosion?"

Yes, but you don't understand, this person was in church every Sunday, he never missed a prayer meeting. Saturdays he spent at hospitals praying for the sick. Weeknights he was casting out demons. He did the most wonderful works, he was a god-fearing man. Surely this is proof that he must be in heaven.
Well, what do scriptures say?

> *Mat 7:19 Every tree that bringeth not forth good fruit is hewn down, and cast into the fire.*
> *Mat 7:20 Wherefore by their fruits ye shall know them.*
> *Mat 7:21 Not every one that saith unto me, Lord, Lord, shall enter into the kingdom of heaven; but he that doeth the will of my Father which is in heaven.*
> *Mat 7:22 Many will say to me in that day, Lord, Lord, have we not prophesied in thy name? and in thy name have cast out devils? and in thy name done many wonderful works?*
> *Mat 7:23 And then will I profess unto them, I never knew you: depart from me, ye that work iniquity.*

There will even be people who declare they have eaten and drunk with Him, but are still told to part from Him.

> *Luk 13:23 Then said one unto him, Lord, are there few that be saved? And he said unto them,*
> *Luk 13:24 Strive to enter in at the strait gate: for many, I say unto you, will seek to enter in, and shall not be able.*
> *Luk 13:25 When once the master of the house is risen up, and hath shut to the door, and ye begin to stand without, and to knock at the door, saying, Lord, Lord, open unto us; and he shall answer and say unto you, I know you not whence ye are:*
> *Luk 13:26 Then shall ye begin to say, We have eaten and drunk in thy presence, and thou hast taught in our streets.*
> *Luk 13:27 But he shall say, I tell you, I know you not whence ye are; depart from me, all ye workers of iniquity.*

I trust you get the point.

In no way am I implying whatsoever that every person who perishes in a disaster will not see heaven, but I very vividly say, not every person who does perish in a disaster will be in heaven.

What about a miscarriage?

This is an event which occurs numerous times every day, around the globe in every country and yet, we are to a large extent, totally oblivious to this fact. According to our source[36] more than 60 babies in SA are born dead every day, called a "stillborn". This figure escalates to 7,300 world wide with a total of 2.6 million per year. In addition to this, another 58 babies die shortly after birth.

The question is: "what to do with the foetus?"
I discus this subject in detail in my book:

"Miscarriage – a biblical perspective on what to do with the foetus"

Please get this book if you are interested in this subject or know someone who is. It also contains a true story of a woman whose first pregnancy ended in miscarriage. This is a heart-rending story as this lady was only prepared to talk about her pain, eight years after the event.

When a miscarriage occurs there is total devastation and turmoil, both physical and emotional for both parents and they tend to make wrong choices in this dreadful nightmare. The truth however is, it's these decisions, taken in the heat of the moment which ends up haunting the parents, especially the mother, for the rest of her life.

However, to summarise in a nutshell what the book teaches is: BURY YOUR BABY! Do not sign it over to the hospital personnel to deal with the little body, however small it is.

(Just for the record – even though the title of the book contains the word: "foetus", this word does not exist in my vocabulary. It is a baby, with body and blood, however small – it's still a little body that needs to be taken care of properly)

Another topic which is briefly discussed in the aforementioned book is: "Biblical advice for pregnant mothers". The core of this message is do what the bible says, deprive yourself the normal luxuries during your pregnancy and don't eat or drink like you did before your pregnancy – this is very valuable advice!

> **_Jud 13:3_** *And the angel of the LORD appeared unto the woman, and said unto her, Behold now, thou art barren, and bearest not: <u>but thou shalt conceive, and bear a son.</u>*
> **_Jud 13:4_** *Now therefore beware, <u>I pray thee, and drink not wine nor strong drink, and eat not any unclean thing:</u>*

Chapter 9

Funeral Cost and The Estate

And I say unto you, Make to yourselves friends of the mammon of unrighteousness; that, when ye fail, they may receive you into everlasting habitations.

Luk 16:9

Funeral cost

A proper funeral costs money and can be very expensive, especially when the relatives are not that well off when it comes to finances – what to do?

My Story

Please afford me an opportunity to first share a true story with you. During the year 1996 in South-Africa, the interest rate came very close to 24%. This of course meant that mortgage payments and the likes skyrocketed. As a family, the only food we had for almost an entire year was just maize-porridge and chicken-eggs. I recall we had a guy at work that kept some chickens at his house and sold the eggs to supplement his income. He only had one customer – ME! Every week I bought all the eggs his chickens produced. When I share this story, people think it is an exaggeration or an analogy, but unfortunately it is the literal truth.

Well, as time went on, we progressed slowly. Many years later we could afford some luxury items like food and household goods. The problem is, to make lots of money takes lots of time, lots of stress and really eats away at your health. This however depends on the kind of person you are. You get two kinds of people in the corporate world – those whom lets everything roll of their backs like water from a ducks back and then you get those who take things more seriously. Those who goes home happy and also has the ability to switch of so to speak, until the next morning and then you get those who wakes up in a cold sweat at night, thinking about what lies ahead the next morning, but the paycheque at the end of the month makes it all worthwhile…right? Money was flowing like water and we were living in luxury.

To make a long story short, I ended up in the intensive medial care unit in hospital for more than a week and remained in hospital for another two weeks. You also get two kinds of bosses, the bad ones and then the ones which qualifies to be Satan's deputy's in hell. Then you get the boss who takes all the flack from his boss, but acts as a buffer between his own boss and his employees – this is usually the boss that ends up in hospital, if he is lucky. I was never the same again since I've been in hospital… well, let me be the first to confess: I am not executive material! Some people have it and some don't and I most definitely don't!

Nonetheless, I decided to resign and take 6 months to a year off – I had saved enough money to finance the latter. This decision was not one taken lightly, and although it was a daunting task, I went ahead and resigned from the corporate world. First I was requested to stay, which I respectfully declined, and then I was requested to stay on for an extended notice period, which I accepted. Once they had to accept my resignation, Satan's deputy's constant grip on my throat immediately disappeared. It was like something severed his hand and I could start breathing again! It was a wonderful feeling. Talking about feeling, when "feelings" started to return I suddenly realised just how far away from God a had drifted. The more time I had, the more I moved closer to God. I've been studying the bible for approximately 25 years, I haven't been in church for more than 12 years, but when the money started rolling in from my executive position at a large company, I forgot all about God, forgot He even existed. When you have a lot of money, you run the risk of becoming your own god because you can fix everything with money. That why scriptures teach us:

> **1Tim 6:10** _For the love of money is the root of all evil:_ _which while some coveted after, they have erred from the faith, and pierced themselves through with many sorrows._

This is exactly what happened to me and the end result was that I pierced myself with many sorrows.

Then I started to write, something I had a coveted since my early childhood. I never knew my dream would come true and never did I even dream of writing books like this. Well, this is my second book (well, actually the 3rd) and the first is as thick as 10 books combined. A few other books have already been started and are nearing completion. The point is: Its almost three years now that I have had zero income. We have sold all the items which we collected while serving the god Mammon…

> **Mat 6:24** _No man can serve two masters:_ _for either he will hate the one, and love the other; or else he will hold to the one, and despise the other. Ye cannot serve God and mammon._

But through the grace of the God of Abraham, Isaac and Jacob, I don't need to "make myself a friend of Mammon" any longer…

> **Luk 16:9** _And I say unto you, Make to yourselves friends of the mammon of unrighteousness; that, when ye fail, they may receive you into everlasting habitations._

A good friend told me once:

> _**"Less is more"**_

And I think this is very true, I am living it!

Forgive me for not remembering who to give credit to for the following quote, but it is so, so true...

"The things you own will own you"

How true is this, think about it dear reader...and think about the absurdity of it all and why? – Because we love this world, follow the majority and need to "fit in"... its absolutely ludicrous! You have nightmares about how you are going to make your payments each month, but once you are in my position, you suddenly and very quickly find out with just how little you can survive and the best is – you don't...

buy things you don't need, with money you don't have, to impress people you don't like...

Once you find yourself in a position where you do not "own" anything, you are also not "owned", especially with Satan's brothers hands clutching at your throat and squeezing the life out of you, 24 ours a day! Well, maybe I owe Satan's brother a big thank you as if it wasn't for him I would not have started writing and I would not be writing this book now. In a sense, if it wasn't for him I would not be living my dream, and what is my dream? I sold everything I had and bought my PEARL!

> **Mat 13:45** *Again, the kingdom of heaven is like unto a merchant man, seeking goodly pearls:*
> **Mat 13:46** *Who, when he had found one pearl of great price, went and sold all that he had, and bought it.*

Why am I sharing this with you? Well, the bible tells us not to collect treasures on earth, but rather in heaven.

> **Mat 6:19** *Lay not up for yourselves treasures upon earth, where moth and rust doth corrupt, and where thieves break through and steal:*
> **Mat 6:20** *But lay up for yourselves treasures in heaven, where neither moth nor rust doth corrupt, and where thieves do not break through nor steal:*

You would very well know by now that my English is not very good, my writing skills neither and I don't even want to mention how bad my spelling and grammar is and even if the latter was the best there was, my books would never sell like hotcakes and even if they do, that will be the first sign that there is something wrong with them, because God tells us:

> *Joh 15:19 If ye were of the world, the world would love his own: but because ye are not of the world, but I have chosen you out of the world, therefore the world hateth you.*

> *1Joh 2:15 Love not the world, neither the things that are in the world. If any man love the world, the love of the Father is not in him.*

Why would I share this story with you? To witness to you that **now that I have nothing, I have everything.** I have nothing, but yet I have a roof over my head, have transport, have enough food, warmth and clothing – how is this possible? It is only possible through God's grace and by His servants, in the form of loving and caring family and friends. Yes, I have nothing of earthly value, but I have never been so happy, so healthy and so immensely grateful towards God, my family and friends and yes, never was I so close to God who blesses me beyond belief with treasures in heaven (and still takes care of me here on earth).

I would argue that:

> *You are only really living when you are at a place in your life where you don't have anything, but also don't need anything and yet you are literally doing what you feel you have been called to do. This dear friend is what I call: Living!*

The best way to summarise my situation would be the following quote:

> *"I have held many things in my hands, and I have lost them all; but whatever I have placed in God's hands, that I still possess."*
> *- Martin Luther*

My apology for digressing with "my story", but I wanted to set the scene that money is not always the first thing we need to be concerned about. I would like to remind you, as it is applicable even in the case of a funeral:

> *You buy things you don't need, with money you don't have, to impress people you don't like...*

This then brings me to the cost of the funeral. What is the very first thought swirling around in our minds? The high cost of the coffin, the printing of the "funeral letter" the expensive reception and lastly the luxurious tombstone etc. etc. etc. We will list what we may call the DIY funeral to make it as cost effective as possible, but please remember; if you do have the necessary finances you can do pretty much what you like. This however is for people who want to bury their dead like scripture tells us to, but can hardly afford to.

Administration

This would include doctor's costs to issue the death certificate, the cost for the grave, the death notice in the local paper etc. These costs you can't really reduce significantly. You can place the notices in the paper yourself at negligible cost, but the biggest cost here and also for the entire funeral is the grave itself. If your local authority does not dictate the burial site, constrained by the residential area you reside in, you can compare costs from different cemeteries, in different areas to find the most cost effective option. Don't however select a cheaper option too far away and end up paying more for fuel to get the body to the required site. Sometime it is worth it to have the grave dug deeper to have the spouse or even child buried in the same grave – there is nothing wrong with this and it is much cheaper in the end. In addition I would suggest purchasing a grave already – although this may cause problems based on future unknowns.

Undertaker's fees

These costs include renting of the chapel, the viewing room, the hearse, the funeral fees and the staff and of course embalming costs. Undertakers normally have a small chapel at their premises for a small funeral service. If you can afford this it is fine, however remember that you do not want a church minister to conduct the funeral. I would suggest as previously stated, leave the chapel and just gather at the cemetery instead. You may want to offer people an opportunity to view the diseased one last time in which case you will have to cover the embalming costs. This is however not compulsory. If this option is chosen one would also need to pay for the viewing room at the undertakers premises. Ask for a cheaper hearse, it needs not be a 50 foot limousine! You even have the option of transporting the body to the cemetery yourself if you so choose. Concerning the funeral staff, you don't even have to have them at the cemetery, but I would suggest that you do as they are professional and also possess the required equipment and skill to lower the coffin into the grave with dignity. If you do this yourself, prepare very carefully as you don't want to have the coffin slipping and falling into the grave.

Ministers fees

You guessed it – none, nada! He is welcome as a friend or family member to attend the funeral like everyone else, but he doesn't speak, he does plenty of that at his own church so don't be concerned that he is missing out on an opportunity.

Flowers

Flowers for what? No really… for what? Or should I say for whom….?
And especially no flowers or rose petals must be thrown into the grave, or
handfuls of sand. This is an ancient pagan practise to "frighten" the evil
demon's out of the grave in order for the departed to continue on their
journey. Here is reality for you, if you neglected to give the deceased
flowers when they were alive, it's too late now! Nope…. No flowers!

The coffin

In our time of grief and sorrow due to, very often sudden, death in the
family, we automatically feel guilty about what could have been. Suddenly
we are confronted with the horrifying reality that we can do nothing about
"what could have or should have been". In an instant we realise that there
are so many things which we have lost, in the blink of en eye. In this state
of mind, it's the feeling of guilt that becomes the driving force behind
wanting to do everything possible for the deceased. Harsh reality is the only
activity left is of course the funeral. In some twisted way, our conscience
would feel better if we do everything in our power to organise the best
funeral ever in a last desperate attempt to assure the deceased that we still
love them dearly. Once my deceased loved one sees the astonishing funeral
we arranged, all past regrets, sins, lost moments and feuds will be forgiven
at once. This will make me happy and it will make my departed loved one
happy. We may almost phrase it as: "The best funeral equal's instant
forgiveness and wellbeing". Although there may be some truth in this and it
may even have a therapeutic effect, the question to ask is: "Who feels
better?" This is not a trick question. The only answer here is: I feel better,
we feel better, but the body in the coffin does not have any "feelings". I am
fully aware of our indoctrination from childhood that the dearly departed is
now a floating soul, in the air above us, looking down at the funeral
proceedings and they are sad to see us weeping and seeing us missing them,
but boy are they happy with the best funeral ever! "**A funeral to die for**",
one could say… This is another fallacy, courtesy of the false churches!

So, what can we possibly do which would prove to be of "value" to the
deceased? Every cost associated with a funeral is non value added, non
permanent so to speak, except for the coffin and the tombstone, these are
more "permanent" or lasting in "value". No surprise then, what lulls our
guilty conscience the most, is an expensive coffin and an even more
expensive gravestone. It is this combination that leads us to answer: "The
best there is!", when we are asked to choose a coffin.

I remember when my dad had died; I was a young man of 26 years old. At
the time, my father had a "live-in-girl-friend", but that status changed from

"girl-friend" to "common law wife", coincidently and very conveniently a few days after my dad died. She commandeered everything – the will, the estate, the possessions and of course the financial portfolio. Nonetheless, when we were at the funeral parlour and had to choose a coffin, I replied: "The very best there is as he (dad) is paying for it himself". She, "the newly appointed common law wife" and "caretaker" of my fathers estate, decided to take the second cheapest coffin in the funeral parlour. I was furious with this because I knew the motive behind this choice was purely to protect her eventual financial benefit with regards to the estate.

Today however I am totally the opposite inclined, convinced in fact! For what reason would we get the best and most expensive coffin. Grandma is not going to see the coffin, contrary to popular theological dogma! The only ones seeing the coffin are the people attending the funeral. Should we then: "**buy something we don't need, with money we don't have, to impress someone we don't like?**" In fact, I believe the more expensive the coffin, the longer it takes for the body to decompose and yes, decomposition is the last thing we want to think about when we lost a dear loved one, but decomposition none the less is part of God's design – not originally intended one may argue to which I would agree, but nonetheless.

In many countries around the world, one is allowed to cover the body in a shroud only. However uncivilised this may seem I would tend to reason this way is more biblical than we realise. I am not trying to say we all have to start burying this way, but for them that have no other means financially – why not? There is absolutely nothing wrong with this, even from a biblical perspective. I would just be careful and speak to my local authorities to familiarise myself with current legislation in this regard. (If there is somebody, familiar with the regulations in South-Africa on this subject, please let me know, I would appreciate it very much) I know that Muslims don't bury in a coffin, but only in a shroud. Can't we do the same?

From Genesis to Revelation the word "coffin" is only mentioned once in the bible. Joseph's body was first embalmed and then placed in a coffin. Unfortunately I cannot prove the following statement, but I suspect the reason for this may be as a result of Joseph's high esteem in Egypt. (This is only an assumption on my part).

> **Gen 50:26 So Joseph died, being an hundred and ten years old: and they embalmed him, and _he was put in a coffin_ in Egypt.**

On the other hand, there is nothing wrong if we quickly purchase some wooden planks and knock together a makeshift coffin, a mere wooden box without any bells or whistles. (Again, check with local legislation first).

In the old days on the farms, and maybe this is still practiced – I am not sure – the farmer would build his own coffin and even lie in it to see if it fits, test drive it, so to speak. Once happy with his handiwork, the coffin would be stored in the attic and used as a storage container, until D-day of course. I cannot see any reason why we cannot practise this today, absolutely nothing wrong with it! (I am giving it a lot of thought to manufacture my own coffin in time to come)

Not to go into detail, but I want to share my own preferences with you, useless information if you will. I would like to be buried in a makeshift wooden coffin, but I also have no problem if it is just a shroud, however – the coffin must not, I repeat…must not have wooden or rope handles and it must be held together with steel screws. This may sound like useless information, but those who know, knows what this is all about….One other thing is, it must be a box with 4 sides, not 6 sides. Ditto….

The Church

What church? Granma may have not even been a congregation member and all the children are in different churches, what to do? My advice? Stay far, far away from a church funeral! The purest funeral you can arrange is one that is not conducted by an unclean church. Period! How would I know which church is pure and which is not, you may ask? There is a simple answer, none of them are pure. Once a church is registered as a church, with a minister who studied theology, it is tainted and can not and will not bring you the true gospel. They are all harlots of the mother harlot!

Rev 17:5 And upon her forehead was a name written, MYSTERY, BABYLON THE GREAT, THE MOTHER OF HARLOTS AND ABOMINATIONS OF THE EARTH.

I can assure you that I am not shooting from the hip here, like Rambo… You only need the bible to prove this shocking statement!

> *"Every step away from church, is two steps closer to God"*
> - *Piet Wilsenach*

Rev 18:4 And I heard another voice from heaven, saying, Come out of her, my people, that ye be not partakers of her sins, and that ye receive not of her plagues.

That which applies to the coffin also apples to the funeral letter. Ah…. But the departed was such a wonderful person who deserves nothing but the best. The funeral letter must be once again: "something to die for…" It must have quite a few pages, it must be brilliant, it must be beautiful, with bells and whistles, gold frills, colour photos and it must be varnished so it shines in sunlight! May I ask a stupid question? To impress who - exactly? Are we again spending money we don't have on things we don't need to impress someone we don't even like?

I have an aunt who, in my opinion, is addicted "weddings" and "funerals". If she finds out that a wedding or for that matter a funeral has been conducted and she was not invited, there is hell to play! It simply does not matter how far down the friend or family –tree she resides, she wants to be there. She showed me a briefcase once, filled almost to the brim with funeral letters she collected from attending funerals. I paged through these and I must tell you, I found some of the most beautiful pieces of paper mankind have ever laid eyes on. I can't even image what some of them must have cost. What is the point? Here is a woman who collects them, but they gather dust in a briefcase anyway. Where are all the other funeral letters which were distributed on the day of the funeral? Thrown in the garbage the next day? Now and then you find the odd funeral letter in a display cabinet, and then only because it was very close family, like a mother or father, brother or sister or even a child, but where the rest of the hundreds of letters are, printed at astronomical cost, no one knows – gone!

My advice: Print one page only, black and white – containing:

- *A black and white photo of the deceased.*
- *Birth date and date of death.*
- *Pallbearers at the cemetery – no church pallbearers as no church involved.*
- *The family may compile a section, dedicated to the memory of the departed, not to impress other people, but of importance to the family, and print this on the back.*

Good advice is: it is not a wedding invitation and the person for whom it was compiled cannot see it, nor read it. Ask yourself this question: "Are you really going to frame the funeral letter in a gold frame and display it in your living room until the end of days? Am I really going to look at the funeral letter every morning before I go to work? Or am I going to put it somewhere, only to be seen again when I have to de-clutter the house?

Leave those fancy funeral letters to the rich people and don't worry about the printing business collapsing, the rich people will keep them going…. :-)

Who conducts?

Who is going to conduct the funeral if there is no church minister? This is easier than you think, a believer from within the family or close friends, someone who follows Christ and not the church. The bearers carries the coffin from the hearse to the grave, the chosen spokesperson reads a few scriptures and says a few words about the departed. The close family may also say a few words if they choose to do so, at the grave. The coffin will be lowered and then covered by the family as described earlier. No rose petals and handfuls of dirt to be thrown onto the coffin, as described earlier.

What if there is no one in the family to "conduct" the funeral at the grave? You can speak to the undertaker, they normally have someone who can fill in and usually they are not affiliated to any specific church or denomination – this is if all else fails, so to speak. Remember however that even if no one says a word and the coffin is just lowered into the grave, it is still fine, because trust me, nothing said at the funeral or thereafter makes one iota difference to the deceased in terms of the afterlife, nothing, nada!

The funeral reception

They say: You have to show respect by attending the funeral. That may be so, but I avoid funerals like the plague. I only attend the closest possible family funerals and if I quickly calculate, this happens about once every 10 year's or so. One could argue that I have no respect for the dead, but hold on a minute, please allow me to explain: I don't attend funerals because the people attending the funeral don't know how to behave themselves at a funeral. So, you have a family who lost a loved one about three days ago, maybe even parents who lost their child. Then, the proverbial John and Jane arrives from 600 miles away to attend the funeral and the family is in total ecstasy to see John and Jane again, so much so they forget the event is actually a funeral – where somebody died you know…! Its greetings, conversations, loud laughter and merriment, before they even made it into house where the grieving family is at. At the grave, the chattering about the good old times and keeping up to date is so bad, they have to be silenced before for the mister can start speaking. They are so happy to see each other again; they completely forget they are attending a funeral, totally oblivious to the fact that they are standing a few feet away from an open grave.

Right, so the funeral is complete and everybody is on their way to the reception, the place where it really becomes jolly and cheerful! (I even attended a funeral where the family, dressed in their suits, just before we left the house for church, took a few drinks – and when I say drinks I mean alcoholic drinks. Now, I have nothing against anyone taking a drink now and then, even the bible says we must take a little wine now and then, but that day I was stunned and flabbergasted beyond belief – it's a funeral for Pete sake!)

Many people will agree when I say the following: When an unknown or uninvited person accidently walks into a funeral reception by mistake, the only tell-tale lead that it may be a funeral reception, is (and only sometimes) one or two lonely people are sitting in a corner somewhere, grieving about the deceased, and oh yes… usually there's more black garments, compared to a wedding. Other than that it is a jolly time. Laughter fills the room, chattering about current events, promotions at work, and getting up to speed with who is richer and better off nowadays… Photographs are taken, addresses are written down and promises made…. "Now that we have each others addresses we must visit soon…they would reassure one another of their good intensions" Now and then they spot the grieving person, really sad and in no mood to join the jollification – "I wonder what's with him?" they would say in a whispery voice, while nodding their heads in the direction of the grieving person.

This begs the question – Is it a funeral or is it a family reunion with free food and drinks? No really…I can't tell the difference, can you? Ask yourself another question – how many people will attend the funeral, if they know that there will be no reception afterwards?

My advice: No reception!
Let's apply some logic here. Why must we have a reception? Well, people have to be at church half an hour before the time, then an hour worth of church, then driving time to the cemetery and the funeral itself and this is excluding viewing the body. Many hours are accumulated in this activity, hours where people get hungry and thirsty.

When we drastically reduce the time, we don't need to have a reception. Family and friends are informed that the body may be viewed at the undertaker's premises, if the relatives choose this option. The funeral will then be conducted at the cemetery. After the coffin has been lowered and the grave covered by the family, anybody can stay behind at the cemetery to "catch-up". Some of them may go to the relatives home for a visit and some of the others can go to a local hotel or bar where they can really have a jovial time and "catch-up", drinks and all. But a reception where 1% is heartbroken and the other 99% are on a free trip down "memory lane", courtesy of "compassionate leave" from work, with free food and drinks, is not what I would describe as a funeral, and I sure as hell would not describe this as "paying last respects" neither!

What is the point? (Remember that we are focussing on costs). If finances are not an issue, you can have a massive reception with the greatest of pleasure. There is nothing wrong with that. From a cost effective point of view however the reception is nothing more than a reunion, and believe me, all those addresses and telephone numbers which were exchanged and all those promises of visiting one another don't mean a damn thing. Those same people will only see each other again... yes you guessed it, at the next family and friend –reunion, codenamed: "funeral". Here and there someone made some remarks about the departed loved one, how good they were, how they will be sorely missed and so on, but even that is gone when the reception has ended. If family or friends want to reunite and catch-up, they must do it because they desire to do so, from their own free will and not wait for the funeral reception. What is the point? In any event, I am willing to bet the attendance would drop considerably if there is no reception...

Anyhow, talking about receptions where there are always sandwiches to eat, the next verse is rather interesting:

Eze 24:17 Forbear to cry, make no mourning for the dead, bind the tire of thine head upon thee, and put on thy shoes upon thy feet, and cover not thy lips, and eat not the bread of men.

The tombstone

We have looked at the gravestone in detail already, but all it will cost is a bag of cement, a bit of building sand and a few drops of sweat to make a tombstone yourself. Just consider the memorial value and emotional gratification if you created the tombstone yourself. Would this not be far more valuable than a tombstone which costs thousands? It seems to me, the cheapest is also the most dignified and honourable.

This is also a very good example:

In summary

- *The cheapest coffin money can buy, or a DIY coffin*
- *No church*
- *No minister*
- *No flowers*
- *Black and white, one page funeral letter*
- *No reception.*
- *The cheapest tombstone money can buy, or a DIY tombstone*

What do you have? You have a funeral, according to scripture and possibly even cheaper than a cremation. You have to remember, the moment the departed exhales their very last breath, or like scripture says: "yielded up the ghost", that is it! There is nothing, absolutely nothing that anyone on this earth can do to change that person's judgement. It does not matter what the Catholics teach, it does not matter what your own church teach, its all false teachings – there is absolutely no way whatsoever that you can benefit the departed with any action you take, much less "a funeral to die for…"

Are my loved ones in heaven?

Dear reader, this is a question which has a standard answer in almost all forms of theology and I specifically call it "theology" because the standard answer is not compatible with the teachings of scripture. This standard teaching is: Yes, your loved one is with Jesus in heaven. Our good doctor Isak Burger even sent his departed father a message by asking another dying person to relay the message. The doctor was sure that the dying person will be in heaven with Jesus, and the doctor's late father obviously is in heaven as well. Of course this is what every relative wants to hear, it makes them feel good inside to know that the minister (a man of God) assures them that their dearly departed is in heaven, with Jesus.

People accuse me, the author, of being judgemental. They say: "The bible says you must not judge, but you (the author) are judging in your books" One clergymen whom was shown one of my books, paged through it quickly and proclaimed: "the author of this book is "judging", therefore a book like this does not belong in a Christian home – Burn it!" May I be so bold as to ask: Are you not judging my book then, without even reading it? Who is judging now?

The next issue that tickles my mind is this: If the puppet behind the pulpit states that our loved one is with Jesus in heaven, is this not judging? Who is the minister to take the place of God and "judge" a person into heaven? Is this not judging in the highest possible degree? What do they base this judgement on – well, the person was a good little Christian, attended church regularly, gave lots of money to the church etc. etc. etc. But what does God say: (This is Jesus speaking – Red letter in the KJV)

> **Mat 7:21** __Not every one that saith unto me, Lord, Lord, shall enter into the kingdom of heaven__; __but he that doeth the will of my Father which is in heaven.__
> **Mat 7:22** __Many will say to me in that day, Lord, Lord, have we not prophesied in thy name? and in thy name have we cast out devils? and in thy name done many wonderful works?__
> **Mat 7:23** __And then will I profess unto them, I never knew you: depart from me, ye that work iniquity.__

Please take careful note: Jesus is not talking to Satanists here, he is talking to so-called "Christians", people who basically demand to be in heaven. It is vitally important that you understand this dear reader!
Can you now understand why Jesus says people are "pressing" into the kingdom of God? Demanding to be in heaven!

> **Luk 16:15** *And he said unto them, __Ye are they which justify yourselves before men__; but God knoweth your hearts: for that which is highly esteemed among men is abomination in the sight of God.*

> **_Luk 16:16_** *The law and the prophets were until John: since that time the kingdom of God is preached, <u>and every man presseth into it.</u>*
> **_Luk 16:17_** *And it is easier for heaven and earth to pass, than one tittle of the law to fail.*

He, Jesus states further that heaven and earth will pass before the law fails, this is scriptures -and yet we have the good theologians calling these very same statutes of scriptures, "Jewish Culture" not applicable today! Well then, let me not judge, but rather state that I do not wish to be part of this cesspool of vile crap which only descends into DIRE consequences!

Let's assume for argument sake the following scenario: Not those that are good little church members will enter into the kingdom, but those who do the will of the Father. This is what Jesus Himself says. Let's assume the funeral service is a cremation service, which if we study scriptures, is totally against the will of the Father, but yet the minister overrides what Jesus says and commits the deceased to heaven, judge, jury and executioner style no less! Who is judging now? Who is yanking God's judgement away from Him and playing "god" themselves?

The truth is a bit different from this teaching, but here is my humble request to you dear reader:
Please allow me answer this question in great detail in a book to follow shortly. Please visit my website every so often to see when the book is available. (You can also subscribe on my website so that I am able to inform you when this book is available)

The truth however, regardless of the above question, badly in need of a proper scriptural answer, is when the person died, there is nothing, absolutely nothing you or I can do to change their fate. Even if we bury them in a solid gold coffin, from the biggest church in the world, by the highest possible theologian professor, it changes nothing – NADA! Even the dead person cannot pray for forgiveness anymore!

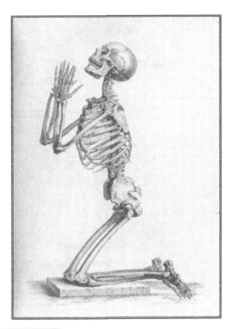

Dear reader, the most unfortunate but nonetheless true reality is this: When you die you've had your proverbial chips and your hourglass has run out. There is nothing you or any living relative can do for you.

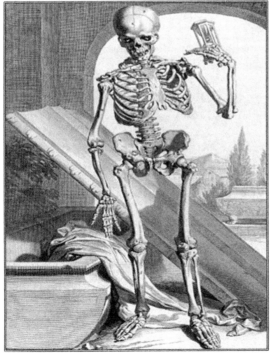

You can't even relay messages to someone's dearly departed father!

The Estate

Someone asked me once: "Should I fight for what is rightfully mine from the estate?"

My answer? Yes! If you are a very good Christian and loyal churchgoer, then yes, fight! Fight tooth and nail for what is yours! Stuff them up!

If however you are a true child of God, you will not do this. Why not? Because your life is solidly and fundamentally based on God's Will and you trust Him to decide what is best for you. You trust Him in your cause for justice and not yourself. If God wants you to inherit a large sum of money, He will allow it based on His will and in His time. When you start fighting for it yourself, you are stepping across a boundary where He may very well not be present. Also be very careful, you should be familiar with the saying: "easy come, easy go". This saying gets a new meaning when it comes to an inheritance!

Off the topic, there are those qualified theologians on the pulpit who teaches the congregation members that when they pray, they must be very specific. For example, you must not merely pray for a bicycle, you must specify the model, the colour and remember to describe all the accessories in detail. I have acquaintances that actually do this and the best is, sometimes they get exactly what they specified, much to their dismay when it does not work out like they hoped it would!

My bible however, yes the same bible they use in church, teaches me that before I even ask, God knows what I need:

> **Mat 6:7 But when ye pray, use not vain repetitions, as the heathen do: for they think that they shall be heard for their much speaking.**
> **Mat 6:8 Be not ye therefore like unto them: for your Father knoweth what things ye have need of, before ye ask him.**

I suspect my God and the Churches "god" is not the same "god". Why do preachers teach their members they have to be specific if my bible states that God knows already what I need before I ask? I think it may be that their "god" is perhaps dyslexic and runs the risk of getting the "order" wrong....? No I don't know why they do this. I do know one thing though, to submit yourself to God's Will is to trust Him in everything and to be assured that His answer, His plans and His Will is always the best for you, even though sometimes it does not look or feel like it in the heat of the moment, just be patient and you will see…

The churches love to quote this verse:

> **_Rom 8:28 And we know that all things work together for good to them that love God..._**

There are however two problems with their context. Firstly, it states "for those who love God", which they don't because they don't even know what it means and secondly: The verse has another portion to it...

> **_Rom 8:28 And we know that all things work together for good to them that love God, to them who are the called according to his purpose._**

This simply means: "Not all things work out together for good" – for ALL people! Only for those

CALLED ACCORDING TO HIS PURPOSE!

The vultures

How do you transform a bunch of heartbroken, grieving, broken people in black mourning garments in an instant into a ferocious, brutal swarm of vultures with blood dripping beaks?

Just throw the last will and testament of the deceased into the bunch.

Foto: Lip Kee Yap

It is so horrific and sad to see how the "holier-than-thou" Christian zips open his mourning garment from top to bottom and out climbs a Jurassic monster vulture, when the deceased's possessions comes into play.

I knew a man for many years, who was much older than me and a good Christian. More than once I witnessed how he took his own children to court for the most trivial and insignificant issues. The end result was that the children also started taking each other to court when one borrowed money from the other and the first one didn't pay up. Truly a sad state of affairs!

Trust God to be your judge, with the floor as your cause and your knees on it as your defence.

> *1Cor 6:3 Know ye not that we shall judge angels? how much more things that pertain to this life?*
> *1Cor 6:4 If then ye have judgments of things pertaining to this life, set them to judge who are least esteemed in the church.*
> *1Cor 6:5 I speak to your shame. Is it so, that there is not a wise man among you? no, not one that shall be able to judge between his brethren?*
> *1Cor 6:6 But brother goeth to law with brother, and that before the unbelievers.*
> *1Cor 6:7 Now therefore there is utterly a fault among you, because ye go to law one with another. Why do ye not rather take wrong? why do ye not rather suffer yourselves to be defrauded?*
> *1Cor 6:8 Nay, ye do wrong, and defraud, and that your brethren.*
> *1Cor 6:9 Know ye not that the unrighteous shall not inherit the kingdom of God? Be not deceived: neither fornicators, nor idolaters, nor*

How dare two, so-called Christians take each other to court, to appeal their case in front of unbelievers, to have unbelievers preside over a believers cause? No, a true follower of God does not indulge in this kind of behaviour.

Please note another important lesson from scriptures:

> *1Cor 6:4 If then ye have judgments of things pertaining to this life, set them to judge who are least esteemed in the church.*

This does not mean: NOT the highly educated theologian, the scribe, the Pharisee, the preacher, the priest, the pastor or doctor and the professor, but he whom is the least esteemed!

(By the way – the word church has not been correctly translated in the bible. The correct translation should have been something like "an assembly of the very elect", and this is not the church my friend. Never confuse this meaning with the word "church" as we know it today.)

A word of caution

The "live-in-girlfriend" of my dad which suddenly became the "common law wife" after his death, really did well. She proved to be very cunning in this regard. How would you feel if your dad is very ill and he summons all the children and tells them the following: "Kids, you don't have to worry, everything has been taken care of, my last will and testament has been compiled and also signed. My "live-in-girlfriend" does not want anything from the estate; everything I have I leave to you, my children…" The first thought you have is – wow, I can't believe this woman does not want anything because you know she is a nasty piece of work. Suddenly you feel guilty because you realise that all the guerrilla warfare she practised towards the kids is now gone. She doesn't want anything from the estate? Can this be true? Oh how bad I feel now about myself, unbeknown to us she actually turned out to be a wonderful person.

Shortly after this event, your dad passes away. The same day, a last will and testament is produced which states that she, the now "common law wife" gets half of everything. This will and testament is a copy, the original was nowhere to be found, even unto this day which is some 20+ years later, very convenient don't you think. Ah…but wait, you say – if there was no original will, how could she have commandeered the estate and gone wild? That is a good question, but did I mention how cunning she was? The best of all is, the signature on this "copy" of the will is so dodgy and wobbly, it looked like a child had forged it. And that's not all, when we consulted the hospital and checked my dad's bed-records, it stated that in the week preceding the signature date and on the day of the signature, my dad was "confused", "hallucinating", "not himself", "did not know who he was" and kept falling out of bed, walking around in a daze…. etc.

There were other documents forged as well – my dad's pension fund for example had a letter, sighed by us, the children who stated how we loved this woman and how she cared for my dad, day and night at his bedside etc. What is the problem with this? We never, ever wrote that letter, and never ever signed it – that I can promise you. We would not have written such vile crap even if you paid us to do it!

Anyhow, armed with all the documents and evidence we went to see a lawyer. The lawyer looked at the evidence and arranged an appointment with an advocate. The advocate looked at the evidence and said: "You have a watertight case – there is no way she can possibly get away with this, but….." and then came the bad news – "you will spend all the money in your dad's estate and then owe some more, before the case is complete, so just let it go and take what she is offering". This is the proverbial "half an egg is better than an empty shell".

I can't stress this enough – please get your last will and testament in order, and most importantly, keep it up to date, make it an on-going priority. This is an especially serious matter where two divorcees married, maybe with each coming into the marriage with kids, and please kids; watch out for that "common law wife", nasty business I tell you! (Of course I am not implying that everybody is the same, there are wonderful "common law wife's" as well)

Hate is poison

I just need to share something else with you. I hated this woman so much it was unbelievable. I found my every waken moment was dedicated to hating this woman, and when I say hate, I mean HATE! The "hate" had nothing to do with earthy possessions or money or even the estate, it had everything to do with the injustice of it all, what she got away with and nobody could do a damn thing about it. This carried on for months on end and suddenly, one day out of the blue, a thought struck me like a ton of bricks – this woman has, amongst others, bought a brand new car and is spending my dad's money, having the best time of her life and I am ruining my life by dedicating all my thoughts towards my hate to her and she isn't even aware of it. When I realised this I knew at once that hate like this poisons you and eats away your insides, piece by piece. On that day I stopped thinking about her and made peace with what happened. After that, to this day I never wished her anything bad. I have forgiven her… however; I will not sit down and drink a cup of tea with her though. It also helps that I haven't seen her again after the events surrounding my dad's affairs. Remember that forgiveness does not necessarily imply that punishment is automatically removed…

> *2Sam 12:13 And David said unto Nathan, I have sinned against the LORD. And Nathan said unto David, The LORD also hath put away thy sin; thou shalt not die.*
> *2Sam 12:14 Howbeit, because by this deed thou hast given great occasion to the enemies of the LORD to blaspheme, the child also that is born unto thee shall surely die.*

> **2Sam 12:18** *And it came to pass on the seventh day, that the child died...*

The moral of this true story is; don't hate, it only devours yourself from within, while the person you hate doesn't even think about your existence, never mind what he or she did to you. Forgive, make peace and leave it be. Place it in God's hands and forget about it, believe me, you will feel so much better! (By forgiving I don't necessarily mean hugging, kissing and making up...)

> **Rom 12:19** *Dearly beloved, avenge not yourselves, but rather give place unto wrath: for it is written, Vengeance is mine; I will repay, saith the Lord.*

Words of caution though, don't be asking God to punish the person you "hated" now – this will be disastrous on your account – I trust you get the point.

Always remember this: We ourselves are not blameless angels now are we?

> **Tit 3:3** *For we ourselves also were sometimes foolish, disobedient, deceived, serving divers lusts and pleasures, living in malice and envy, hateful, and hating one another.*

Last will and testament

A friend told me, he doesn't want to be cremated, but he is sure his family is going to cremate him. Another husband and wife want their father to be buried according to scripture, but he refuses – he demands to be cremated and so we can carry on...

What to do in these cases? The best is to put your wish in writing in your last will and testament. Do you recall that the cremation may not take place if it is against the wishes of the deceased? Well, I would not bargain on this little legality because if they throw the bones in a mass grave behind the crematorium together with animal bones, why would a last will and testament stop them? It does however make it legal. Let's look at what I regard as the very first will regarding these issues in scriptures:

> **Gen 47:29** *And the time drew nigh that Israel must die: and he called his son Joseph, and said unto him, If now I have found grace in thy sight, put, I pray thee, thy hand under my thigh,*

> *and deal kindly and truly with me; <u>bury me not, I pray thee, in Egypt:</u>*
> *<u>Gen 47:30</u> But I will lie with my fathers, and thou shalt carry me out of Egypt, <u>and bury me in their buryingplace.</u> And he said, I will do as thou hast said.*

The twelve patriarchs of Israel (12 sons of Jacob) each left us a testament. These scripts are available for us to read and they are indeed very informing and enlightening writings. The cores of these testaments are mostly based on morals, how we should live, what to avoid and so on.

Todays last will and testaments are different. Last wills where the dead attempts to rule the living, especially by means of financial do's and don'ts are dreadful document's. Nevertheless, it is still the last "say" we have on this earth, even if we exhaled our last breath already. If we judge by this book, the very last say we have is in fact how we want our loved ones to deal with our remains. Therefore we are subject to our loved one's promises because after we died, there's nothing we can influence anymore.

Ensure your last will and testament states clearly that you must not be cremated.

The promise

It so happens that many people die without a last will and testament. We will attempt to provide an alternative option here.

> *<u>Gen 50:25</u> And Joseph took an oath of the children of Israel, saying, God will surely visit you, and <u>ye shall carry up my bones from hence.</u>*

We will not be asking our loved ones to take an oath, but just to make a promise that they would do everything in their power to fulfil our last wish.

Just take any old piece of paper and write your particulars on it, your names, appropriate identification numbers, address etc. and give it a heading, for example: **"My Last Wish"**. Then write down how you would like to be buried and stipulate that cremation is out of the question. Have your children or spouse, loved ones etc. sign the document with their own names and signatures, signifying their acknowledgement of your Last Wish.

Obviously, if by the time you die, cremation became compulsory, then the loved ones have no choice, but only when they have done everything in their power to prevent it without success. If they go against your wishes you will not be held accountable, but they must be very careful:

> **Deu 23:23** _That which is gone out of thy lips thou shalt keep and perform; even a freewill offering, according as thou hast vowed unto the LORD thy God, which thou hast promised with thy mouth._

> **Rom 14:12** _So then every one of us shall give account of himself to God._

The other side

Now the big question, what if dad says he wants to be cremated because mom was cremated, no matter how we try to convince him that it is unscriptural? This is a nasty affair! What if he stipulates this wish in his last will and testament? After all, it is a legal document which we have to abide by, but what must we do if this "legal" document is violating the scriptures?

I don't have all the answers my friend, but the scripture below is very important:

> **Mat 10:36** _And a man's foes shall be they of his own household._
> **Mat 10:37** _He that loveth father or mother more than me is not worthy of me: and he that loveth son or daughter more than me is not worthy of me._

My opinion?
Formulate a document, the same as the previous document, but with a twist. After all the names and legal numbers have been inserted, write something like this down: (formulate your own words of course)
"Herewith I (name) declare that I refuse to cremate (name) when he or she passes away. I have tried to reason with them from scriptures, but to no avail. I further declare that even if this person stipulates this wish in their will or other legal document, I still distance myself from having anything to do with such an unscriptural act whatsoever…." Or "I will go ahead and bury them anyway, regardless of their will. You get the point.

Then have the person (who wants to be cremated) as well as two witnesses and yourself sign the document – don't forget to date the document! Remember, if you found the truth regarding cremation and you still have anything to do with it because you respect mom, dad or anybody else's wishes to be cremated, you are choosing them above God and this is very dangerous. And if it so happens that you know the person wanted to cremate and you go against their wishes and bury them instead, you are following scripture, because you are choosing God above man, no problem with that.

Truth is hard and truth hurts! But God has given us a choice to either stand for truth or reject it. It's always easier to follow the majority and find excuses as to why we cannot make a stand for God's truth. Just look at the churches and you will see what I mean.

> *Mat 19:29   And every one that hath forsaken houses, or brethren, or sisters, or father, or mother, or wife, or children, or lands, for my name's sake, shall receive an hundredfold, and shall inherit everlasting life.*

What if I am asked to attend a cremation service? What if it is close family? The answer is hard, but simple – don't attend, but tell them why you cannot possibly attend – it's against your religion! Period! They will hate you for a while, but hey…. guess what:

> *Joh 15:18 If the world hate you, ye know that it hated me before it hated you.*

> *Mar 13:13 And ye shall be hated of all men for my name's sake: but he that shall endure unto the end, the same shall be saved.*

I wish you all the best in this difficult, but very important issue...

*But please, don't do this to yourself and don't do it to
anyone else...*

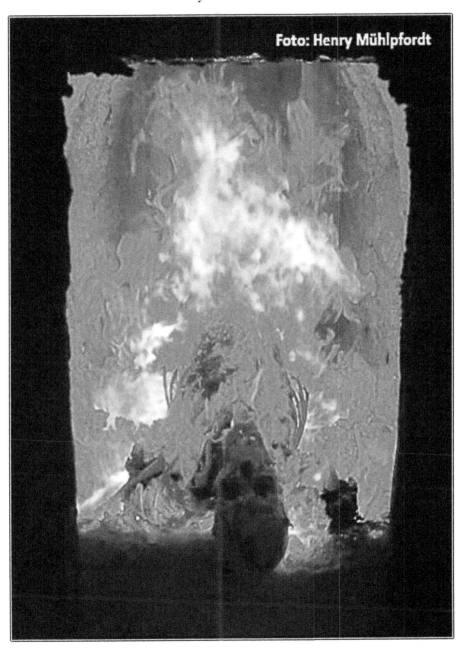

Foto: Henry Mühlpfordt

What do I do with the ash?

It will happen that some of us would have the "ash" of a loved one in the house. We may even have inherited the ash. Some of us may even have "ash" of pets that we keep in the house. The question is: "May wee keep it? What do we do with it?

Again, I don't have all the answers and what I am about to say is just my own opinion, I cannot prove this from scripture, therefore you will have to consult with God, as always.

The first fact we have to accept is: The abomination has been committed already, maybe due to ignorance but still. The second fact is what we read in scriptures:

> *Eze 22:26 Her priests have violated my law, and have profaned mine holy things: they have put no difference between the holy and profane, neither have they shewed difference between the unclean and the clean, and have hid their eyes from my sabbaths, and I am profaned among them.*

This tells us in plain English: The priest have violated the law – profanes God's holy things – they don't differentiate between holy and profane – they don't tell us what clean and unclean is etc. One only has to look at the churches to see this in action, every day, in every church, around the globe. According to the churches, everything goes, everything is fine, everything fits and everybody is going to heaven! They who should teach us what is unclean don't do it. Once again we must search the scriptures ourselves:

> *Eze 39:12 And seven months shall the house of <u>Israel be burying of them, that they may cleanse the land...</u>*

If burying cleanses the land, then not burying UN-cleanses the land, not so? This then should also indicate, to not bury the bones (as it is not ashes, but bones) is also to UN-cleanses the land.

Therefore, a statement which may be supported by scripture would be to bury the bones (ashes). Human or animal, makes no difference, bury it! Do not flush it down the toilet, do not throw it in the refuse bin and **please do not scatter it** – BURY IT! It is perfectly legal to bury "ashes". You can even bury it in your garden if you wish and even put a little headstone on it, or bury it at any other appropriate place of your choice. I would suggest in addition, <u>to keep it in the house is to make the house unclean</u> as well. Don't however believe a word I say, search the scriptures yourself. Consult with God once again on this issue. I just want to warn you regarding the answer you get: In my first book I wrote about a pastor in South-Africa who claims God told him in a dream to which casino he must go to win money. This is the stuff people want to hear. They love it, because how can gambling be wrong when God himself tells the pastor where to go and the best of all is, he won quite a large amount as well, R46,000 I believe! The problem here is very simple – God will never ever let you do something or give you an answer which violates His Word, never!

God can't state the following:

> *Isa 65:11 But ye are they that forsake the LORD, that forget my holy mountain, that prepare a table for that troop, and that furnish the drink offering unto that number.*
> *Isa 65:12 Therefore will I number you to the sword, and ye shall all bow down to the slaughter: because when I called, ye did not answer; when I spake, ye did not hear; but did evil before mine eyes, and did choose that wherein I delighted not*

In order to understand this passage better, the quote below is from Good News Bible[37]

> *Isa 65:11 "But it will be different for you that forsake me, who ignore Zion, my sacred hill, and worship Gad and Meni, the gods of luck and fate.*
> *Isa 65:12 It will be your fate to die a violent death, because you did not answer when I called you or listen when I spoke. You chose to disobey me and do evil.*

It states, if you worship the god of luck (e.g. gambling and such) at the same time you pour the cup for fate or destiny, but in a bad way – it will be your fate to die…

How can God say this and then guide the pastor, in a dream, to the nearest "god of luck"? This is not from God, but it is from "god", the god of this world, no one else but Satan himself! How many Christian clergymen and even good Christian's equally claim that "god" told them this, and made them to that, but these things are all impious when compared to what scripture says? I'm sorry, if what you believe is against what scripture tells me; your belief is vested not in the God of Abraham, Isaac and Jacob! And the truth is, there is one other "god" and that is Satan.

So then, please ensure that when you do get your answers that they are not from the "god" of this world, remember he is the master UDT teacher, the

Unsound Doctrine Teacher, he is the ultimate expert and master artist in "soothing the ears" by telling the congregation members what they want to hear….. and all who teaches his doctrine's are under his authority!

"and ye shall be as gods"
Satan Gen 3:5

A lie gets halfway around the world before the truth has a chance to get its pants on.

Winston Churchill

More about the bone

How much do you think do the bones of an average individual weigh? This is the skeleton with all the associated bones. Our source[38] supplies a figure of between 14% - 20% of the total body mass. A common figure for men is estimated at ±18%. The actual figure obviously varies with age, gender, race and other factors. As we age, our bone-mass decreases.

I don't want to bore you with the functions of the bones in our bodies, but this is very interesting information. The bone is not merely a frame to keep us from falling to the floor like a jelly-fish – please do your own research and you will be astonished about the complex and sophisticated role our bones contribute to our bodies and heath in general. In summary – if we assume for argument sake that the body will remain in its current composure in the absence of our skeleton and bones, the body will die! Our bones contribute such and intricate part in our survival, that without them we will perish.

We now know from scriptures how important our bones are after death. We also now know how important our bones are prior to death. The question now is: How much of the bone remains after cremation?

After cremation

We know that the remains or rather "cre-mains" is not "ash". This is a misleading and deceiving term, but I can understand how it became known as "ash". It sounds much better to say: "Here are your loved ones "ashes", as opposed to: "Here is your loved ones crushed bones, "hot off the industrial blender".

Even though there are tiny bones of which nothing remains after cremation, the majority of bones do remain, even after the intense heat and flames of the cremation oven. How many bones remain? Sources[39] estimate about 3.6 kilograms for an average male and 2.6 kilograms for an average female. To put this in perspective we can compare it to an average babies weight at birth which is ± 3kilograms and remember, these bones we are referring to here are totally dehydrated, not one drop of moisture, no flesh, sinews, or any other bodily fluids – they are totally dried out bones!

Even if you never had the opportunity to hold an urn with the ash of a deceased, you should know that the ash does not weigh even close to 3+ kilograms. So, where do the rest of the bones go? Well, as you know by now, one location (of many) is behind the crematorium, in a mass grave together with cats, dogs and the like!

Are your bones destined for that same hole?
You do have a choice my friend!

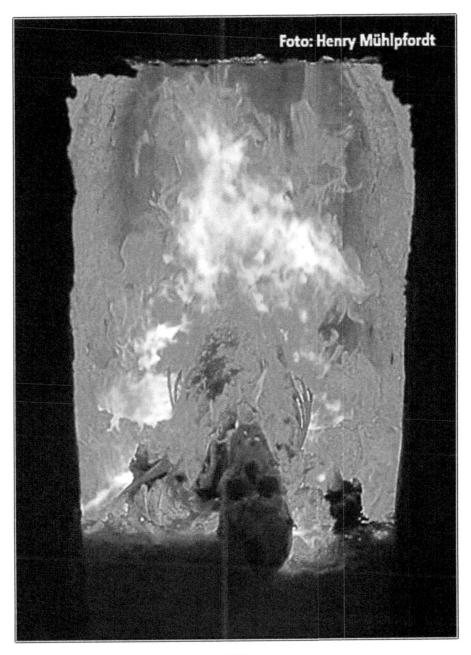

The indestructible bone

Even the most intense heat as well as the most ferocious and violent acid cannot destruct our bones. God designed our bones this way for a specific purpose dear reader. If you believe this, then ask yourself: "how in hell can we develop an industrial blender with hardened steel balls, purposefully designed to crush our bones to little pieces, when no other process is capable of achieving this feat?" No, no and NO! This is no good – no argument can ever justify this inhumane, ungodly act. Leave this for the "good Christian" who serves and trusts his LORD – the one behind the pulpit every Sunday (or Saturday in other cases), which he worships so faithfully, but we whom chooses to trust God and the Word he gave us, let us do everything in our power to avoid this grievous sin at all costs.

I would rather be cremated, than be cremated!
- **Piet Wilsenach**

Let us submit to the Will of our Creator, never mind family, parents and children alike!

> _**Mat 10:34**_ _**Think not that I am come to send peace on earth: I came not to send peace, but a sword.**_
> _**Mat 10:35**_ _**For I am come to set a man at variance against his father, and the daughter against her mother, and the daughter in law against her mother in law.**_
> _**Mat 10:36**_ _**And a man's foes shall be they of his own household.**_
> _**Mat 10:37**_ _**He that loveth father or mother more than me is not worthy of me: and he that loveth son or daughter more than me is not worthy of me.**_
> _**Mat 10:38**_ _**And he that taketh not his cross, and followeth after me, is not worthy of me**_

Please don't be mistaken, you will, just like me also be made a "gazingstock"! This means "publicly insulted and mistreated…"

> _**Heb 10:32**_ _**But call to remembrance the former days, in which, after ye were illuminated, ye endured a great fight of afflictions;**_
> _**Heb 10:33**_ _**Partly, whilst ye were made a gazingstock both by reproaches and afflictions; and partly, whilst ye became companions of them that were so used.**_

Yes, they mock you and end up hating you, but stand fast!

> *Mat 10:22 And ye shall be hated of all men for my name's sake: but he that endureth to the end shall be saved.*

> *Mat 19:29 And every one that hath forsaken houses, or brethren, or sisters, or father, or mother, or wife, or children, or lands, for my name's sake, shall receive an hundredfold, and shall inherit everlasting life.*

When we use the term "heathen" we are basically describing a person who is not of the same faith or religious conviction of ours. For example – a Muslim will regard me as a heathen and I regard a Muslim as a heathen, but I can tell you this – when it comes to a Muslim, in terms of cremation as just one example, the majority of Christians are "heathens" to both myself as well as the Muslim! You must decide where you stand my friend…there is no grey area – only God vs. Satan!

Value of bone – more than gold

I mentioned before that I would insist on seeing the body when the coffin arrives at the cemetery, just before it goes into the grave. The reason for this is – you cannot trust anybody, especially when it has to do with human remains. If you though we have exhausted the shocking events with regards our remains, then I apologise, because like the advertisement on TV says: But wait, there's more…..! Do you recall the Tristate Affair, where the judgment was that a cadaver has no monetary value, well guess again…

Organ donation

Most of us are aware that we have a choice to donate our bodies after we die to serve as "spare-parts". This is so that other people can continue living or improve their quality of living. The question is: Do we really know what's going on in this multi-billion-dollar-industry?

As an ignorant man, I though these included organs such as heart, lungs, kidneys, skin and even eyes, but boy was I surprised to learn that bones are also "harvested" and used. The best, or maybe the worst in this case is – the bone of a dead person is used to manufacture implants for another person's mouth…. Yuk!

When the jawbone was damaged or eroded over time, it must be "rebuilt", so to speak prior to a new tooth being inserted or implanted into the bone. This is called a "dental implant", and bone is used in this process of rebuilding. Bone of the patient may also be used such as part of the jawbone or the hipbone.

Another rude awakening

A dentist by the name of Michael Mastromarino[40] decided to "harvest" approximately 1000 bodies from various mortuaries, for "parts" and generated approximately 4.6 million US dollars and this without the consent of the deceased nor their relatives, according to our source. These events took place from 2002 – 2005. The age of the deceased as well as the cause of death of these bodies was falsified. There was the case of a man who died at age 79, from cancer of the bladder which the dentist falsified to death at age 64 and cause of death to heart attack. Bodies were exhumed and it came to light that instead of bones, the bodies had plastic pipes (PVC) inserted into the legs in place of the leg bones just to keep the normal shape of the body intact. The source estimates that up to 50,000 potential people received these illegal implants. Organ transplant's which includes dental implants already generates more than 1 billion US dollars, just in the United States of America alone!

Other sources also allege that patients developed conditions such as syphilis and HIV due to contaminated organs. The estimated value of a body, "harvested" for organs and bones can generate up to $250,000. William Sherman, the journalist who was instrumental in uncovering this fraudulent mess, alleges that the cost of 1 ounce of bone, in terms of dental implants, is more than the cost of 1 ounce of gold.

Below is an x-ray taken of such an exhumed body where PVC pipes have been inserted to retain the normal body posture.

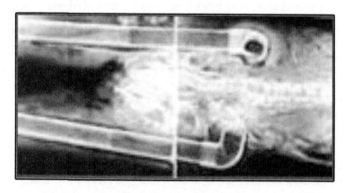

Let's consider for a moment the act of cremation. No evidence exists after the cremation. No "body" to be exhumed to verify foul play. The family is very happy to receive a bit of saw dust and cement in an "ash-urn" or wooden box, believing wholeheartedly that its grandma's ash, but grandma's body is decomposing under a bush at the Tristate crematorium, while the family scatters grandmas ashes at her favourite spot. The possibility that nothing will ever happen to reveal the truth is quite huge.

Now, I am not implying that this sort of thing happens when bodies are cremated, but just think about it, nobody goes to witness the cremation, they just want the ashes. Certainly there is huge a financial motive for "harvesting" a complete body, with neither the deceased, nor the relatives none the wiser. I did not research the possibility of this, but I would not be surprised if it is possible – it will just be another vile act on the list of cremation atrocities!

Spare parts

Here I have no scriptural evidence – yet, but for myself I am declaring – I am not a junkyard with spare parts! No cremation and no organ donation for me thank you very much!

Christians and others will be fuming at the mouth when they read this, they will claim that God is blessing science and medicine; therefore it would be an honourable deed to donate your organs. My opinion and -only my opinion? I see this in a totally different light. From scriptures I understand the "value" of the body, in life and in death, especially the bones and therefore, for me it's totally against scripture to serve as spare parts for someone else, in life or in death! People will say I am not a good Christian, and I will say you are right; I am not even a bad Christian. They would also perhaps ask me: "What if you need an organ one day?" My answer is: I am always open to conviction and I submit myself to God's will – if I am wrong I will apologise and ask for forgiveness and correct my statement, but until then I feel that if God has drawn my line, I must accept it and not try to stay alive at all costs by inserting someone else's body parts into my own body. However, this is something between yourself and God – I can't prove my conviction from scripture, therefore I will stand corrected if I am wrong.

Judging?

Am I "judging" cremation? You bet your behind I do! In the strongest possible most brutal form! I judge it as pagan, unscriptural, idol worshipping, satanically inspired and one of the worst ever abominations against our living God! A barbaric practice which is condoned, promoted and practiced by the very priests, the PBP's (Puppet Behind the Pulpit) who is supposed to lead God's flock of elected children and teach them what is clean and unclean, but they instead teach us that we may indulge in this practice and none may judge us, what a despicable shame!

So, who am I, the unlearned and ignorant man, to judge when the good theologian doctor clearly demand that none may judge you in terms of cremation? I'm glad you are asking. In this book we have truly evaluated and assessed the so-called traditional funeral and cremation, not only from scriptures, but also current events and facts and we clearly learned what is acceptable to God and what isn't. Therefore I choose to reprove and also to have no fellowship with those whom choose and promote what is not acceptable to God.

> *Eph 5:10 <u>Proving what is acceptable unto the Lord</u>.*
> *Eph 5:11 And <u>have no fellowship</u> with the <u>unfruitful works of darkness, <u>but rather reprove them.</u>*

No really…Muslims don't even partake in this abomination – the same abomination that Christian clergyman promotes and practices with their Christian fellowmen! Let it never come into our hearts to burn our sons and daughters, something that that never even came into God's heart…

> *<u>Jer 7:31</u> And they have built the high places of Tophet, which is in the valley of the son of Hinnom, <u>to burn their sons and their daughters in the fire; which I commanded them not, neither came it into my heart.</u>*

> *<u>1Cor 10:20</u> But I say, <u>that the things which the Gentiles sacrifice, they sacrifice to devils, and not to God: and I would not that ye should have fellowship with devils.</u>*
> *<u>1Cor 10:21</u> Ye cannot drink the cup of the Lord, and the cup of devils: ye cannot be partakers of the Lord's table, and of the table of devils.*
> *<u>1Cor 10:22</u> Do we provoke the Lord to jealousy? <u>are we stronger than he?</u>*

ARE YOU STRONGER THAN GOD?
SHALL YOU TEACH GOD KNOWLEDGE?

> *<u>Job 21:22</u> Shall <u>any teach God knowledge?</u> seeing he judgeth those that are high.*

<u>*Knowledge of truth*</u>

I make no comments here; it's up to you to ponder over the following passages from scriptures…

> *<u>Eze 22:26</u> Her priests have violated my law, and have profaned mine holy things: they have put no difference between the holy and profane, neither have they shewed difference between the unclean and the clean, and have hid their eyes from my sabbaths, and I am profaned among them.*

2The 2:10 And with all deceivableness of unrighteousness in them that perish; because they received not the love of the truth, that they might be saved.
2The 2:12 That they all might be damned who believed not the truth, but had pleasure in unrighteousness.

2Tim 3:13 But evil men and seducers shall wax worse and worse, deceiving, and being deceived.

2Tim 3:7 Ever learning, and never able to come to the knowledge of the truth

2Tim 4:3 For the time will come when they will not endure sound doctrine; but after their own lusts shall they heap to themselves teachers, having itching ears;
2Tim 4:4 And they shall turn away their ears from the truth, and shall be turned unto fables.

Heb 10:26 For if we sin wilfully after that we have received the knowledge of the truth, there remaineth no more sacrifice for sins,
Heb 10:27 But a certain fearful looking for of judgment and fiery indignation, which shall devour the adversaries.
Heb 10:28 He that despised Moses' law died without mercy under two or three witnesses:
Heb 10:29 Of how much sorer punishment, suppose ye, shall he be thought worthy, who hath trodden under foot the Son of God, and hath counted the blood of the covenant, wherewith he was sanctified, an unholy thing, and hath done despite unto the Spirit of grace?

2Tim 3:14 But continue thou in the things which thou hast learned and hast been assured of, knowing of whom thou hast learned them;
2Tim 3:15 And that from a child thou hast known the holy scriptures, which are able to make thee wise unto salvation through faith which is in Christ Jesus.
2Tim 3:16 All scripture is given by inspiration of God, and is profitable for doctrine, for reproof, for correction, for instruction in righteousness:
2Tim 3:17 That the man of God may be perfect, throughly furnished unto all good works.

Chapter 11

TRUTH above all

If ye were of the world, the world would love his own: but because ye are not of the world, but I have chosen you out of the world, therefore the world hateth you.

Joh 15:19

Book burning

Why is the truth of scripture so vehemently despised?

> *Joh 3:19 And this is the condemnation, that light is come into the world, and men loved darkness rather than light, because their deeds were evil.*
> *Joh 3:20 For every one that doeth evil hateth the light, neither cometh to the light, lest his deeds should be reproved.*
> *Joh 3:21 But he that doeth truth cometh to the light, that his deeds may be made manifest, that they are wrought in God.*

In my very first book I stated that people will not accept the truth, they will despise me for bringing them the scriptural truth and they will label me as a madman. Am I a prophet, a type of Nostradamus? Not by any means - I wrote these things because that is what scripture tells me. In fact – if any of my books becomes a best seller it will be proof that I strayed far away from God, as once the world starts to love you, you are part of this world:

> *Joh 15:19 If ye were of the world, the world would love his own: but because ye are not of the world, but I have chosen you out of the world, therefore the world hateth you.*

Just think: If I were to strip this book of truth and promote cremation as a viable option for Christians, pastors would recommend this book to their congregation members and the book would sell like hotcakes, but by now you know that no preacher with his senses still intact will ever recommend this book to anyone, in fact he may label it as a satanic book and warn his congregation to avoid it at all costs.

Close family members as well as good friends completely severed all ties with me because of my books. All this I knew beforehand, but I never expected to be honoured to such high level where Christians, yes - Christians would burn my books. Some comments from Christians – of course staunch churchgoers – who burnt my books:
"Your books do not belong in a Christian home!"
"If you are looking for the books you gave me, go look for them in the depths of hell as I burnt them!"

Yes, this book you are reading now was also burnt. (The Afrikaans version was published first)

How does this make me feel? From the bottom of my heart, this is one of the greatest honours I have ever experienced in my life. I will tell you why. When you have time, please read the full chapter 36 of Jeremiah, but in short, this is why:

> *Jer 36:2 Take thee a roll of a book, and write therein all the words that I have spoken unto thee against Israel, and against Judah, and against all the nations, from the day I spake unto thee, from the days of Josiah, even unto this day.*
> *Jer 36:18 Then Baruch answered them, He pronounced all these words unto me with his mouth, and I wrote them with ink in the book.*
> *Jer 36:19 Then said the princes unto Baruch, Go, hide thee, thou and Jeremiah; and let no man know where ye be.*
> *Jer 36:22 Now the king sat in the winterhouse in the ninth month: and there was a fire on the hearth burning before him.*
> *Jer 36:23 And it came to pass, that when Jehudi had read three or four leaves, he cut it with the penknife, and cast it into the fire that was on the hearth, until all the roll was consumed in the fire that was on the hearth.*

I always though that book burning only started after Gutenberg invented the printing press, how surprised was I to find it happened in Jeremiah's time already!

Take my advice: Don't believe a word I have written in this book, in fact I need you to reject me and everything I said in this book, but please be careful not to reject scriptures together with me. As they say: don't throw out the baby with the bathwater! Distinguish between your rejection of me and rejection of the Word of God. I always have an open invitation to direct me where I am wrong, but all I ask is that you show me from scripture where I am wrong – the truth however is, they never once attempt to tell me where I err, burning the book is easier – but hold on a minute there, are you not burning all the passages in this book as well? More than 800 of them? The fact that you never saw these passages before or heard them in church does not mean it is not written in the bible. It's also not my fault that you never heard these passages before: Do you hate me for telling you the truth?

> *Gal 4:16 Am I therefore become your enemy, because I tell you the truth?*

People say they will ask their pastor etc. and the pastor will tell them the truth, he knows as he has studied theology for many, many years. Well, the truth dear reader is this – if a pastor etc. dares tell the truth he is FRIED on the spot, sorry I meant FIRED on the spot. This is not a myth, this is fact, and I know some of them personally! So please, don't ask your pastor, reverend, priest etc. as they are in a massive people pleasing cesspool filled to the brim with conflict of interest!

The scale of evidence

So, how then do we know what the truth is when there are so many interpretations of scripture?

The only way to find the truth is:

"Let scripture, interpret scripture"

2Pet 1:20 Knowing this first, that no prophecy of the scripture is of any private interpretation.

Scripture can never contradict scripture! Let me say that again: Scripture can never contradict scripture! Let's put everything we have learned thus far from scripture on one side of the scale. Then decide what a vast amount of contradictory bible passages the UDT preachers must place on the other side of the scale to contradict, cancel out and nullify what we have learned so far. Even if it is possible (which it is not) then scripture would contradict scripture, which is also impossible! I cannot choose God for you my friend; you have to do that on your own…

We are taught that church is the bride of God, we have been indoctrinated from childhood that church is the "house of God". One pastor even said: "God is waiting to meet you at His house, this Sunday" This is FALSE, untrue, deceitful, and dishonest and a fabricated lie! The pastor must bury, the pastor must marry, the pastor must baptise, and the pastor must pray for me, the pastor must, must, must.......... Well, I agree, the pastor MUST collect money yes! And that's what it's all about. As soon as he starts spreading truth, he's income dries up!

Church is a business where the "word of the preacher is the product" and provided "the product" soothes the ears, the customers (congregation members) will pay and pay and pay even more...

God does not dwell in temples (churches) made with hands dear reader:

> _Act 17:24_ **God that made the world and all things therein, seeing that he is Lord of heaven and earth, _dwelleth not in temples made with hands;_**

> _Isa 66:1_ **Thus saith the LORD, The heaven is my throne, and the earth is my footstool: _where is the house that ye build unto me? and where is the place of my rest?_**
> _Isa 66:2_ **For all those things hath mine hand made, and all those things have been, saith the LORD: _but to this man will I look, even to him that is poor and of a contrite spirit, and trembleth at my word._**

In fact, don't be deceived with the term: "This is the house of the Lord" it's a lie!

> _Jer 7:4_ **_Trust ye not in lying words, saying,_ The _temple of the LORD, The temple of the LORD, The temple of the LORD,_ are these.**

If God is not in temples, where is He?

> _1Cor 3:16_ **Know ye not that _ye are the temple of God,_ and that the _Spirit of God dwelleth in you?_**

Your body clearly does not belong to you and you have no right whatsoever to take that which is God's property and pass it through fire for Molech where the body (the temple of God) spasms and contracts and burns to a crisp in the cremation oven! Please act according to God's will because he paid dearly for us.

> *1Cor 6:19 What? know ye not that your body is the temple of the Holy Ghost which is in you, which ye have of God, and ye are not your own?*
> *1CoR 6:20 For ye are bought with a price: therefore glorify God in your body, and in your spirit, which are God's.*

Don't listen to the hireling; listen to God, as the hirelings do not fulfil their tasks...

> *Mal 2:7 For the priest's lips should keep knowledge, and they should seek the law at his mouth: for he is the messenger of the LORD of hosts.*

> *Luk 11:52 Woe unto you, lawyers! for ye have taken away the key of knowledge: ye entered not in yourselves, and them that were entering in ye hindered.*

These hirelings keep us from knowledge and they will run away. Their false teachings will not save you on the day of reckoning...

> *Joh 10:12 But he that is an hireling, and not the shepherd, whose own the sheep are not, seeth the wolf coming, and leaveth the sheep, and fleeth: and the wolf catcheth them, and scattereth the sheep.*
> *Joh 10:13 The hireling fleeth, because he is an hireling, and careth not for the sheep.*

I am not kidding, I have a book of one of the biggest churches in South-Africa which states clearly that the minister is the mediator between the congregation (man) and God; You decide for yourself how this blends with scripture.

> *1Tim 2:5 For there is one God, and one mediator between God and men, the man Christ Jesus;*

The fruit

We shall know them by their fruits, says scriptures. What kind of fruit is it when the hireling and servants of corruption tell us the bible does not explicitly condemn cremation and therefore we can choose? We must be wide awake and alert to detect and recognise this kind of vile fruit.

> *2Pet 2:17 These are wells without water, clouds that are carried with a tempest; to whom the mist of darkness is reserved for ever.*
> *2Pet 2:18 For when they speak great swelling words of vanity, they allure through the lusts of the flesh, through much wantonness, those that were clean escaped from them who live in error.*
> *2Pet 2:19 While they promise them liberty, they themselves are the servants of corruption: for of whom a man is overcome, of the same is he brought in bondage.*

We must discern between good and evil:

> *Heb 5:14 But strong meat belongeth to them that are of full age, even those who by reason of use have their senses exercised to discern both good and evil.*

One of the gifts of the Spirit is to "EXHORT", but we are told NO! … You shall not!

> *Rom 12:6 Having then gifts differing according to the grace that is given to us, whether prophecy, let us prophesy according to the proportion of faith;*
> *Rom 12:7 Or ministry, let us wait on our ministering: or he that teacheth, on teaching;*
> *Rom 12:8 Or he that exhorteth, on exhortation: he that giveth, let him do it with simplicity; he that ruleth, with diligence; he that sheweth*

Why then are they doing this to us? They are merely fulfilling what is written scriptures and dishonest gain is only one of many reasons.

> *Eze 22:25 There is a conspiracy of her prophets in the midst thereof, like a roaring lion ravening the prey; they have devoured souls; they have taken the treasure and precious things; they have made her many widows in the midst thereof.*

Eze 22:26 *Her priests have violated my law, and have profaned mine holy things: they have put no difference between the holy and profane, neither have they shewed difference between the unclean and the clean, and have hid their eyes from my sabbaths, and I am profaned among them.*
Eze 22:27 *Her princes in the midst thereof are like wolves ravening the prey, to shed blood, and to destroy souls, to get dishonest gain*

The dog's vomit

When God, only by grace alone, brings truth across our path and we choose to go back, turn from the holy truth to go back to our previous convictions, the politically, socially and theologically correct majority view, we are compared to a dog that turns to its own vomit! In this case it would have been much better for you if you had never crossed paths with the truth.

2Pet 2:20 *For if after they have escaped the pollutions of the world through the knowledge of the Lord and Saviour Jesus Christ, they are again entangled therein, and overcome, the latter end is worse with them than the beginning.*
2Pet 2:21 *For it had been better for them not to have known the way of righteousness, than, after they have known it, to turn from the holy commandment delivered unto them.*
2Pet 2:22 *But it is happened unto them according to the true proverb, The dog is turned to his own vomit again; and the sow that was washed to her wallowing in the mire.*

Eph 6:4 *And, ye fathers, provoke not your children to wrath: but bring them up in the nurture and admonition of the Lord.*

I can assure you that this book which is an exhortation from cover to cover has not been written in deceit, uncleanliness or guile.

1The 2:3 *For our exhortation was not of deceit, nor of uncleanness, nor in guile:*

1Tim 4:13 *Till I come, give attendance to reading, to exhortation, to doctrine.*

A preacher which is worth his salt, will resign and sever all ties with church, no matter what the dogma is, and a preacher who is only worth half his salt, will refuse point blank to partake in any action whatsoever related to any form of cremation.

> *Rev 22:14 Blessed are they that do his commandments, that they may have right to the tree of life, and may enter in through the gates into the city.*

> *Rom 1:21 Because that, when they knew God, they glorified him not as God, neither were thankful; but became vain in their imaginations, and their foolish heart was darkened.*
> *Rom 1:22 Professing themselves to be wise, they became fools,*
> *Rom 1:23 And changed the glory of the uncorruptible God into an image made like to corruptible man, and to birds, and fourfooted beasts, and creeping things.*
> *Rom 1:24 Wherefore God also gave them up to uncleanness through the lusts of their own hearts, to dishonour their own bodies between themselves:*
> *Rom 1:25 Who changed the truth of God into a lie, and worshipped and served the creature more than the Creator, who is blessed for ever. Amen.*

Am I my own god?

When the bible is clear regarding a certain matter or subject and the pastor says we may choose (just look at the almost total acceptance of homosexuality today, by Christians, theologians and the church nonetheless!) and nobody must judge us; this is code-word for "you are god". Are you aware, dear reader who the very first preacher was who preached the sermon of "you will be as gods"? The very First UTD teacher who perfected the art of "soothing the ears" Let me quote him:

> *"then your eyes shall be opened, and ye shall be as gods"*
> -   *Satan Gen 3:5*

Never heed to these seducing spirits dear friend...

> *1Tim 4:1 Now the Spirit speaketh expressly, that in the latter times some shall depart from the faith, giving heed to seducing spirits, and doctrines of devils;*
> *1Tim 4:2 Speaking lies in hypocrisy; having their conscience seared with a hot iron;*

> *2Tim 4:3 For the time will come when they will not endure sound doctrine; but after their own lusts shall they heap to themselves teachers, having itching ears;*
> *2Tim 4:4 And they shall turn away their ears from the truth, and shall be turned unto fables.*

Let's talk explicit!

> *Rom 1:19 Because that which may be known of God is manifest in them; for God hath shewed it unto them.*

Is this true? Does God really reveal the truth in His Word related to "cremate or bury"? Does He give us the ability to distinguish between right and wrong in this regard? Some say you can choose, others say cremation is not explicitly forbidden in the bible. All right then, let's see then if God provides an explicit answer to this "fiery" debate:

> *Gen 3:19 In the sweat of thy face shalt thou eat bread, till thou return unto the ground; for out of it wast thou taken: for dust thou art, and unto dust shalt thou return.*

Did you see it? Not? Let's have another look:

"till thou return unto the ground; for out of it wast thou taken"

This is the explicit command: **You will return to the ground, for out of it you were taken!** More explicit than this I cannot give. Let us then, also in our death, die unto God, in other words, let us in life, do it to the glory of God and let us in death, also die in the glory of God.

> *Rom 14:8 For whether we live, we live unto the Lord; and whether we die, we die unto the Lord: whether we live therefore, or die, we are the Lord's.*

> *Rom 12:1 I beseech you therefore, brethren, by the mercies of God, that ye present your bodies a living sacrifice, holy, acceptable unto God, which is your reasonable service.*

Now you tell me – how does one combine "**present your living body**" as a holy sacrifice by putting it through a cremation oven? How can we, whether we live or **DIE** be the Lord's, when we in death, pass through the fire?

> *Joh 5:28 Marvel not at this: for the hour is coming, <u>in the which all that are in the graves shall hear his voice,</u>*
> *Joh 5:29 And shall come forth; they that have done good, unto the resurrection of life; and they that have done evil, unto the resurrection of damnation.*

Does it say that all those in the ash-urns will hear his voice, or all those scattered in the ocean? Or does it say:

"Everyone in the graves shall hear His voice"

I state: When a person, claiming to be a Christian, says that a Christian may cremate and will be with Christ forever, it is a doctrine of devils!

> *1Ti 4:1 Now the Spirit speaketh expressly, that <u>in the latter times some shall depart from the faith, giving heed to seducing spirits, and doctrines of devils;</u>*

Appeal denied

You see dear friend, you cannot change what God says just because we are modern man with modern cremation ovens and modern bone-crushing industrial blenders. God's word is settled in heaven, for ever!

> *Psa 119:89 LAMED. For ever, <u>O LORD, thy word is settled in heaven.</u>*

Whether you like it or not, whether you believe in Gods existence or not – you will appear before the judgement seat:

> *2Cor 5:10 <u>For we must all appear before the judgment seat of Christ; that every one may receive the things done in his body, according to that he hath done, whether it be good or bad.</u>*

Did you notice: it says to receive the things done in your body, whether good or bad?

> *Mat 16:26 For what is a man profited, if he shall gain the whole world, and lose his own soul? or what shall a man give in exchange for his soul?*

> *Mat 16:27 For the Son of man shall come in the glory of his Father with his angels; and then he shall reward every man according to his works.*

Don't lend your ears to anyone, especially me (the author), but please listen to YAHSHUA!

> *Col 3:23 And whatsoever ye do, do it heartily, as to the Lord, and not unto men;*
> *Col 3:24 Knowing that of the Lord ye shall receive the reward of the inheritance: for ye serve the Lord Christ.*
> *Col 3:25 But he that doeth wrong shall receive for the wrong which he hath done: and there is no respect of persons.*

And if you acted as follows:

> *Amo 2:1 Thus saith the LORD; For three transgressions of Moab, and for four, I will not turn away the punishment thereof; because he burned the bones of the king of Edom into lime:*
> *Amo 2:2 But I will send a fire upon Moab, and it shall devour the palaces of Kerioth: and Moab shall die with tumult, with shouting, and with the sound of the trumpet:*

You will have to give account of yourself…

> *Rom 14:12 So then every one of us shall give account of himself to God.*

Why?

> *Jam 2:19 Thou believest that there is one God; thou doest well: the devils also believe, and tremble.*
> *Jam 2:20 But wilt thou know, O vain man, that faith without works is dead?*

Your defence that you listened to your preacher, after you received the truth, but turned like the dog to its own vomit, will not be accepted and furthermore, the big stunner - when God says:

> *Mat 7:23 And then will I profess unto them, I never knew you: depart from me, ye that work iniquity.*

THAT'S IT!
THERE IS NO APPEAL PROCESS!

If you still don't believe that cremation is evil, then do yourself a favour and look up the verses we quoted in this book an tear those pages from you bible – this way you can truly declare there is nothing in YOUR bible against cremation.

> *Rev 21:7 He that overcometh shall inherit all things; and I will be his God, and he shall be my son.*
> *Rev 21:8 But the fearful, and unbelieving, and the abominable, and murderers, and whoremongers, and sorcerers, and idolaters, and all liars, shall have their part in the lake which burneth with fire and brimstone: which is the second death.*

> *Eph 5:6 Let no man deceive you with vain words: for because of these things cometh the wrath of God upon the children of disobedience.*
> *Eph 5:7 Be not ye therefore partakers with them.*
> *Eph 5:8 For ye were sometimes darkness, but now are ye light in the Lord: walk as children of light:*
> *Eph 5:9 (For the fruit of the Spirit is in all goodness and righteousness and truth;)*

Follow His example

> *1Pe 2:21 For even hereunto were ye called: because Christ also suffered for us, leaving us an example, that ye should follow his steps:*

God can get you out of trouble, every single time, even if it you committed the most abominable sins. I know -I am living proof!

TRUST HIM

Lastly on the "judgement" issue, for those accusing me of judging, the following verse talks about hell, but also see "pulling them out of the fire" as pulling one from the cremation fire, and the method – save them with fear!

> *Jud 1:22 And of some have compassion, making a difference:*
> *Jud 1:23 And others save with fear, pulling them out of the fire; hating even the garment spotted by the flesh.*

There is so much more to be said, but I will conclude with the words of Yahshua:

Joh 16:12
I have yet many things to say unto you, but ye cannot bear them now.

Just as God and Mammon are direct opposites, so is God and cremation and yes, so is God and church

Gal 4:16
Am I therefore become your enemy, because I tell you the truth?

Please don't choose the same punishment for yourself as God had preserved for Satan!

Eze 28:18
...therefore will I bring forth a fire from the midst of thee,
it shall devour thee, and I will bring thee to ashes...

****

One final question

Ask yourself one last question:
If it is true that once we die, our bodies are mere, good for nothing remains which may be cremated, why would God, and we are talking about GOD here dear reader, why would GOD have Josiah exhume bones from a grave and pollute them and burn them to ashes, by order of GOD? Why? Why? Why?

> **_2Kin 23:16_** **And as Josiah turned himself, he spied the sepulchres that were there in the mount, and sent, _and took the bones out of the sepulchres, and burned them upon the altar, and polluted it, according to the word of the LORD_ which the man of God proclaimed, who proclaimed these words.**

Foto: Henry Mühlpfordt

CREMATE or BURY
What Saith The Bible?

The Bible Saith:

Cremation is one of the biggest Sins we can possibly commit!

And also the very last sin you will ever commit…

Regards and Best Wishes
Piet Wilsenach

"When a well-packaged web of lies has been sold gradually to the masses over generations, the truth will seem utterly preposterous <u>and it's speaker a raving lunatic.</u>"

Dresden James

Chapter 12
Appendage

Man is least himself when
he talks in his own person.
Give him a mask, and he
will tell you the truth.

Oscar Wilde

For whom was this book written?

This book was not written for all of humanity. It was written for truth seekers, those who CAN hear the truth, God's elected children, not for those who can not hear!

> **Joh 8:43** *Why do ye not understand my speech? even because ye cannot hear my word.*

This book is not written for every kindred, and tongue, and people, and nation; it is written for the elected children of God only. (Please do not think for one moment that I consider myself an elected child of God and that my name has been written in the book of life. This I do not know and if I weigh myself, I find myself too light, before God even weighed me)

This book is for those whose names are written in the book of life, those who **CAN** listen to the truth, and those who have an unquenchable hunger to be unbound from the lie. This book has not been written for those who my Father did not plant.

> **Joh 14:17** *Even the Spirit of truth; whom the world cannot receive, because it seeth him not, neither knoweth him: but ye know him; for he dwelleth with you, and shall be in you.*

Furthermore, it is only for people who truly believe the following:

> **2Tim 3:16** *All scripture is given by inspiration of God, and is profitable for doctrine, for reproof, for correction, for instruction in righteousness:*
> **2Tim 3:17** *That the man of God may be perfect, throughly furnished unto all good works.*

People, who do not believe that the Bible is the inspired Word of God and became flesh among us, can discard the book, because this book contains more than 800 verses from scripture and scripture cannot be broken!

> **Joh 10:35** *If he called them gods, unto whom the word of God came, and the scripture cannot be broken;*

My Doctrine

If one listens to the spiritual leaders of today, one finds the new buzz word is: "Leave the dogma, it's not important..." I, dear reader am very sensitive about my dogma. I will never abandon my dogma and I will defend it to the ends of the earth. What is my doctrine?

Scripture, Scripture, and Scripture!

As I write, I sometimes listen to radio broadcasts of sermons. Recently I heard a pastor pray the following during one of these broadcast: "Lord, make people go to church, it does not matter what church, as long as it is a church". I think this is a very brave pastor, who practically commands God, during prayer that false doctrine does not matter. This is the same God who warns us time and time again, against the ravenous wolves in sheep's cloth, the false Christ's and the false prophets, but the pastor basically instructs God, under prayer, that every church is holy. Utterly disgusting! Well, one can clearly identify the fruit of such a person, just like scripture tells us:

> *Mat 24:24 For there shall arise false Christs, and false prophets, and shall shew great signs and wonders; insomuch that, if it were possible, they shall deceive the very elect.*

Jer 29:9 For they prophesy falsely unto you in my name: I have not sent them, saith the LORD.

Luk 11:52 Woe unto you, lawyers! for ye have taken away the key of knowledge: ye entered not in yourselves, and them that were entering in ye hindered.

Jesus says in Mat 15:14, after he offended the Pharisees:
"Let them alone: they be blind leaders of the blind"

The Bible will never fit into church. The church Pharisees have to scrape cut and saw scriptures to suit the teachings of the church!

I am not a Christian! But I believe IN God and I BELIEVE God, the God of Abraham, Isaac and Jacob, the **"I AM THAT I AM"** of:

> **Exo 3:14** **And God said unto Moses, _I AM THAT I AM_: and he said, Thus shalt thou say unto the children of Israel, I AM hath sent me unto you.**

I believe IN His Word and I BELIEVE His Word, from Genesis to Revelation! The word of God is an embarrassment for Christianity and there is no way that Christianity will ever fit into the Word of God, without scraping, cutting and sawing scriptures! (If you find this comment distasteful, I have proven this in my book "Kinderdoop...". Unfortunately this book is currently not available in English. The translation is in the pipeline. However, the pipe line is a bit long at the moment. The book is almost a 1000 pages and I also offer a R1m (one million ZAR) reward if you can biblically prove infant baptism as doctrine from scripture. The book contains the rules, terms and conditions for the reward. The reward money may just as well be $1m USD because it can never be proven from scripture and this is the very beginning of the destruction of the spirit of the child and subsequent adult, right there during infant baptism. The English title will be "Infant baptism vs. believer's baptism")

Do not be ashamed of Gods Words as the churches are ashamed of His Words!

> **Mar 8:38** **Whosoever therefore shall be ashamed of me and of my words in this adulterous and sinful generation; of him also shall the Son of man be ashamed, when he cometh in the glory of his Father with the holy angels.**

Uncompromised Truth

This book is intended to bring uncompromised truth. Truth which God gave us in His scriptures. Did you know that even in the New Testament, there were people who were afraid of the truth, not children or ordinary men, but Chief Rulers, those who we should be trusting to bring us truth. We observe exactly the same today. It is the highly educated theologians who reject the truth in favour of the praise of men! And ordinary people like us? Well, we love the praise of the pastor, minister, preacher and priest (Pharisees and scribes) more than God also, and that's why we are also afraid of the truth.

> *Joh 12:42 Nevertheless among the chief rulers also many believed on him; but because of the Pharisees they did not confess him, lest they should be put out of the synagogue:*
> *Joh 12:43 For they loved the praise of men more than the praise of God.*

Do you also love the praise of men, more than the praise of God?

When we refuse to accept the truth, but rather accept the teachings of the false prophets with their signs and lying wonders, God will send us a delusion to believe the lie and then my friend, we are in a really bad state indeed. This is not fun and games, this is serious.

> *2Ths 2:9 Even him, whose coming is after the working of Satan with all power and signs and lying wonders,*
> *2Ths 2:10 And with all deceivableness of unrighteousness in them that perish; because they received not the love of the truth, that they might be saved.*
> *2Ths 2:11 And for this cause God shall send them strong delusion, that they should believe a lie:*
> *2Ths 2:12 That they all might be damned who believed not the truth, but had pleasure in unrighteousness.*

The old wise man says: **"He that believeth the lie is not as bad as he who refuses to believeth the truth"**

> *Jas 4:17 Therefore to him that knoweth to do good, and doeth it not, to him it is sin.*

How do we interpret scripture?

I've heard the following phrase:

"You must not dig too deep into scriptures, it will make you crazy". I am in agreement with this statement, with one very important condition however. There are many wise men, top notch theologians who study the bible very deeply, for many years, but they still can't make heads or tails from Genesis to Revelation. Their years of studies bring forth no biblical sense at all. Why do we see this?

Actually, the answer is very simple and we find it in the following verse:

> *Luk 24:44 And he said unto them, These are the words which I spake unto you, while I was yet with you, that all things must*

> *be fulfilled, which were written in the law of Moses, and in the prophets, and in the psalms, concerning me.*
> *Luk 24:45 Then opened he their understanding, that they might understand the scriptures,*

Dear reader, the last thing I want to do is insult your intelligence, but can you read? If you can, what does Jesus tell us in this verse? Does it not state very clearly end very comprehensibly that He (Jesus) opened their understanding so that they may understand the scriptures? This single verse tells us that you can study for 40 years and make absolutely no biblical sense? Why? Because no theological university or institution can open your mind to understand scripture!

If God does not "open" the scriptures for you, the following happens:

> *Isa 29:11 And the vision of all is become unto you as the words of a book that is sealed, which men deliver to one that is learned, saying, Read this, I pray thee: and he saith, I cannot; for it is sealed:*

Does this mean that we suddenly understand the entire Bible when God "opens our understanding". No, we understand "here a little and there a little".

> *Isa 28:10 For precept must be upon precept, precept upon precept; line upon line, line upon line; here a little, and there a little:*

Allow me to repeat:
Must we be highly educated theologians, doctors and professors before God can "open" the scriptures for us? Is this Bible really locked for ordinary people like you and me? Absolutely not! Jesus says:

> *Luk 10:21 In that hour Jesus rejoiced in spirit, and said, I thank thee, O Father, Lord of heaven and earth, that thou hast hid these things from the wise and prudent, and hast revealed them unto babes: even so, Father; for so it seemed good in thy sight.*

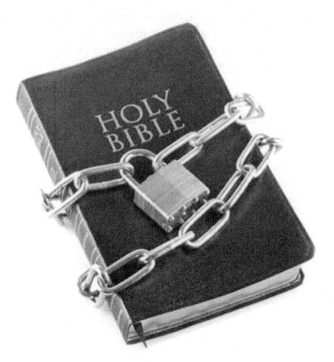

Our Father hides (locks) scriptures for the wise and opens it for little children, ordinary little children like you and me. If we teach a child that a tree is green, the child believes that the tree is green. He accepts it; he does not say "no, the tree is light green with a red shine". If then we read the Word of God, we read what is written and we understand that which we read. Hart and soul I believe the following:

The Bible interprets the Bible!

This means: If you have a number of versus which portrays a certain teaching throughout scripture, you cannot take one verse, completely out of context, to nullify or wipe out all the preceding verses.

Remember: The Bible is not merely and old out-dated book. It is our living God's Word!

> **_Joh 1:14_ _And the Word was made flesh, and dwelt among us, (and we beheld his glory, the glory as of the only begotten of the Father,) full of grace and truth._**

It is true that there are sections of scripture which is really tough to understand, but mostly, the Bible is written in clear comprehensible language. The principle is to study that which is easily comprehensible first to form a frame of reference. This enables us to search and study the more difficult portions and add it to the existing framework.

Example as follows:
When we have, say five verses from Genesis to Revelation which clearly teaches that a tree is green and we then find a verse that suggests a tree to be brown, then we have to somehow add the "brown" verse to the "green" verses to compliment the "green" verses. This is because the Word never ever contradicts the Word! We can do a bit if study and then find that the writer of the "brown" verse is referring to a tree in autumn, when the leaves are in fact brown.

What we cannot do is quote the "brown" verse to prove that scripture is wrong or incorrect in terms of the "green" verses, nor can we just ignore the "green" verses to formulate a "brown" doctrine teaching only, just because it does not fit the churches dogmatic "green verse" belief system, like some of the highly educated theologians do. If we however find a verse that states the tree is "blue", in other words totally against the grain of the entire scriptural teaching, we need to seriously study and try and identify the problem, which may very well be a mistranslation, addition or even an omission. I trust you get the point.

Which Bible?

There are people who can speak 13 languages fluently, really clever people, but when you want to know what a persons native language is, just ask him in what language he prays. Since I pray in my native language which is Afrikaans, there are only two Bibles for me. One is the very first Afrikaans translation of 1933 and the other is the:

The 1611 King James Version

For English speaking people I recommend the 1611 King James Version and the 1769 King James Version of the Holy Bible (also known as the Authorized Version). Studying should be done with the 1611 and only where difficult words are encountered should they be looked up in the 1769 version, which is very, very close to the 1611 version.

This does not suggest that these bibles are 100% accurate, they are just more accurate than any other Bible we have available today. Unfortunately, present in these bibles are omissions, additions and also deliberate and unintentional translation errors. This however is brought to the surface with good bible study (exegesis). The 1611 is however the most accurate Bible we have available today.

Any other bibles should be used for comparison purposes only.
I use the 1769 version in this book purely because it's the only version I have containing Strong's Word Numbers.

The Names

I don't want to elaborate on the names in this book. I use the name "Jesus" in this book for your convenience only, but I do not use this name when I pray. I also never use the name or rather the title "Lord". To call the God of the scriptures, the God of Abraham, Isaac and Jacob by the name, or rather title of "Lord" is an abomination. Yes, I am aware that it is written in your Bible, but it is still an abomination.

Illustrations

All illustrations and images in this book do not necessarily portray the view of the author or owner of said illustration or image, nor do the authors agree with the content of this book. Those images or illustrations which have not been credited are used according to the rules of Wikimedia Commons, are in the public domain, are used under the free licence agreement, purchased for commercial use or they are images I have taken myself. The cut-out cremation illustration on the cover of the book is credited to Henry Mühlpfordt.

What readers say about this book

"Knowledge is Power", or so we are told by the wise men since childhood. This slogan never really claimed its rightful place in my mind. Subconsciously, I may have regarded this more as a clever sales stunt to ensure full classrooms.

When I finished this book, I realised the severity of the very clear warning we receive from Scripture in *Hos 4:6* that we are truly being destroyed because of the lack of knowledge, not knowing or not understanding. Maybe we are too busy to ask, too busy to enquire and too busy to make our own decisions. We have come accustomed to our spiritual leaders to guide us on our path. They are the educated, the highly qualified and the experts when it comes to Gods Word. We trust them to lead us down the spiritual path and serve us with pure Scripture and undiluted truths. With sadness, but also joy, we find that no one loves the sheep as much as the SHEPHERD Himself! With utter shock and dismay that we suddenly realise the horrible truth; we cannot and must not trust anyone other than the true Shepherd and his wonderful Word, especially not the false prophets which come to you in sheep's clothing, but inwardly are ravenous wolves!

As long as I am alive and in control of this decision, I will not allow myself, or anyone of my loved ones to burn in this man made hell (sorry, I mean crematorium). Never will I allow the bones of my loved ones to be discarded in a waste bin, hole in the ground or any other place, like the colonel's chicken bones. Never before have I realised just how gruesome and also unscriptural a cremation is, yet again imported from paganism, by our own spiritual leaders whom we entrust so much, without any form of protest, where all of us are made to believe that our Creator has no problem with this utterly gruesome and idolatrous act.

Read this book and find out what Scripture truly says about cremation and what abomination it is in the eyes of our God. You will be flabbergasted by the truth and you will never be the same!
N. Kelbrick

The decision with regards to cremate or bury was never an issue for me. In fact, I had made my decision long ago and that was to cremate, based on two reasons namely: Cremation is less costly and the last thing I want is to wake up in a coffin underneath six feet of soil. Every person has the right to decide for themselves in terms of their remains, not so? This book crossed paths with me and I decided to read it, although I was not looking for answers as my decision was already set in stone.

I was so wrong and blind in my decision making process. The author, in a very fitting manner, pointed out just how far from the truth I have strayed. Even though this book quotes more than 800 verses, there are a few that I will never forget. One of them is: *"Isa 28:10 For precept must be upon precept, precept upon precept; line upon line, line upon line; here a little, and there a little".* Little by little, verse by verse, I started seeing how my thought pattern was directly in opposition to the Word of God, in terms of cremation.

The information and research in this book is inspirational, revealing and also bewildering, to say the least. I cannot believe that humanity is so cruel at times. I was shocked, dumbfounded, flabbergasted and thunderstruck and yes, also ashamed as my eyes rolled over the pages of this book. I saw my own religious conviction tumbling down like a house of cards, card by card, page by page. The more I read, the more a gorge developed between my very definition of Christianity and the Word of God. As time passed, my Christian-coloured glasses disappeared and suddenly I could clearly see and also understand the beautiful truths of scripture, not due to what the author said, but what is really written in the Bible!

It's very important and I will say it over and over again: This book is of value and worth and should not be taken lightly. By the authors own admission, don't believe him, but confirm for yourself by reading these truths in the Word of our Wonderful Heavenly Father. To the author I would like to say, this book is the most precious gift you could have possibly given me on this earth and I thank him for writing this book, he transferred me to the right track again, the scriptural track of undiluted truth with no compromise. After this book I confirm with every cell in my body that I never ever want to be cremated!
D. van den Berg

Support the author

If you read this book and you are susceptible to the content in light of what the Bible teaches, you are probably only part of an estimated 3%; the remaining 97% will either not read the book in its entirety or burn the book because the content is totally against their indoctrination by their churches or upbringing. If you are part of the 3% I would appreciate it very much if you could take two minutes and just write a review on Amazon.com, regarding your feeling about the book and if any, what you have learned, not from me, but from scriptures. If you could rate the book with 5 stars it would help me a great deal as a large portion of the 97% will probably write derogatory reviews and rate the book with the lowest possible degree. This I don't mind, because as I have sated, be careful about the direction of your resentment. You may resent me by all means, but please do not resent scriptures.

I would like to thank all of you who CAN listen and accept scripture and your time to rate this book – THANK YOU!

Sign-up

Please remember to go to my website and sign up to be notified when new or updated publications are launched.

Love to hear from you

Please send me an email - I love corresponding about issues related to constructive criticism, new convictions and rectifications, because no matter what, I always learn something new from you, the reader, the critic and yes, even the theologian. Let me know where I am in error. I appreciate every email, even if you just email me to tell me that you decided to burn my book! – Thank you.

Bible challenges, questions and your vote

I would appreciate it if you would visit my website where I have listed a few "Bible challenges". Some of these "challenges" are held very dear by Christians and they totally believe this is what scripture teaches due to their church indoctrination, but in fact most of them are nowhere to be found in the bible. All I ask is that someone directs me to the scripture which proves or disproves the "challenge".

In addition there are a few statements which I ask the reader to simply vote "true" or "false" according to their belief system. It is very interesting indeed to see how the majority of people vote completely the opposite of what scripture teaches and yet regard themselves as "Christians destined for heaven".

I also have a "questions" section where I list personal difficulties in understanding scripture. This is where I humbly request the reader to assist me in finding answers for some of these complex issues which I don't understand yet. This really helps a great deal as we need to help each other in this regard. Again – Thank you for your contributions!

****

Contact Details

Website:
www.pietwilsenach.com

Contact the author:
piet@pietwilsenach.com

Please visit the website every so often for new publications and updates or subscribe so I can inform you when new books are published.

• •

Even Elvis Presley said:

Truth is like the sun. You can shut it out for a time, but it ain't goin' away.

16 Augustus 1969 - RIP
(Peter Henry Wilsenach)

1Timothy 4:14-16

Neglect not the gift that is in thee, which was given thee by prophecy, with the laying on of the hands of the presbytery.

Meditate upon these things; give thyself wholly to them; that thy profiting may appear to all.

Take heed unto thyself, and unto the doctrine; continue in them: for in doing this thou shalt both save thyself, and them that hear thee.

(AG714)

Sources and References:

[1] Little Oxford Dictionary © Oxford University Press, eighth edition 2002

[2] google.co.za/publicdata/explore?ds=d5bncppjof8f9_
&met_y=sp_pop_totl&idim=country: ZAF&dl=en&hl=en&q=
population+of+south+Africa

[3] en.wikipedia.org/wiki/Mortality_rate

[4] blog.funeralone.com/grow-your-business/cremation-rate-rising/

[5] en.wikipedia.org/wiki/Cremation

[6] wardsbookofdays.com/18january.htm

[7] en.wikipedia.org/wiki/Druid

[8] en.wikipedia.org/wiki/Gauls#Religion

[9] everlifememorials.com/v/urns/urns-history.htm

[10] en.wikipedia.org/wiki/Cremation#Hinduism_and_other_
India_origin_religions

[11] en.wikipedia.org/wiki/Bhagavad_Gita

[12] Brown-Driver-Briggs' Hebrew Definitions

[13] Strong's Hebrew and Greek Dictionaries
Dictionaries of Hebrew and Greek Words taken from Strong's
Exhaustive Concordance by James Strong, S.T.D., LL.D., 1890.

[14] en.wikipedia.org/wiki/List_of_Christian_denominations

[15] en.wikipedia.org/wiki/Bone#Organic

[16] news.discovery.com/animals/dinosaur-buried-alive.html

[17] en.wikipedia.org/wiki/Red_Lady_of_Paviland

[18] msnbc.msn.com/id/33110809/
ns/technology_and_science-science/t/worlds-oldest
-human-linked-skeleton-found/

[19] en.wikipedia.org/wiki/Ossuary

[20] looklocal.co.za/looklocal/content/en/middelburg
/middelburg-news-section?oid=6430728&sn=Detail&pid=
4979893&Mass-grave-shocker-

[21] dailymail.co.uk/news/article-427368/
Cremation-costs-rise-tooth-fillings-poison-living.html

[22] msnbc.msn.com/id/16656749/ns/us_news-
environment/t/cremation-pollution-neighbors-ervous/#.
UKeEV3p4PQ8

[23] mercuryexposure.info/environment/
release-pathways/cremation/item/856-crematory-emissions-data

[24] mercuryexposure.info/environment/
release-pathways/cremation/item/855-crematory-
outcry-has-minnesota-cities-weighing-risks

[25] quigleyscabinet.blogspot.com/2009/07/creative-remains.html

[26] ehow.com/how_7852858_make-tattoo-inks-out-ashes.html

[27] en.wikipedia.org/wiki/Alkaline_hydrolysis

[28] livescience.com/15980-death-8-burial-alternatives.html

[29] resomation.com/index_files/Page1485.htm

[30] africanbusinessreview.co.za/money_matters/how-south-africas-carbon-tax-may-affect-businesses

[31] google.co.za/url?sa=t&rct=j&q=vehichle%20carbon%20tax%20south%20africa&source=web&cd=3&cad=rja&ved=0CDsQFjAC&url=http%3A%2F%2Fcoursemain.ee.ukzn.ac.za%2Fenel2enh2%2Fnotes%2FCarbon_Tax_for_Motor_Vehicles.doc&ei=9L2wUJ3mM4OD4gTA44DICA&usg=AFQjCNFAkLe30FEfrkacIyHMnsRXkldWVQ

[32] resomation.com/index_files/Page347.htm

[33] uitvaartvlaanderen.be/Resomeren-Resomatie-Resomatieproces-vlaanderen.php

[34] news.bbc.co.uk/2/hi/africa/3818833.stm

[35] en.wiktionary.org/wiki/oxymoron

[36] news24.com/SouthAfrica/News/60-babies-stillborn-every-day-in-SA-20110415

[37] Scriptures marked as "(GNB)" are taken from the Good News Bible – Second Edition © 1992 by American Bible Society.

[38] wiki.answers.com/Q/How_much_do_the_bones_weigh_in_the_human_body

[39] answers.com/topic/how-much-of-the-body-remains-after-cremation

[40] theglobeandmail.com/technology/science/raiders-of-the-lost-parts/article1096601/?page=all

Notes

Printed in Great Britain
by Amazon